M000267455

Charting Reform, Achieving Equity in a Diverse Nation

A Volume in
Research in Educational Policy:
Local, National, and Global Perspectives

Series Editor:
Kenneth K. Wong,
Brown University

Research in Educational Policy: Local, National, and Global Perspectives

Kenneth K. Wong, Editor

Improving Results for Children and Families: Linking Collaborative Services With School Reform Efforts (2001)
edited by Margaret C. Wang and William Lowe Boyd

Cross-National Information and Communication: Technology Policy and Practices in Education (2003)
edited by Tjeerd Plomp, Ronald E. Anderson, Nancy Law, and Andreas Quale

System-Wide Efforts to Improve Student Achievement (2006)
edited by Kenneth K. Wong and Stacey Rutledge

The Testing Gap: Scientific Trials of Test-Driven School Accountability Systems for Excellence and Equity (2007)
by Jaekyung Lee

Partnering for Progress: Boston University, the Chelsea Public Schools, and Twenty Years of Urban Education Reform (2009)
edited by Cara Stillings Candal

Cross-National Information and Communication Technology Policies and Practices in Education (Rev. 2nd Ed.) (2009)
edited by Tjeerd Plomp, Ronald E. Anderson, Nancy Law, and Andreas Quale

Charting Reform, Achieving Equity in a Diverse Nation

Edited by

Gail L. Sunderman
Center for Education Policy,
University of Maryland

Information Age Publishing, Inc.
Charlotte, North Carolina • www.infoagepub.com

Library of Congress Cataloging-in-Publication Data

Charting reform, achieving equity in a diverse nation / edited by Gail L.
Sunderman.
   pages cm. — (Research in educational policy.)
  ISBN 978-1-62396-271-5 (paperback) — ISBN 978-1-62396-272-2 (hardcover) —
ISBN 978-1-62396-273-9 (ebook) 1. School improvement programs—United
States. 2. Critical pedagogy—United States. 3. Education and state—United States. I.
Sunderman, Gail L.
  LB2822.82.C433 2013
  371.2'07—dc23

                                            2013006342

Printed in the United States of America

CONTENTS

PART III: EDUCATIONAL ACCOUNTABILITY: EFFECTS ON STUDENT OUTCOMES AND EQUITY

PREFACE

Gail L. Sunderman

What does equity mean in a nation where the schools are becoming more diverse? And, perhaps more importantly, how well are our educational reform policies, often framed in the language of equity and opportunity, measuring up to the challenges of achieving equity in a diverse nation? There is reason to be concerned. Over the past decade, education policy and demographic changes have brought renewed attention to inequalities in student achievement. The federal No Child Left Behind Act of 2001 (NCLB), by requiring schools and districts to disaggregate data by subgroups, increased attention on disparities in student outcomes based on race and other categories. However, this type of disaggregation can be misleading by masking within-group differences and tells us very little about the sources of inequities or how to address them. Nor has the NCLB accountability framework directed attention to the complexity of the issues facing education. Questions about the success of NCLB at narrowing the achievement gap or improving student achievement have lingered (Lee & Reeves, 2012; National Research Council, 2011), even as the federal government intensified it focus on performance based accountability as the driver of reform.

At the same time, demographic data indicates that once homogeneous districts are diversifying, both racially and economically. Already, over half of minority students in large metropolitan areas now attend suburban schools (Orfield & Frankenberg, 2008), and there are more poor people living in suburbs than in cities (Berube & Kneenone, 2006; Metropolitan Policy Program at Brookings, 2012). There is widening income inequality

Charting Reform, Achieving Equity in a Diverse Nation
pp. vii–xiii
Copyright © 2013 by Information Age Publishing

in America as well and a concomitant rise in the income-based achievement gap. Recent research finds that the achievement gap between children from high- and low-income families has grown substantially in recent decades, and that the income gap is considerably larger than the Black-White gap (Reardon, 2011).

This current context—increasing diversity within formerly homogeneous communities coupled with continuing inequities between different racial, ethnic, and socioeconomic groups—was the impetus for this book. In this book, the authors explore the challenges and opportunities emerging from the dynamics between increasing diversity in our nation's schools and the challenges of school reform through the lens of equity. Central themes include the critical examination of how equity is conceived under the law and in policy, the experiences of minority students in suburban schools, and the impact of current reform policies and strategies for achieving greater educational opportunities for all students.

Sunderman begins by tracing the evolution of how equity and opportunity are defined under federal education policy and the kinds of reforms these policies articulated to address equity and increase opportunity. Central to this evolution are the assumptions behind the policies. While policies and reforms in the 1960s recognized the influence of structural inequalities and underresourced schools on educational outcomes, more recent reforms operate under very different assumptions. The now dominant reform paradigms—accountability for performance, choice, and governance reform—downplay the influence of these broader societal factors on student achievement, concentrating instead on accountability for performance. Arguing that the increasing diversity of the nation's schools and the limited impact of many current reform strategies on improving equity calls for a new approach to school reform, she lays out an equity perspective on school reform that focuses on schooling conditions and the within school policies and practices that are relevant to facilitating the learning of racially and ethnically diverse students.

There is no doubt that our nation is becoming more diverse. Demographic data on public school enrollment changes indicate that nationwide the proportion of White students in the nation's public school population is declining while non-White enrollment is increasing. In 1960, the percentage of students enrolled in elementary and secondary schools that were White was 86.6% (National Center for Educational Statistics, 2006). By the 2009-10 school year, it was 54.1% (National Center for Educational Statistics, 2011). This trend is projected to continue, with Latinos—already the largest minority group in public schools—increasing at a greater rate than other racial/ethnic groups (Orfield & Lee, 2007). What is less well understood is how demographic changes are transforming suburban school districts, arguably, the frontier of racial and economic change. Frankenberg provides a systematic analysis of racial and socioeconomic change in major metropolitan areas using census data and NCES Common Core of Data on student enrollment. She also uses data from NCES Schools and Staffing Survey (SASS) to assess teacher composition and segregation in suburban schools. She argues that the migration of large numbers of low-income and minority families to the suburbs have made definitions of poverty and racial equity as urban problems obsolete. At the same time, her analysis shows that increasing diversity in suburban schools may be replicating urban patterns of school segregation on a wider geographic scale and that the segregation of students extends to the segregation of students from teachers of different races. She argues that even as suburban schools have become more diverse, the effect of these trends has largely escaped the attention of educational reformers, who remain focused on urban school reform. The richness of the data presented in this chapter illustrates differing patterns of suburban racial change that are important to understand when thinking about equity within the context of diversifying suburban schools.

As our schools become more diverse, the mix of legal and legislative legacies that inform educational policy have promoted a narrow view of how to address social inequality and achieve equitable public education. Recognizing that the nation has long had competing visions of what constitutes equal opportunity, Croninger and Hoyer trace the progression of these legacies from early 20th century attempts at promoting social and political equality within the broader society to the emergence of the education contract in the mid- to late-20th century. Using a social contract perspective, they argue that achieving equity in public education has been hindered by policies and legal decisions that place the primary responsibility for achieving social equality and fairness in our society onto the public school system. At the same time, educational opportunities that are increasingly seen as individual, as opposed to public goods make it more difficult for the courts, governmental agencies or policymakers to claim a compelling interest in creating equitable schools. The consequences of these two trends suggest that the nation will need a broader perspective if educational opportunities are to improve.

The tension between school based and non-school-based remedies for achieving equity is highlighted in Schwartz's chapter. As the U.S. Supreme Court has backed away from using racial classification for achieving equity, reform is less about achieving racial integration, and more about school improvement and improving student achievement. Still, as Schwartz shows, inclusionary housing, which provides access to low-poverty neighborhoods and schools, leads to better educational outcomes than providing additional resources in segregated schools in high poverty neighborhoods. Using data from suburban Montgomery County,

MD, she finds that by the end of elementary school, low-income children who attended the district's low-poverty schools and lived in low-poverty neighborhoods outperformed students who attended less advantaged schools that were provided additional resources. She also tests whether the findings from Montgomery County hold for 11 additional jurisdictions with inclusionary zoning programs. Her findings that inclusionary zoning programs do provide access to low-poverty schools and neighborhoods make it a compelling policy for diversifying suburban communities.

While attention to narrowing the achievement gap dominates the reformers' agenda, most studies on the achievement gap have been based on Black urban and low-income settings. To understand why racial and socioeconomic achievement gaps persist in integrated suburban communities, Sunderman examines race, opportunity, and student achievement in an integrated suburban school district. In a case study of Oak Park, IL, she shows how multiple forms of disadvantage, both inside and outside the schools, shape students' experiences, and access to learning opportunities. Structural inequalities outside the schools, such as persistent income inequalities, extend to institutional patterns within schools that influence how race and income affect access to educational resources and learning opportunities within schools. Exacerbating the failure to adopt strong equity policies was the inability of the community to come together around a common agenda. There was a commitment in principle to the idea of equity, but less commitment to accepting the deeper changes necessary for achieving equity when those goals were seen as competing with parental pressure for demanding and rigorous education.

Foundations often play a crucial role in setting the education policy agenda. They can commit resources and provide proactive thinking to advance an agenda. In a case study of the Ford Foundation's education reform activities designed to improve school finance equity, Bott examines how an external entity can affect funding inequities. Using historical analysis and theories associated with persistent inequity in U.S. school finance, Bott traces the evolution of Ford's strategy from the 1960s into the present. She shows how a strategy that combined litigation with support for social science research, public engagement, and advocacy worked to reduce spending disparities. Ford was most successful early on when public engagement of low-power constituents was a prominent element of the strategy. Long-term sustainability, however, proved vulnerable to powerful political constituencies who, fearing that further reform would harm their constituents, countered Ford's efforts. Nonetheless, Ford achieved a measure of financial equity that endured, suggesting their efforts were more than quixotic tilting.

Test-based accountability has been a primary tool for improving student achievement and reducing racial and socioeconomic achievement gaps since the 1970s. Yet this approach has not been an unqualified success and has resulted in a variety of undesirable side effects. Holcombe, Jennings, and Koretz examine how accountability tests can create the illusion of reduced racial or socioeconomic inequality on state tests when teachers and administrators respond strategically to increase test scores without increasing overall learning. State actors often argue that racial gaps have "closed by half" on state tests, while scores on other assessments such as the National Assessment of Educational Progress remain unchanged. The authors outline a framework of opportunities for score inflation on state tests to explain how these two different stories can arise. Using examples of tests from New York and Massachusetts, they show how these opportunities manifest themselves and discuss the implications of teachers' responses to them for equity.

While all states have emphasized performance-based accountability to reduce academic achievement gaps, fewer states have adopted standards for socioemotional skills education and less attention has been given to narrowing the social skills gaps among diverse racial and socioeconomic status groups. Liu and Lee provide a snapshot of children's social skills developmental trajectories from kindergarten through fifth grade. Using data from the Early Childhood Longitudinal Study, they apply hierarchical linear models to track two sets of social skills—work related skills and interpersonal skills. The study finds significant gaps in work related skills and interpersonal skills based on race and socioeconomic status, suggesting the need for interventions to enhance educational opportunity. To this end, the study provides evidence for the types of parent-child interactions and school-based strategies most suitable for improving the social skills of different racial groups.

There also are dramatic changes underway in the Federal role on increasing access and opportunity for students living in poverty. Acosta, Burch, Good, and Stewart examine the paradoxes of federally funded compensatory policies that incorporate market-based accountability strategies. On the one hand, compensatory policies are intended to redistribute resources to improve the educational opportunities of low-income students. From another perspective, these policies rely on theories of market-based accountability as a central mechanism for improving the quality of education. In this mixed-method, multisite study, the authors consider how the Supplemental Educational Services provisions of the No Child Left Behind Act play out for advancing equity. Drawing on focus group data from students and parents, the chapter provides voice for the perspective of those at the receiving end of the changes, in particular students with disabilities and English language learners. Based on these voices, the authors identify the core issues that policymakers must wrestle with if current forms of privatization are to strengthen ties between parents and schools.

Access to college is a critical barometer for the equitable distribution of opportunities in the U.S. Educators and policymakers have explored a number of strategies to increase access from adopting need-based aid policies to administering precollege outreach programs, mentoring initiatives, and ratcheting up academic expectations. However, the results have been mixed. One approach that has excited educators and policymakers but raised concerns over equity is the adoption of place-based college access strategies. Two approaches—the Kalamazoo Promise and the statewide Michigan College Access Network—offer two separate strategies for leveraging resources to address the postsecondary needs of local communities. Barrett and Holohan-Moyer examine the contours of these place-based college access strategies, compare the features of each, and discuss the implications of local access strategies on the distribution of postsecondary opportunities in the state of Michigan.

What do these chapters suggest for the direction of equity and school reform in a diverse nation? It is hard to argue that current education reform policies are up to the task of addressing either the inequities in American education or the growing diversity of the country. Current reforms, if they work at all, merely tinker at the edges of equity, more often benefiting the majority population than the disadvantaged they purport to serve (Glass, 2008). Since inequities in education tend to mirror the inequalities in the larger society, efforts at addressing these broader societal issues will need to be incorporated into the political discourse on education reform. The authors identify policies and reforms that can advance an equity agenda in a diverse nation while also showing the shortcomings of many current reforms. At the same time, they acknowledge the broader challenge of developing the leadership and commitment that is required to confront the growing diversity of the nation's schools.

REFERENCES

Berube, A., & Kneebone, E. (2006). *Two steps back: City and suburban poverty trend 1999-2005*. Washington, DC: The Brooking Institution Center on Urban & Metropolitan Policy.

Glass, G. V. (2008). *Fertilizers, pills, and magnetic strips: The fate of public education in America*. Charlotte, NC: Information Age.

Lee, J., & Reeves, T. (2012). Revisiting the impact of NCLB high-stakes school accountability, capacity, and resources: State NAEP 1990-2009 reading and math achievement gaps and trends. *Educational Evaluation and Policy Analysis, 34*(2), 209-231.

Metropolitan Policy Program at Brookings. (2012). *State of metropolitan America: On the front lines of demographic transformation.* Washington, DC: The Brookings Institution.

National Center for Educational Statistics. (2006). Digest of education statistics, 2006. Retrieved February 14, 2008, from http://nces.ed.gov/programs/digest/ d06/table/dt06_040asp

National Center for Educational Statistics. (2011). Digest of education statistics, 2011. Retrieved from http://nces.ed.gov/programs/digest/d11/tables/ dt11_044.asp

National Research Council. (2011). *Incentives and test-based accountability in education.* Washington, DC: The National Academies Press.

Orfield, G., & Frankenberg, E. (2008). *The last have become first: Rural and small town America lead the way on desegregation.* Los Angeles, CA: The Civil Rights Project, UCLA.

Orfield, G., & Lee, C. (2007). *Historic reversals, accelerating resegregation, and the need for new integration strategies.* Los Angeles, CA: The Civil Rights Project, UCLA.

Reardon, S. F. (2011). The widening academic achievement gap between the rich and the poor: New evidence and possible explanations. In G. J. Duncan & R. J. Murnane (Eds.), *Whither opportunity? Rising inequality, schools, and children's life chances* (91-115). New York, NY: Russell Sage Foundation.

PART I

CONCEPTIONS OF EQUITY

CHAPTER 1

EDUCATIONAL EQUITY AND REFORM

Have We Achieved Our Goals?

Gail L. Sunderman

Reform is a staple of our public schools. The later half of the 20th century saw an array of reforms designed to improve the educational system and achieve other, often ideological, goals. Equity is often a stated aim of these reforms, but how equity is defined and the goals that policy aim to achieve in the name of equity has evolved. This chapter examines that evolution while making the argument that if schools are to improve, it will be necessary to focus more than is often the case on improving those within school policies and practices that are particularly relevant to facilitating the learning of racially and ethnically diverse students.

EVOLUTION OF EQUITY IN FEDERAL EDUCATION POLICY

Two important pieces of federal legislation—the 1965 Elementary and Secondary Education Act (ESEA) and the related 1964 Civil Rights Act—forced the opening of schools to previously excluded groups of students and provided additional resources to schools to improve the educational

Charting Reform, Achieving Equity in a Diverse Nation
pp. 3–25
Copyright © 2013 by Information Age Publishing

opportunities of underserved students. Title I of ESEA has been the primary federal education program designed to assist educationally and economically disadvantaged students. Since its inception in 1965, Title I
targeted additional resources to high poverty schools with the express
purpose of reducing the disparities in educational achievement between
at-risk students and their more advantaged peers.

During this period, the phrase "equal educational opportunity" was
adopted as the keystone of federal educational policy and there was the
recognition that the public schools played an important role in the education of low-income and minority students (Graham, 1993). These reforms
were based on assumptions that structural inequalities, resulting from
racial discrimination, underresourced schools, and the racial isolation of
Black students in urban schools, contributed to the poor educational outcomes of a particular group of people (Kaestle & Smith, 1982; Kantor,
1991; Thomas, 1983). There was the recognition that differences between
the educational experiences of minority urban students and their White
counterparts derived from very different schooling conditions available to
students—inequalities in resources and racial isolation of Black students
in urban schools (Council of Economic Advisors, 1964; Harrington,
1962).

Subsequent reauthorizations of ESEA sustained a focus on achieving
equity, albeit under different assumptions. The 1994 Improving America's Schools Act was notable for mandating that challenging standards
apply to all students, including those receiving Title I services. States were
required to develop content and performance standards, adopt annual
assessments that measured student progress against those standards, and
hold schools accountable for the achievement of all students. The basic
idea behind the standards movement was that structural factors mattered
far less than systemic school reform that would bring about instructional
change at the classroom level (Smith & O'Day, 1993). Performance-based
accountability was seen as the linchpin for insuring the quality of public
education and achieving equity. When Congress passed the No Child Left
Behind Act of 2001 (NCLB), both parties agreed to continue along the
path of performance-based reform and accountability for student achievement. There was general agreement on the principle of racial and ethnic
equity and support for subgroup accountability as a means to achieve that
goal. NCLB raised the expectations and goals of Title I policy by empha-
sizing equal educational outcomes, regardless of differences in students'
backgrounds. Indeed, an important goal of NCLB was to close "the
achievement gap between high- and low-performing children, especially
gaps between minority and nonminority students, and between disadvantaged children and their more advantaged peers" (P. L. 107-110, Sec.
1001, (3)).

NCLB and the accountability systems that preceded it are driven by performance on standardized achievement test tied to incentives and sanctions. Under this regime, state and federal accountability systems hold a tight grip over schools and teachers through the emphasis on test-based accountability tied to quotas—in this case, reaching a certain percentage of students scoring at a predefined cut off score on standardized tests. For the most part, outcome-based accountability systems do not pay attention to so-called opportunity to learn standards and do not incorporate indicators of schooling conditions when calculating school performance. Instead, incentives place responsibility for improving school performance on teachers and administrators. At the same time, they incorporate differential goal setting as a mechanism for improving schools, with higher growth demands placed on lower performing schools (Mintrop, 2004a).

Ten years after the passage of NCLB, the nation is embarking on another set of reform elements—still within the performance-based accountability framework—where educator evaluation systems will drive the system. Driven in part by the failures of NCLB to achieve its stated goals of 100% proficiency by 2014 and closing the achievement gap (Lee & Reeves, 2012), dysfunctionalities in the system (Mintrop & Sunderman, 2013) and political intransigence when it came to reauthorization of ESEA, these new initiatives share many common elements.

Beginning with the American Recovery and Reinvestment Act of 2009, the Obama Administration articulated its vision and approach for reforming America's schools (U.S. Department of Education, 2010a). This vision evolved to include developing college and career-ready standards for all students, establishing longitudinal data systems to track every student's progress, improving teacher and principal effectiveness, and turning around the lowest performing schools. The Administration used competitive grants to leverage state education agencies to adopt the federal priorities. With slight variations, the Administration's three grant competitions, including the Race to the Top grant competition in January 2010, followed by the School Improvement Grants (SIG) in November 2010, and the ESEA Flexibility waiver requests in September 2011, reinforced the key elements of its approach to school reform (U.S. Department of Education, 2009, 2010b, 2011). States that applied for and could demonstrate their commitment to the federal priorities were provided federal funds. Even though it is not clear if this package of initiatives will survive state-level or congressional politics, it does suggests that the nation has entered a new phase of performance-based accountability.

While equity goals figure prominently in the Administration's rhetoric, the outcomes of the Administration's policy on equity are less clear. Support for subgroup accountability as a means to achieve broad-based equity has been replaced with an intense focus on the bottom 5% of the neediest schools. States will no longer be required to disaggregate test-score data by subgroups, lessening the pressure on racially diverse schools to address disparities in student outcomes. Investment in support and intervention will be concentrated on the bottom 5% of the neediest schools, which must adopt federally mandated interventions.[1] While it may make sense to concentration on the lowest performing schools given the states' limited intervention capacity (Mintrop, 2004b; Sunderman & Orfield, 2006), this approach forces unproven intervention strategies on the nation's most vulnerable students. The other key component, which seems to have bipartisan support, is to shift from holding schools (except for the lowest performing) accountable to holding individual educators (teachers and principals) accountable based on data on student growth on standardized tests and measures of professional practice. This approach shifts accountability back to local administrators, who must evaluate teachers, but makes no new investments in capacity and uses a metric—standardized test scores—prone to error and other problems (Baker et al., 2010; Kelly, 2011). At this point, we can only speculate on how the combined approach of holding educators accountable and concentrating a prescribed set of interventions on the lowest performing schools will work to advance equity goals. However, the preponderance of research offers little support for the efficacy of these approaches and considerable evidence to suggest they are dubious at best, particularly for achieving equity.

THE DEMISE OF INTEGRATION STRATEGIES

As the population has become more diverse, public schools have become more separated by race and ethnicity (Orfield & Lee, 2007). This increasing racial isolation has corresponded to significant increases in Black-White and Latino-White test score gaps (Berends & Penaloaz, 2010; Lee, 2002, 2008). While scholars agree that integrated schools helped to raise the educational opportunities of both Black and White students and increased interracial contact (Frankenberg & Orfield, 2007; Mickelson, 2003; Mickelson & Bottia, 2010), the tools available to school districts to promote integrated schools have been sharply curtailed. The courts have retreated from addressing racial segregation and inequality (Boger & Orfield, 2005; Orfield & Eaton, 1996), beginning with the decision that confined remedies to individual school districts (rather than allow cross-district plans) in 1974[2] and then to rejecting the use of racial classifications, even in voluntary integration plans 30 years later[3] (Frankenberg, 2008; Minow, 2010; Orfield & Lee, 2007). As Minow (2010) has argued,

Neither legitimacy nor efficacy concerns explain the Court's rejection of voluntary desegregation plans, enacted by school boards fully subject to the approval and disapproval of their electorates. Instead, the rejection of these voluntary plans seems part of an abstract political project to equate equal protection with colorblindness and to terminate affirmation action. The result favors White anxieties in an increasingly multiracial nation. (p. 30)

Colorblind policies, which emphasize treating everyone as individuals rather than recognizing and valuing the different perspectives and resources that people from different backgrounds bring (Steele, 2010), ignore how highly segregated schools and broader societal inequities impact learning. Lin and Harris (2008) argue that the effects of poverty and segregation on student learning outcomes derive less from any one source, but from the cumulative process where "any type of disadvantage makes one vulnerable to other disadvantages. Conversely, advantages insulate, allowing those with fewer vulnerabilities to buffer themselves from cascading disadvantage" (Lin & Harris, 2008). Likewise, in a review of the effects of neighborhoods on the education of African Americans, Johnson (2012) suggests that higher resourced and integrated areas better explain the educational trajectory of poor African American children than the influence of particular neighborhood conditions (Johnson, 2010). Johnson concludes that the most important measures for estimating the differences in educational attainment between the most and least advantaged areas are resources rather than poverty (p. 567). In other words, it is the advantages that better resourced communities provide that matter most.

While integrated schools provide the foundation for equity, other issues factor into achieving better outcomes for minority students. Diamond (2006) argues that racial achievement gaps in integrated suburban school districts persist because of racial inequality on structural, institutional, and symbolic levels. "Limited school integration in an unequal society, has not, in and of itself, meant higher educational achievement for Black students" (Diamond, 2006, p. 501). While desegregation may be associated with some modest achievement gains for Black students, with no negative impact on White achievement, and more tolerant racial attitudes, "integrated schools (to the extent that they have existed) have failed to created equal opportunity for all students, in part, because racial inequality in the society as a whole or within the schools, in numerous cases, has not been directly confronted" (p. 502).

Even as scholars continue to unpack the influence of structural, institutional, and symbolic mechanisms on the achievement of minority students, education policy has retreated from acknowledging their role. Instead, reformers focus on improving schools for minority students apart from addressing other sources of inequities, even though this strategy has yielded little in way of school improvement for impoverished schools serving minority students (Berends & Penaloaz, 2010; Lee, 2007; Lee & Reeves, 2012; Natriello, McDill, & Pallas, 1990). The idea, most forcibly articulated by the *all students can learn* formula, is that with additional funding tied to clearly articulated performance standards that are the same for all students, schools can ameliorate disadvantages attributable to social isolation and poverty (Orfield & Eaton, 1996). These ideas were visible in the Obama Administration initiatives, which provided school improvement grants (of considerable amounts) to the lowest performing schools to support the implementation of federally prescribe intervention models.

APPROACHES TO SCHOOL REFORM AND IMPLICATIONS FOR EQUITY

Since the 1990s, the dominant reform paradigm has been accountability systems driven by performance monitoring and assessments, measurable goals, incentives, and consequences for low performance. These systems are based on assumptions that recalcitrant local actors often block reform and the lack of motivation on the part of employees is responsible for poor performance and that the provision of performance information (i.e., test score data), clear goals, rewards and sanctions would lead educators to search for new ways of improving performance (Fuhrman, 1999). These policies also assumed that by centralizing rules and educational policy, institutions, and practice could be rapidly changed to accommodate new requirements (Mintrop & Sunderman, in press). While the primary unit of accountability targeted for reform has changed—NCLB incentivized schools as the unit of change and the Obama Administration policies incentivized educators—the underlying assumptions remained the same. This framework emphasized the importance of teachers' instructional skills, principal leadership, and the implementation of a predetermined set of comprehensive instructional reforms over other approaches. The importance of evidence-based instruction, improving teaching through professional development, and engaging in data-driven decision making, most often focused on test scores on standardized achievement tests, are key reform strategies.

Also prevalent are strategies to change the governance of the public schools through public school choice, charters, vouchers, or site-based governance. These policies are framed in the language of equity and equality and promised to open new avenues for students of different races and income levels to mix. For example, charter schools were sold as a way to improve and expand the schooling options of disadvantaged students and, as such, have been limited to underperforming urban areas. However, as charters have become more established and charter interests gained influence, charter operators are beginning to market in areas where schools are generally successful (suburban communities) as a means to increase market share. Charters often engender strong opposition as suburban communities—happy with their public schools—question the rationale for charter schools in their communities (Hu, 2011; Mooney, 2011).

Evidence has accumulated that accountability and choice reforms have had little impact on improving educational equity. As already noted, standards-based and accountability policies have failed to achieve their stated goal of eliminating the achievement gap. While scores on most state tests tended to rise under NCLB[4] (Center on Education Policy, 2008, 2011; Lee, 2006), these gains were not confirmed by gains on low-stakes tests such as the National Assessment of Educational Progress. National Assessment of Educational Progress scores demonstrated that the achievement gap, some modest improvements in achievement notwithstanding, remained (Hanushek & Raymond, 2005; Lee, 2006, 2007, 2008; Lee & Reeves, 2012; National Research Council, 2011). Research also suggests that improving average achievement as well as narrowing the achievement gap was associated with long-term statewide instructional capacity and teacher resources rather than fidelity of NCLB policy implementation, the rigor of performance standards, or state data-tracking capacity (Lee & Reeves, 2012).

The promise that choice would foster integration has resulted in charter schools that are more racially and economically segregated than their respective districts (Frankenberg, Siegel-Hawley, & Wang, 2011; Miron, Urschel, Mathis, & Tornquist, 2010), and evidence that school choice, either vouchers or charter schools, has improved student achievement or resulted in school improvement is mixed, depending on data sources, research design (e.g., lack of adequate controls), and statistical controls used. However, for the most part, charter schools perform no better than public schools (Bettinger, 2005; Center for Research on Education Outcomes, 2009; Zimmer et al., 2009). Finally, the focus on "all students can learn" can mask enduring racial and economic inequalities and move responsibilities for inequities from the state to the individual.

Other reforms emphasize the importance of local control and the governance of schools by locally elected boards or mayors. Proponents of these reforms argue that mayoral control promotes efficiency, comprehensive rationality, accountability, and democratic participation and that it can create the institutional pressure and support necessary to promote academic improvement systemwide (Wong, Shen, Anagnostopoulos, & Rutledge, 2007). Wong et al. (2007) contend that mayoral control is a means to integrate school governance with city government and is characterized by a strong political will to improve the operations of the city's school system through partnerships between city hall, the schools, teachers' unions, and civic groups dedicated to systemwide improvements. The impact of mayoral control on educational issues varies widely, depending on local context, capacity constraints, and political will of mayors. Mayors have been most successful at improving the fiscal management and stability of schools districts by using their power to address fiscal crises, launch capital improvement efforts, and if they choose, buying labor peace through favorable labor contracts (Wong et al., 2007). Mayoral control also brought greater emphasis on district wide standards tied to outcome-based accountability policies that placed low-performing schools under district intervention.

Who benefits and who loses from the direction of current reform? The effect of these policies has been to shift power upward and responsibility downward. NCLB altered the distribution of power among federal, state, and local officials by expanding federal power to regulate education (Sunderman & Kim, 2007). The increased federal role in education strengthened state education agencies as regulatory and monitoring agencies, resulting in greater bureaucratization of the educational system rather than greater centralization where an organizational center dominates the system (Meyer, Scott, Strang, & Creighton, 1994; Rowan, 1990). In this system, the federal government has become an important arbitrator in establishing the contours of the educational debate and setting national educational policy priorities. The Obama Administration has taken this a step further by requiring that states meet certain requirements in order to win funding. By using a competitive grant process, the Administration bypasses Congress and promotes its policy priorities without following the usual policy process. This strategy has been very effective during a time of budget shortfalls at enticing states to adopt the Administration's priorities, as evidence by the almost universal adoption of the Common Core State Standards and moves to join regional assessment consortiums to develop common assessments. At the same time, the use of competitive grants raises questions about equity and whether this process gives some states advantages over others and undermines an equitable system for the distribution of funds.

RETHINKING EDUCATIONAL EQUITY IN A DIVERSE NATION[5]

The increasing diversity of our schools[6] and the limited impact of many current reform strategies and policies on improving outcomes for diverse students suggest a need to rethink educational equity and how to achieve it. Defining the goal as equity, as opposed to equality as is often the case, offers a way to identify specific factors that contribute to unequal outcomes. Equality refers to equal opportunities or, sometimes, equal outcomes. It may also mean comparability in funding where schools receive equal resources. In contrast, the term equity refers to perceptions of fairness and is often used to describe fair treatment when the application of rules is involved (e.g., due process in disciplinary actions). Equity also relates to the distribution of resources needed to address issues of inequality, such as unequal student outcomes. However, the elimination of differences in outcomes may require unequal allocation of resources. In this context, "equity" means the allocation of resources based on the need to achieve a measure of equality. This is most readily seen in cases involving students with disabilities, but also in cases involving low-income and minority students. Inevitably, achieving equity is difficult because of limited resources and the uncertainty of the effects of different remedies to address the academic and developmental needs of students. It can also engender political opposition when it is viewed as taking resources from one group of students to benefit another.

An equity perspective on school reform would also focus more than is often the case on schooling conditions and the within school policies and practices that facilitate the learning of racially and ethnically diverse students (Hawley & James, 2012; Hawley & Skyes, 2007; Sunderman, Hawley, Brown, Hicks, & Kirton, 2011). While it may seem obvious that schooling conditions matter, the search for school improvement strategies gives inadequate attention to that reality. For example, the focus on measuring teacher effectiveness and holding teachers accountable virtually ignores the fact that schooling conditions, particularly factors such as schedules, materials, students, institutional incursions into the classroom, and a range of reforms that teachers must accommodate, influence teaching quality (Kennedy, 2010). Another common strategy for addressing diversity is to improve teaching through professional development. While the quality of teaching students receive is an important indicator of student learning, professional development that targets improving the teaching of diverse students quite often focuses on teacher beliefs rather than pedagogical skills. And, even when teaching strategies are dealt with and designed for meeting the needs of racially and ethnically diverse students, this is seldom integral to efforts to improve the teaching of core academic subjects.

Two other frequently heard remedies for reducing racial and ethnic achievement gaps are "strong leadership" and an inclusive school culture. Nevertheless, neither of these provides much guidance for programmatic school improvement. Effective leadership is usually described in terms of heroic personal attributes—charismatic, committed, intolerant of failure, inspirational, and indefatigable. The complexity of school culture is often reduced to "high expectations." Other approaches to equity analysis frequently focus on a narrow set of resources—such as the allocation of teacher expertise and financial resources (Odden, 2003; Sklar, McKenzie, & Scheurich, 2009) or the characteristics of effective schools in which race and ethnicity are not usually implicated (Bryk, Sebring, Allensworth, Luppescu, & Easton, 2010; Murphy, 2010; Scott, 2009). These approaches do not examine many of the other school sources of inequities and differences in opportunities to learn such as access to and support for success with rigorous curriculum, fair and sensible disciplinary practices, and grouping for instruction, among others.

An equity approach to school reform would focus on those within school policies and practices that maximize learning opportunities for all students, but are particularly important for enhancing the learning of diverse students (Hawley & James, 2012). In laying out an equity agenda for school reform, this chapter identifies those factors that will increase access to learning opportunities and that address barriers which remove students from classrooms. This approach incorporates empirical evidence on sources of inequities and uses data on things that schools and districts can do.

Access to Multiple Forms of Disaggregated Data

While collecting and analyzing student test score data and dropout rates are commonplace, there is much less data collected on differences in opportunities to learn such as grouping practices, enrollment in different curricular programming, attendance, and discipline. Data on these areas are needed to make problem solving possible and engage educators in issues related to race. Disaggregated student data has raised awareness of disparities in student outcomes based on race, but it needs to be much more detailed because there are large differences in performance within subgroup categories such as Latino and Asian. Providing access to disaggregated data, both by subgroup and within subgroups, on a variety of indicators is critical if inequities related to race are to be addressed.

Access to Quality Teachers and Teaching

The single most important school-based influence on student learning is the quality of teaching that students experience (Darling-Hammond, 2000; Darling-Hammond & Youngs, 2002; Goe, 2007; Rice, 2003; Wayne & Youngs, 2003). At the same time, there is substantial evidence that access to quality teaching varies by the racial and socioeconomic composition of schools (Boyd, Lankford, Loeb, Rockoff, & Wyckoff, 2008; Lankford, Loeb, & Wyckoff, 2002; Marvel, Lyter, Peltola, Strizek, & Morton, 2007; Scafidi, Sjoquist, & Stinebrickner, 2008). Closely related are teacher attrition and the constant "churn" of faculty, which make it difficult to develop programmatic coherence and productive school environments. Since teacher turnover is much higher in schools serving non-White and students from low-income families (Barton & Coley, 2009), schools and districts need to pay attention to both developing the professional expertise of their teachers and turnover if they are to achieve equity in access to quality teaching.

Equally important to access to quality teaching is the relevance of the professional development teachers receive to the teaching of diverse students. Most often, professional development that targets improving the teaching of diverse students focuses on teachers' cultural awareness and dispositions, rather than on pedagogical skills. To narrow the achievement gap requires that schools and districts ensure that teachers have skills and knowledge that are particularly relevant to their students' racial, ethnic, cultural, and linguistic diversity (Gay, 2010). This includes providing professional development that helps teachers incorporate culturally responsive pedagogical skills and knowledge, including those that are content specific, into their teaching practice. It also means developing teachers' abilities to build productive interpersonal relationships across student subgroups, which are essential to student motivation.

Access to Rigorous Curricula and the Provision of Adequate Support

Students from low-income families are more likely to get a larger proportion of their learning opportunities from school than students from higher income homes (Raudenbush, 2008). In addition, English language learners are heavily dependent on schools for their academic learning opportunities. However, for a host of reasons—some the consequences of well-meaning instructional practices that effectively dumb-down the curriculum, some related to biases and misconceptions, and some because students are sometimes reluctant to seek rigorous curricula—students of color are often less likely than White students and many Asian-descent students to be engaged in rigorous coursework.

Among the issues here is how students are selected for gifted and talented programs, honors courses, or Advanced Placement courses (Barton & Coley, 2009; Payne, 2011) as well as access to mathematics (Gamoran & Hannigan, 2000). Insuring access to rigorous courses requires reviewing referral processes and assessment practices used to identify and place students in rigorous courses and adopting measures that develop the talents of potentially gifted students from an early age by providing them with additional enrichment and quality instruction (Payne, 2011).

Many students need additional support to succeed. Schools that successfully address the needs of struggling students have a well-defined and ongoing process for identifying those at risk of academic failure. To support students who struggle, schools must recognize factors that place students at serious risk for academic failure. Students are at risk for academic failure when they are achieving at least one grade level below in math or reading; failing or at risk of failing one or more courses in middle or high school; and they are reporting low attendance rates and/or demonstrating behavior problems (Balfanz, Herzog, & Mac Iver, 2007). Closely monitoring those indicators allow schools to intervene early, before it is too late. Second, schools need to put in place supports that address the needs of struggling students. Ambitious programs have the following characteristics: sufficient monitoring of students to identify and support those who are struggling; in-school supports that are evidence-based and well implemented to meet the needs of struggling students; and out of school (after school and summer) programming of sufficient intensity and duration to enable struggling students to advance academically.

Reducing Policies and Practices That Remove Students From Classrooms

Policies and practices affecting access to a rigorous curriculum that get less attention include misassignment to special education, retention strategies, and how students are grouped for instruction within classrooms.

Historically, students who are not representative of the majority culture of a school have been overidentified and placed in special education classrooms (Losen & Orfield, 2002; U.S. Department of Education Office of Special Education and Rehabilitative Services Office of Special Education Services, 2006). Reasons for this include: (1) inadequate classroom instruction prior to referral to special education; (2) inconsistent, vague, or arbitrary assessment and placement policies and processes; and (3) the lack of effective schooling options (Harry & Klingner, 2006). The complexity of the reasons for disproportionality in special education suggests the need for multifaceted and comprehensive approaches to identification and intervention, including ongoing examination and interpretation of data, prevention and early intervention, and attending to educational inequities (Artiles, Klingner, & Tate, 2006; Skiba et al., 2008).

Minority and low-income students are more likely to be retained than their White and more affluent peers (Texas Education Agency, 1996). Retaining students in grade as a method of remediating poor academic performance has become increasingly popular with the emphasis on standards, testing for promotion, and accountability. Nonetheless, research has consistently shown that retention has a negative impact on achievement and socioemotional adjustment and that it does not help students "catch up" (Jimerson, 2001). There is also a relationship between retention and dropping out: students who are retained in elementary grades have a higher probability of dropping out of high school (Balfanz, et al., 2007; Ou & Reynolds, 2010). Since there are multiple factors that influence a student's poor achievement, simply having a student repeat a grade is unlikely to address all of them.

One of the more common ways that students experience different levels of academic rigor is that they are tracked and grouped by "ability" (students are invariably grouped by prior achievement, not ability). Grouping is a common and often necessary practice. How it is done—whether it is targeted to specific goals with progress assessed continuously and whether students are held to high standards of performance—is key to student success. Research is clear that tracking (formal or informal) and inflexible ability grouping disadvantages most students (Hawley, 2007). On the other hand, there is persuasive evidence that very high achieving students can benefit from learning in academically homogeneous groups. The resolution of this conundrum resides in flexibility and teacher expertise in managing the instruction of diverse students.

Managing Disruptive Behavior

Student motivation and opportunities to learn are affected by how teachers and administrators manage disorderly and disruptive behavior (Gregory, Skiba, & Noguera, 2010). Students of color are much more likely than their White peers to be disciplined (Gay, 2006; Losen & Gillespie, 2012; Skiba et al., 2011; Skiba, Michael, Nardo, & Peterson, 2002). Students of color may be more distrustful of authority and respond defensively to criticism and disciplinary action (Carter, 2008; Cohen, 2008; Noguera, 2008). Many disciplinary practices effectively reduce student-learning time and this is especially true of suspension. Providing well-understood processes to adjudicate school rules, identifying perceived inequities and interpersonal conflict, and ensuring that disciplinary policies and practices remove students from learning opportunities only as a last resort are essential to managing student behavior. Tracking discipline data can help ensure that minority and special education students are not disproportionally affected by disciplinary measures.

Many districts have adopted zero tolerance policies, which rely on punishment and security measures to deter unwanted behavior. However, these policies tend to increase student suspension and expulsion rates, often for behaviors that are not severe, even trivial, such as disrespect, attendance problems, and classroom disruption (Wald & Losen, 2003). They disproportionally affect minority students (Skiba et al., 2011) and are not very effective at creating safe school environments or reducing misbehavior (American Psychological Association Zero Tolerance Task Force, 2008). Schools need to consider replacing these policies with policies and programs that emphasize prevention and encourage the development of appropriate behaviors.

Policies and Practices That Foster an Inclusive School Environment

Student connectedness to school and a positive school climate have been identified as two factors that support academic performance and behavior (Weiss, Cunningham, Lewis, & Clark, 2005). Students who feel connected to the school are more likely to attend school regularly, stay in school, and have higher school grades and test scores (U.S. Department of Health and Human Services Division of Adolescent and School Health, 2009). Student disengagement is linked to limited student involvement in the school, few leadership opportunities, and little or no recognition of student accomplishments. For example, school policies, practices, or traditions may inadvertently impose requirements that limit the number of students who can compete for elected positions or serve in leadership positions. This can result in decreased levels of student connectedness and negatively impact school climate (McNeely, Noonemaker, & Blium, 2002)

Schools that provide opportunities for student leadership and recognize student contributions to the school enhance school connectedness. Schools in which student leadership is valued and cultivated by the staff are more likely to have a climate that is conducive to student leadership and learning. Celebrating student contributions to the school on a regular basis provides numerous opportunities for recognition by the staff and peers and reinforces school connectedness.

Fostering Racial and Socioeconomic Integration

Social science research and experiences of school districts suggest that students—White and non-White students alike—benefit from being in racially diverse schools and classrooms (Brief of 553 Social Scientists as

Amici Curiae in Support of Respondents, Parents Involved in Cmty, Sch. v. Seattle Sch. Dist. No. 1, 127 S. Ct., 2007; Mickelson & Bottia, 2010).[7] They develop dispositions and skills that will help them learn from and work with people who are different from them. These proficiencies have social, economic, and political benefits for individuals and for society in our increasingly diverse nation. Research also shows that school integration has a positive effect on the academic performance of students of color, with no negative effects on White students (Mickelson & Bottia, 2010). Promoting integrated schooling is a challenge in the wake of Supreme Court decisions overturning the use of race in student assignment plans. But there are approaches that districts and schools can legally do to promote racial diversity and address racial isolation in the public schools (NAACP Legal Defense and Educational Fund, 2008; Tefera, Frankenberg, Siegel-Hawley, & Chirichigno, 2011).

It has long been known that an individual's poverty level has a detrimental impact on academic achievement. Indeed, recent research finds a widening achievement gap between high- and low-income students (Reardon, 2011). However, less widely acknowledged is that high levels of poverty schoolwide—or concentrated poverty—create additional educational challenges for the systems and students they serve. Research shows that tests scores for all students, both poor and nonpoor, decline as school level poverty increases. The U.S. Department of Education's report on Title I (Puma, Jones, Rock, & Fernandez, 1993) found a "tipping point" where school poverty negatively effects student performance. "School poverty depresses scores of all students in schools where at least half the children are eligible for subsidized lunch and seriously depresses the scores when more the 75% of students live in low-income households" (Puma, et al., 1993). This suggests that schools and districts should focus not just on educational improvements (such as improving teachers' skills) but also on alleviating the concentration of students by poverty.

There are a number of reasons that concentrated poverty puts the school and or system at a disadvantage. Most systems with high levels of poverty do not have the resources needed to overcome the effects of poverty. Also important is the ability of a district to attract middle class students. Once poor students become a majority, middle class families find the schools less attractive and usually leave. Thus, it is important that rapidly diversifying districts, many of which are in the suburbs, pay attention to how low-income students are distributed across the system.

Racially and socially integrated schools foster greater achievement in a number of ways. Better-qualified teachers are more likely to teach in integrated schools than they are in segregated minority schools or those with concentrated poverty. Students benefit from interactions with peers, both through exposure to values, beliefs, and behaviors that are conducive to academic achievement and by exposure to differences in how people think, solve problems, and interact. For example, research suggests that diverse groups of problem solvers consistently outperform homogeneous groups.

CONCLUSION

Attending to the factors outlined above provide a counternarrative to the predominance of accountability and choice approaches to school reform. They incorporate some important components of current federal education policy—the need to use data to make decisions and the emphasis on improving the outcomes of low-performing students—but go further by focusing on within-school policies and practices that can enhance the learning of racially diverse students. More so than current policies and reforms, they identify research-based sources of inequities that contribute to unequal outcomes. By recognizing the diversity that students bring to school, we can begin to identify and address the school policies and practices that will improve the learning of all students.

Furthering an equity agenda based on these premises will not be easy since they compete for attention and resources with the accountability agenda now dominate. However, by continuing to implement policies and practices that are ineffective, have resulted in a number of unintended and negative consequences, and are unsupported by research evidence we risk perpetuating the current inequalities.

NOTES

1. There are four intervention models: (1) *Turnaround* model where the (local education agency) LEA replaces the principal, rehires no more than 50% of the staff, and gives the principal greater autonomy to implement other prescribed and recommended strategies; (2) *Restart* model where the LEA converts or closes and reopens a school under a charter school operator, charter management organization, or education management organization; (3) *School closure* model where the LEA closes the schools and enrolls students in other schools in the LEA that are higher achieving; (4) *Transformation* model where the LEA replaces the principal, implements a rigorous staff evaluation and development system, institutes comprehensive instructional reform, increases learning time and applies community-oriented school strategies, and provides greater operational flexibility and support for the school (U.S. Department of Education, 2010b).

2. In *Milliken v. Bradley* in 1974, the Supreme Court limited desegregation orders to district boundaries and forbade the inclusion of suburbs in plans to rectify urban segregation.

3. The 2007 Supreme Court decision in *Parents Involved in Community Schools v. Seattle School District No. 1* and *Meredith v. Jefferson County Board of Education* prohibited the use of individual student assignment by race to ensure racial balance in voluntary desegregation plans.

4. For an analysis of the sources of score inflation on state tests, see Holcombe, Jennings, and Koretz in this volume.

5. This section draws from the Equity Planning Tool (http://maec.ceee.gwu.edu/ept/), Sunderman et al. (2011), and Hawley and James (2012).

6. For an analysis of the increasing racial diversity of suburban schools, see Frankenberg in this volume.

7. See also, Schwartz on inclusionary zoning policies in this volume.

REFERENCES

American Psychological Association Zero Tolerance Task Force. (2008). Are zero tolerance policies effective in the schools? *American Psychologist, 63*(9), 852-862.

Artiles, A. J., Klingner, J. K., & Tate, W. F. (2006). Representation of minority students in special education: Complicating traditional explanations. *Educational Researcher, 35*(6), 3-5.

Baker, E. L., Barton, P. E., Darling-Hammond, L., Haertel, E. H., Ladd, H. F., Linn, R. L., et al. (2010). *Problems with the use of student test scores to evaluate teachers*. Washington, DC: Economic Policy Institute.

Balfanz, R., Herzog, L., & Mac Iver, D. J. (2007). Preventing student disengagement and keeping students on the graduation path in urban middle-grades schools: Early identification and effective interventions. *Educational Psychologist, 42*(4), 223-235.

Barton, P., & Coley, R. (2009). *Parsing the achievement gap II*. Princeton, NJ: The Educational Testing Service.

Berends, M., & Penaloaz, R. (2010). Increasing racial isolation and test score gaps in mathematics: A 30-year perspective. *Teachers College Record, 112*(4), 978-1007.

Bettinger, E. P. (2005). The effect of charter schools on charter students and public schools. *Economics of Education Review, 24*(2), 133-147.

Boger, J. C., & Orfield, G. (2005). *School resegregation: Must the south turn back?* Chapel Hill, NC: The University of North Carolina Press.

Boyd, D., Lankford, H., Loeb, S., Rockoff, J., & Wyckoff, J. (2008). The narrowing gap in New York City teacher qualifications and its implications for student achievement in high-poverty schools. *Journal of Policy Analysis and Management, 27*(4), 793-818.

Brief of 553 Social Scientists as Amici Curiae in Support of Respondents, Parents Involved in Cmty, Sch. v. Seattle Sch. Dist. No. 1, 127 S. Ct., Nos. 05-908, 05-915, 2006, WL 2927079(2007).

Bryk, A. S., Sebring, P., Allensworth, E., Luppescu, S., & Easton, J. Q. (2010). *Organizing schools for improvement: Lessons from Chicago*. Chicago, IL: University of Chicago Press.

Carter, P. (2008). Teaching students fluency in multiple cultural codes. In M. Pollock (Ed.), *Everyday antiracism: Getting real about race in school*. (pp. 107-111). New York, NY: The New Press.

Center for Research on Education Outcomes. (2009). *Multiple choice: Charter school performance in 16 states*. Stanford, CA: Stanford University.

Center on Education Policy. (2008). *Has student achievement increased since 2002? State test score trends through 2006-07*. Washington, DC: Author.

Center on Education Policy. (2011). *State test score trends through 2008-09, Part 4: Is achievement improving and are gaps narrowing for TItle I students?* Washington, DC: Author.

Cohen, G. (2008). Providing supportive feedback. In M. Pollock (Ed.), *Everyday antiracism: Getting real about race in school* (pp. 78-81). New York, NY: The New Press.

Council of Economic Advisors. (1964). *The annual report of the Council of Economic Advisors*. Washington, DC: U.S. Government Printing Office.

Darling-Hammond, L. (2000). Teacher quality and student achievement: A review of state policy evidence. *Education Policy Analysis Archives, 8*(1). Retrieved from http://epaa.asu.edu/epaa/v8n1

Darling-Hammond, L., & Youngs, P. (2002). Defining "highly qualified teachers": What does "scientifically-based research" actually tell us? *Educational Researcher, 31*(9), 13-25.

Diamond, J. B. (2006). Still separate and unequal: Examining race, opportunity, and school achievement in "integrated" suburbs. *Journal of Negro Education, 75*(3), 495-505.

Frankenberg, E. (2008). School segregation, desegregation, and integration: What do these terms mean in a post-Parents Involved in Community Schools, racially transitioning society? *Seattle Journal for Social Justice, 6*(2), 533-590.

Frankenberg, E., & Orfield, G. (Eds.). (2007). *Lessons in integration: Realizing the promise of racial diversity in American schools*. Charlottesville, VA: The University of Virginia Press.

Frankenberg, E., Siegel-Hawley, G., & Wang, J. (2011). Choice without equity: Charter school segregation. *Education Policy Analysis Archives, 19*(1). Retrieved from http://epaa.asu.edu/ojs/article/view/779

Fuhrman, S. H. (1999). *The new accountability* (CPRE policy brief RB-27). Philadelphia, PA: Consortium for Policy Research in Education, University of Pennsylvania.

Gamoran, A., & Hannigan, E. (2000). Algebra for everyone? Benefits of college preparatory mathematics for students with diverse abilities in early secondary school. *Educational Evaluation and Policy Analysis, 22*(3), 241-254.

Gay, G. (2006). Connections between classroom management and culturally responsive teaching. In C. M. Evertson & C. S. Weinstein (Eds.), *Handbook of classroom management: Research, practice and contemporary issues* (pp. 343-337). New York, NY: Routledge.

Gay, G. (2010). *Culturally responsive teaching.* New York, NY: Teachers College Press.

Goe, L. (2007). *The link between teacher quality and student outcomes: A research synthesis.* Washington, DC: National Comprehensive Center for Teacher Quality.

Graham, P. A. (1993). What America has expected of its schools over the past century. *American Journal of Education, 101*, 83-98.

Gregory, A., Skiba, R. J., & Noguera, P. (2010). The achievement gap and the discipline gap: Two sides of the same coin? *Educational Researcher, 38*(1), 59-68.

Hanushek, E. A., & Raymond, M. E. (2005). Does school accountability lead to improved performance? *Journal of Policy Analysis and Management, 24*(2), 297-327.

Harrington, M. (1962). *The other America.* New York, NY: Macmillan.

Harry, E., & Klingner, J. K. (2006). *Why are so many minority students in special education? Understanding race and disability in schools.* New York, NY: Teachers College Press.

Hawley, W. D. (2007). *The consequences of tracking and ability grouping in racially and ethnically diverse schools.* Retrieved from www.tolerance.org/tdsi/sites/tolerance.org.tdsi/files/assets/general/SPLC_TrackingandGrouping_8-26pdf

Hawley, W. D., & James, R. (2012). Diversity responsive schools. In J. A. Banks (Ed.), *Encyclopedia of diversity in education.* Thousands Oaks, CA: SAGE.

Hawley, W. D., & Skyes, G. (2007). Continuous school improvement. In W. D. Hawley (Ed.), *The keys to effective schools: Educational reform as continuous improvement* (2nd ed.). Thousand Oaks, CA: Corwin Press.

Hu, W. (2011, July 17). Charter school battle shifts to affluent suburbs. *New York Times.* Retrieved from http://www.nytimes.com/2011/07/17/education/17charters.html?_r=1

Jimerson, S. R. (2001). Meta-analysis of grade retention research: Implications for practice in the 21st century. *School Psychology Review, 30*, 313-330.

Johnson, O., Jr. (2010). Assessing neighborhood racial segregation and macroeconomic effects in the education of African Americans. *Review of Educational Research, 80*(4), 527-575.

Kaestle, C. F., & Smith, M. S. (1982). The federal role in elementary and secondary education, 1940-1980. *Harvard Educational Review, 52*(4), 384-408.

Kantor, H. (1991). Education, social reform, and the state: ESEA and federal education policy in the 1960s. *American Journal of Education, 100*(1), 47-83.

Kelly, S. (Ed.). (2011). *Assessing teacher quality: Understanding teacher effects on instruction and achievement.* New York, NY: Teachers College Press.

Kennedy, M. M. (2010). Attribution error and the quest for teacher quality. *Educational Researcher, 39*(8), 591-598.

Lankford, H., Loeb, S., & Wyckoff, J. (2002). Teacher sorting and the plight of urban schools: A descriptive analysis. *Educational Evaluation and Policy Analysis, 24*, 37-62.

Lee, J. (2002). Racial and ethnic achievement gap trends: Reversing the progress toward equity? *Educational Researcher, 31*, 3-12.

Lee, J. (2006). *Tracking achievement gaps and assessing the impact of NCLB on the gaps: An in-depth look into national and state reading and math outcome trends.* Cambridge, MA: The Civil Rights Project at Harvard University.

Lee, J. (2007). *The testing gap: Scientific trials of test-driven school accountability systems for excellence and equity.* Charlotte, NC: Information Age.

Lee, J. (2008). Is test-driven external accountability effective? Synthesizing the evidence from cross-state causal-comparative and correlational studies. *Review of Educational Research, 78*(3), 608-644.

Lee, J., & Reeves, T. (2012). Revisiting the impact of NCLB high-stakes school accountability, capacity, and resources: State NAEP 1990-2009 reading and math achievement gaps and trends. *Educational Evaluation and Policy Analysis, 34*(2), 209-231.

Lin, A. C., & Harris, D. R. (Eds.). (2008). *The colors of poverty: Why racial and ethnic disparities persist.* New York, NY: Russell Sage Foundation.

Losen, D. J., & Gillespie, J. (2012). *Opportunities suspended: The disparate impact of disciplinary exclusion from school.* Los Angeles, CA: The Civil Rights Project.

Losen, D. J., & Orfield, G. (Eds.). (2002). *Racial inequality in special education.* New York, NY: The Century Foundation.

Marvel, J., Lyter, D. M., Peltola, P., Strizek, G. A., & Morton, B. A. (2007). *Teacher attrition and mobility: Results from the 2004-05 teacher follow-up survey.* Washington, DC: National Center for Education Statistics.

McNeely, C. A., Noonemaker, J. M., & Blium, R. M. (2002). Promoting school connectedness: Evidence from a longitudinal study of adolescent health. *Journal of School Health, 72,* 139-146.

Meredith v. Jefferson County Bd. of Educ., 127 S. Ct. 2738 (2007).

Meyer, J. W., Scott, W. R., Strang, D., & Creighton, A. L. (1994). Bureaucratization without centralization: Changes in the organizational system of U.S. public education, 1940-1980. In W. R. Scott & J. W. Meyer (Eds.), *Institutional environments and organizations: Structural complexity and individualism* (pp. 179-205). Thousand Oaks: SAGE.

Mickelson, R. A. (2003). The academic consequences of desegregation and segregation: Evidence from the Charlotte-Mecklingburg schools. *North Carolina Law Review, 81,* 1513-1562.

Mickelson, R. A., & Bottia, M. (2010). Integrated education and mathematics outcomes: A synthesis of social science research. *North Carolina Law Review, 88,* 993-1089.

Milliken v. Bradley, 418 U.S. 717 (1974)

Minow, M. (2010). *In Brown's wake: Legacies of America's educational landmark.* New York, NY: Oxford University Press.

Mintrop, H. (2004a). High-stakes accountability, state oversight, and educational equity. *Teachers College Record, 106*(11), 2128-2145.

Mintrop, H. (2004b). *Schools on probation: How accountability works (and doesn't work).* New York, NY: Teachers College.

Mintrop, H., & Sunderman, G. L. (2013). Leveraging data-driven accountability systems for good educational practice. In D. Anagnostopoulos, S. Rutledge & R. Jacobsen (Eds.), *The infrastructure of accountability.* Cambridge, MA: Harvard Education Press.

Miron, G., Urschel, J. L., Mathis, W. J., & Tornquist, E. (2010). Schools without diversity: Education management organizations, charter schools, and the demographic stratification of the American school system. Retrieved from http://epicpolicy.org/publication/schools-without-diversity

Mooney, J. (2011, April 25). Charter schools in suburbia: More argument than agreement. *NJ Spotlight*. Retrieved from http://www.njspotlight.com/stories/11/0424/1448/

Murphy, J. (2010). *Understanding and closing achievement gaps*. Thousand Oaks, CA: Corwin Press.

NAACP Legal Defense and Educational Fund, T. C. R. P. (2008). *Still looking to the future: Voluntary K-12 school integration*. Los Angeles, CA: Author.

National Research Council. (2011). *Incentives and test-based accountability in education*. Washington, DC: The National Academies Press.

Natriello, G., McDill, E. L., & Pallas, A. M. (1990). *Schooling disadvantaged children: Racing against catastrophe*. New York, NY: Teachers College Press.

Noguera, P. (2008). What discipline is for: Connecting students to the benefits of learning. In M. Pollock (Ed.), *Everyday antiracism: Getting real about race in school* (pp. 132-137). New York, NY: The New Press.

Odden, A. (2003). Equity and adequacy in school finance today. *Phi Delta Kappan, 85*(2), 120-125.

Orfield, G., & Eaton, S. E. (Eds.). (1996). *Dismantling desegregation: A quiet reversal of Brown v. Board of Education*. New York, NY: The New Press.

Orfield, G., & Lee, C. (2007). *Historic reversals, accelerating resegregation, and the need for new integration strategies*. Los Angeles, CA: The Civil Rights Project, UCLA.

Ou, S., & Reynolds, A. J. (2010). Grade retention, post secondary education, and public aid receipt. *Educational Evaluation and Policy Analysis, 32*(1), 118-139.

Parents Involved in Cmty. Sch. v. Seattle Sch. Dist. No. 1 (PICS), 127 S. Ct. 2738, 2747 (2007).

Payne, A. (2011). *Equitable access for underrepresented students in gifted education*. Arlington, VA: The Mid-Atlantic Equity Center, The George Washington University Center for Equity and Excellence in Education.

Puma, M. J., Jones, C. C., Rock, D., & Fernandez, R. (1993). *Prospects: The congressionally mandated study of educational growth and opportunity: Interim report*. Washington, DC: U. S. Department of Education.

Raudenbush, S. W. (2008). The Brown legacy and the O'Connor challenge: Transforming schools in the image of children's potential. *Educational Researcher, 38*(3), 169-180.

Reardon, S. F. (2011). The widening academic achievement gap between the rich and the poor: New evidence and possible explanations. In G. J. Duncan & R. J. Murnane (Eds.), *Whither opportunity? Rising inequality, schools, and children's life chances*. New York, NY: Russell Sage Foundation.

Rice, J. K. (2003). *Teacher quality: Understanding the effectiveness of teacher attributes*. Washington, DC: Economic Policy Institute.

Rowan, B. (1990). Commitment and control: Alternative strategies for the organizational design of schools. *Review of Educational Research, 16*, 353-389.

Scafidi, B., Sjoquist, D. L., & Stinebrickner, T. R. (2008). Race, poverty, and teacher mobility. *Economics of Education Review, 26*, 145-159.

Scott, C. (2009). *Improving low-performing schools: Lessons from five years of studying school restructuring under No Child Left Behind.* Washington, DC: Center for Education Policy.

Skiba, R. J., Horner, R. H., Chung, C.-G., Rausch, M. K., May, S. L., & Tobin, T. (2011). Race is not neutral: A national investigation of African American and Latino disproportionality in school discipline. *School Psychology Review, 40*(1), 85-107.

Skiba, R. J., Michael, R. S., Nardo, A. C., & Peterson, R. (2002). The color of discipline: Sources of racial and gender disproportionality in school punishment. *Urban Review, 34,* 317-342.

Skiba, R. J., Simmons, A. B., Ritter, S., Gibb, A. C., Rausch, M. K., Curadrado, J., et al. (2008). Achieving equity in special education: History, status, and current challenges. *Council for Exceptional Children, 74*(3), 264-288.

Sklar, L., McKenzie, K. B., & Scheurich, J. J. (2009). *Using equity audits to create equitable and excellent schools.* Thousand Oaks, CA: Corwin Press.

Smith, M. S., & O'Day, J. A. (1993). Systemic school reform and educational opportunity. In S. H. Fuhrman (Ed.), *Designing coherent education policy: Improving the system.* San Francisco, CA: Jossey-Bass.

Steele, C. M. (2010). *Whistling Vivaldi: How stereotypes affect us and what we can do.* New York, NY: W. W. Norton & Company.

Sunderman, G. L., Hawley, W. D., Brown, J., Hicks, B., & Kirton, E. (2011). *Beyond equity assessment: Developing a research based tool for equity planning in schools and districts.* Paper presented at the American Education Research Association.

Sunderman, G. L., & Kim, J. S. (2007). The expansion of federal power and the politics of implementing the No Child Left Behind Act. *Teachers College Record, 109*(5), 1057-1085.

Sunderman, G. L., & Orfield, G. (2006). Domesticating a revolution: No Child Left Behind and state administrative response. *Harvard Educational Review, 76*(4), 526-556.

Tefera, A., Frankenberg, E., Siegel-Hawley, G., & Chirichigno, G. (2011). *Integrating suburban schools: How to benefit from growing diversity and avoid segregation.* Los Angeles, CA: UCLA Civil Rights Project and NAACP Legal Defense and Educational Fund.

Texas Education Agency. (1996). *Grade level retention of Texas students, 1994-95.* Austin, TX: Author.

Thomas, N. C. (1983). The development of federal activism in education: A contemporary perspective. *Education and Urban Society, 15*(3), 271-290.

U.S. Department of Education. (2009). *Race to the top program: Executive summary.* Retrieved from http://www2.ed.gov/programs/racetothetop/executive-summary.pdf

U.S. Department of Education. (2010a). *A blueprint for education reform: The reauthorization of the Elementary and Secondary Education Act.* Retrieved A from http://www2.ed.gov/policy/elsec/leg/blueprint/blueprint.pdf

U.S. Department of Education. (2010b). *School improvement grants; American Recovery and Reinvestment Act of 2009 (ARRA); Title I of the Elementary and Secondary Education Act of 1965, as Amended (ESEA).* Retrieved from http://www2.ed.gov/programs/sif/2010-27313.pdf

U.S. Department of Education. (2011). ESEA flexibility. Retrieved from http://www
.ed.gov/esea/flexibility

U.S. Department of Education Office of Special Education and Rehabilitative Services Office of Special Education Services. (2006). *26th annual report to Congress on the implementation of the Individuals with Disabilities Education Act, Vol. 2*. Washington, DC: Author.

U.S. Department of Health and Human Services Division of Adolescent and School Health. (2009). *Fostering school connectedness*. Washington, DC: Author.

Wald, J., & Losen, D. J. (2003). Defining and redirecting a school-to-prison pipeline. *New Directions for Youth Development, 99*, 9-15.

Wayne, A. J., & Youngs, P. (2003). Teacher characteristics and student achievement gains: A review. *Review of Educational Research, 73*, 89-122.

Weiss, C. L. A., Cunningham, D. L., Lewis, C. P., & Clark, M. G. (2005). *Enhancing student connectedness*. Baltimore, MD: Center for School Mental Health Analysis and Action, Department of Psychiatry, University of Maryland School of Medicine.

Wong, K. K., Shen, F. X., Anagnostopoulos, D., & Rutledge, S. (2007). *The education mayor: Improving America's schools*. Washington, DC: Georgetown University Press.

Zimmer, R., Gill, B., Booker, K., Lavertu, S., Sass, T. R., & Witte, J. F. (2009). *Charter schools in eight states: Effects on achievement, attainment, integration, and competition*. Santa Monica, CA: RAND.

CHAPTER 2

WITHER THE SUBURBAN IDEAL?

Understanding Contemporary Suburban School Contexts

Erica Frankenberg

America is a primarily "suburban" society and suburbs are on the frontier of rapid racial and socioeconomic change (Frey, 2001; Logan, 2003a). In 2008, for the first time Census data indicated that more than half of residents from each major racial/ethnic group in metropolitan areas resided in the suburbs of these metros (Brookings Institution, 2010). Today, between city and suburbs as well as within suburbia, residential areas reflect racial segregation beyond what can be explained by economics alone (Harris & Mcardle, 2004; Shapiro, 2004). The failure to address to address housing segregation in metropolitan areas has resulted in persistently high levels of residential segregation beyond city lines that has major ramifications for public schools. Demographers continue to describe the multiracial diversity and segregation that exists between city and suburbs, and particularly between suburban communities themselves (Farrell, 2008). Other research suggests that there are multiple types of suburban communities rather than a singular model of suburbia (M. Orfield, 2002). However, recognition of how these trends affect suburban schools has largely escaped the attention of educational reformers.

Charting Reform, Achieving Equity in a Diverse Nation
pp. 27–54
Copyright © 2013 by Information Age Publishing
27

This chapter analyzes the diversity of our nation's public schools, with a focus on the suburbs of metropolitan areas. In particular, this chapter examines the district- and school-level enrollment change of students, the diversity of the suburban teaching force, and the segregation of students *and* teachers in these suburban areas in large metropolitan areas using data from several national data sources.

UNDERSTANDING SCHOOLING PATTERNS IN METROPOLITAN AREAS

Contemporary Forces Shaping School Segregation: Demographic, Economic, and Housing

Relatively little attention has been paid in educational literature to examining the twin impacts of suburbanization and growing diversity on the public schools, although it seems likely that adapting biracial urban models of racial and economic changes from a generation ago may not be entirely helpful. In our nation, and in suburbia as well, Latinos today outnumber Black students, resulting in a multiracial school enrollment in most metropolitan areas. Further, many, but not all, metropolitan areas are balkanized into dozens or hundreds of school districts. This means that a given suburban district has a very small share of the entire metro enrollment, and, in essence, is but a small player in the suburban competition for households and students. Within suburbia, researchers find "gradations" in terms of racial composition with further flung, exurban areas tending to have a higher percentage of White residents while older, inner suburbs have a much higher percentage of non-White residents (Brookings Institution, 2010, p. 62; see also M. Orfield, 2002). School districts are among the most important amenities in a suburban community (Berkman & Plutzer, 2005, Bischoff, 2008; Frankenberg, 2009a), but suburban school districts differ from urban districts in key ways that may leave them especially vulnerable to multiracial transitions within metropolitan areas.

Just as demographic change is affecting the racial diversity of suburban communities, so too is the growing number of people living below the poverty line affecting the economic composition of the suburbs. In a recent analysis of the largest 95 metropolitan areas, Kneebone and Garr (2010) found that from 2000 to 2008 poverty increased at a much more rapid rate in the suburbs than in cities. Although the suburban poverty rate (9.5%) was roughly half that of the cities (18.2%) (Kneebone & Garr, 2010), the greater number of suburban residents means that the suburbs contain more people who are poor (almost 12.5 million in 2008). These trends varied across regions; the Midwest, for example had the highest increase in suburban poverty rates due to industrial decline. In some metros the majority of poor residents shifted during this time from the city to the suburbs. The authors suggest that, if anything, these numbers might underreport the increasing suburban poverty rates. They speculate that suburban communities are likely to continue to experience increasing poverty due to the decentralization of jobs and the lack of social safety nets in communities that have traditionally had fewer lower-income residents.

Analysis of Census data through 2010 finds that residential segregation has decreased slightly, but it remains quite high, particularly for Black and White residents. Economic and racial residential segregation persists for a number of reasons (e.g., Massey & Denton, 1993; M. Orfield & Luce, 2012). Discrimination in the housing market is prevalent in a number of ways. Studies consistently find that minority homeseekers are steered to different neighborhoods than similar White homeseekers (e.g., Galster & Godfrey, 2005). One analysis found that after accounting for income, minority homeowners were much more likely to be subject to predatory lending than were White homeowners, which makes them more likely to default (Bocian, Li, & Ernst, 2010); minority mortgage applicants are also denied at higher rates. In addition, policies such as school district jurisdiction or exclusionary zoning can structure the ways in which residents settle within metropolitan areas (Frankenberg, 2009a; Rothwell & Massey, 2009). Likewise, the placement of low-income housing in segregated neighborhoods can reinforce existing segregation and, although this is prohibited by the Fair Housing Act, analyses find that this still occurs, and has, in fact, exacerbated resegregation in racially changing suburbs (M. Orfield & Luce, 2009).

Private preferences—albeit preferences shaped by our existing segregated, unequal society—also play a role in decisions about home buying, and research indicates that different racial groups have varying levels of diversity with which they are comfortable, which may destabilize neighborhoods that begin to show initial diversity (Charles, 2005). In addition, as some central cities gentrify, rising home prices in these urban cores displace families of color to suburban areas where real estate might be more affordable. Despite what gentrification might portend for positive outcomes for school integration in central cities, for many reasons, it has not necessarily resulted in increased diversity in city public schools to date (Stillman, 2013).

It is important to note that the last year of data on suburban schools and districts reported in this chapter falls at the beginning of the economic crisis, which resulted in the collapse of housing prices, and, among other impacts, revealed the extent to which non-White homeowners—and the communities with high percentages of such residents—are still subjected to different housing forces than White homeseekers. Thus, while the mortgage crisis may have limited the mobility of groups, it may also have disproportionately devastated some suburban communities where Black and Latino families had settled. Understanding the implications of these trends on housing segregation, and therefore school segregation, will be important.

Suburbanization and Diversification in the Nation's Schools: What's at Stake

As the demographic transformation of the United States is well underway (e.g., Whites now constitute a minority of babies born), social science evidence continues to describe the myriad of ways in which integrated K-12 schools are important for students' social and academic success. Students of all races benefit from attending racially diverse educational environments in terms of reducing prejudice, challenging stereotypes, and presenting different perspectives that can enhance critical thinking (Orfield, Frankenberg, & Garces, 2008). Students of color are also more likely to persist to graduation and have higher postgraduation outcomes than their peers in less diverse schools (Orfield et al., 2008). There are externalities that accrue from integrated schools for communities. Research finds that students from integrated schools are more likely to live and work in diverse settings and to participate as citizens (Mickelson & Nkomo, in press).

Further, with growing shares of students from historically disadvantaged groups, the U.S. risks producing future generations of students with lower educational attainment than preceding generations if schools remain segregated. Decades of social science research document the harms for students who attend racially isolated non-White schools, most of which are also schools of concentrated poverty that have fewer educational resources such as advanced curricular offerings and experienced, high-quality teachers (Linn & Welner, 2007). Not surprisingly, students in such schools, on average, have lower achievement; additionally many "drop out factories" have high concentrations of students of color (Balfanz & Letgers, 2004).

Data

After briefly reviewing Census data on demographic changes in the nation's largest metropolitan areas, the bulk of this chapter analyzes data from the National Center for Education Statistics (NCES) Common Core of Data and NCES Schools and Staffing Survey. The NCES Common Core of Data includes data on virtually every district since the late 1980s in its public school universe. This chapter draws on the Common Core of Data from 1990-91, 1999-2000, and 2006-07. Importantly, this dataset has counts for students by racial/ethnic group and a measure of low-income status (eligibility for free or reduced priced lunch), as well as demographic composition and other details for each school.[1] NCES's Schools and Staffing Survey (SASS) is a sample of public school districts, teachers, and schools are selected for participation via a stratified sampling procedure (Tourkin et al., 2010). The 2007-08 school and teacher files from a restricted-use version of SASS are used in this chapter to assess teacher composition and segregation in suburban schools. The files have data from more than 38,000 teachers and their schools. Together, these two data sources provide information on thousands of suburban schools, students, and teachers that help us understand the demographic context of suburban schools.

Before describing this context, it is important to define terms used in this chapter. According to the U.S. Census Bureau, a metropolitan area is "a large population nucleus, together with adjacent communities having a high degree of social and economic integration with that core" (U.S. Census, n.d.). Data analyzed in this chapter were constructed using the 2003 Office of Management and Budget's definition of what places are included in each of the nation's (MSAs). The OMB regularly updates such definitions and defines new MSAs as needed. I selected the 25 most populous MSAs (out of more than 300) for most of the analysis in this chapter, representing schools in 25 states and the District of Columbia. Districts and schools located in principal cities (defined by the U.S. Census) were coded separately from all other districts and schools, which, for these purposes are designated as "suburban." Metropolitan areas were also categorized, using the principal/central city, into five regions according to definitions used in school segregation research (Clotfelter, 2004).[2] Additionally, I examined large and small metropolitan areas using definitions from the federal government. Large MSAs were defined as metropolitan areas where the population of the central city was greater than 250,000 and small MSAs as those where the city population was less than 250,000. All of the largest 25 MSAs were classified as large MSAs (e.g., the 25th largest, Sacramento, had more than 400,000 central city residents in 2000).

CHANGING METROPOLITAN AREAS: THE INTERSECTION OF SUBURBANIZATION AND GROWING DIVERSITY

The population of each of the nation's largest metropolitan areas became more suburban since 1990, although the extent of change varied widely.

Growth in most Midwestern and Northeastern metropolitan areas was less than 5% over the decade. In 1990, a majority of residents in all but one (Phoenix) of the largest 25 metros lived in the suburbs (see Table 2.A-1 in the Appendix). Atlanta had the highest percentage of suburban residents, where more than 90% of all metro residents in 2010 lived outside of the metro's principal cities. Census data reveal that the move to the suburbs in the nation's largest metropolitan areas remained strong between 1990 and 2010, particularly outside of the Northeast and Midwest. Many of the largest increases in the number of suburban residents during the last decade were in the South and West regions. Atlanta, and Los Angeles all gained more than a million new suburban residents in the last decade, and Atlanta and Los Angeles both had gained an additional 1 million suburban residents from 1990 to 2000. Many of the metrowide changes in population since 1990 reflect the suburban changes during this time period.

Since 1990, the racial composition of the entire suburban population in the largest 25 metropolitan areas has become much more heterogeneous. In 1990, sixteen of the metros had suburban populations that were at least 80% White; seven, in fact, had 90% or more White residents. Los Angeles had the highest percentage of non-White suburban residents but still maintained a majority of Whites in suburbia in 1990. As of 2010, four metros have majority non-White suburban populations, and only one is 90% White (see Table 2.A-2 in the Appendix).

Racial transition was significant in the suburban rings of the largest metros during the 1990s, particularly among metros that already had a more diverse suburban population in 1990. Ten metros had a decline in suburban White percentage of at least 10 points from 1990 to 2010. The largest declines were in Atlanta and Houston, where the White share of the suburban enrollment declined approximately 25 percentage points in 20 years. While more than half of the decline in Atlanta's White suburban population is due to the increase of Black suburban residents (increase of 11 percentage points), the rapid increase among the Latino population in suburban Houston accounts for the suburban transition in that metro since 1990. The large declines in the percentage of White suburban residents in metro Los Angeles and Miami have transformed the suburban parts of these metros into majority non-White areas where Whites are only one third of the suburban population. Since 1990, both of these metros experienced a sharp growth of Latinos in suburbia, and they now outnumber suburban Whites.

Although the White homogeneity of suburbia has lessened in the largest metropolitan areas over the past two decades, the declines in the percentage of White residents were lower within those metro areas that were overwhelmingly White at the time period (1990). The White percentage of residents in the suburbs of Pittsburgh declined by five percentage points respectively over the decades, and the total population remained 90% White in 2010. Of all metros that had a suburban population that was at least 90% White in 1990, Portland experienced the largest decline in the share of White suburban residents: 15 percentages points decline from 1990-2010.

The 1990s witnessed economic prosperity,[3] which is reflected in the Census statistics measuring the share of poor residents in the nation's largest metropolitan areas. Somewhat unexpectedly, central cities and suburban residents alike shared in this prosperity. Across the largest 25 metropolitan areas, the percentage of poor residents declined in the majority of central city and suburban regions. In the suburbs of fifteen metropolitan areas, the percentage of poor residents declined; in another, the percentage remained the same in 2000 as it was in 1990. Yet, because of the increasing *number* of suburban residents, the number of poor residents actually increased in the suburbs of all but four Midwestern metropolitan areas,[4] mostly places in which there was slower population growth during the 1990s.

Student Patterns of Racial Change and Segregation in Suburbia

Though the tradition of local control of schools means that school composition is affected by—and in turn, affects—neighborhood composition, considerably less is known about how patterns of suburbanization are affecting the racial and economic composition and segregation of schools in suburban communities. Elementary schools, in fact, are often the first sign of community transition (M. Orfield, 2002). This section explores the aggregate composition of suburban students, as well as racial change in students over time, before turning in subsequent sections to understanding whether students are evenly (or not) distributed between districts and schools.

The spread of students of color into suburbia is evident, particularly in suburban areas of the largest metropolitan areas (G. Orfield & Frankenberg, 2008). For example, in 2006 nearly 40% of Asian students in the largest metros (e.g., metropolitan areas where the central city had 250,000 or more residents) attended suburban schools, as did more than 30% of Latino students—in comparison to only 28% of White students and one quarter of Black students (G. Orfield & Frankenberg, 2008). By contrast, smaller metros (e.g., metropolitan areas where the central city had fewer than 250,000 residents) had considerably smaller shares of students of color. Latinos experienced surprisingly high racial isolation in suburban schools regardless of metro size and more than one in three

Latino and Black students in suburban schools of large metros also attended racially isolated non-White schools (G. Orfield & Frankenberg, 2008).

Suburban students in the 25 largest metropolitan areas combined to account for one fourth of all public school students in the United States in 2006-07, including approximately 30% of Latinos, Blacks, and Asians. Likewise, the percentage of low-income students has grow in suburbia, since the beginning of the 21st century (Kneebone & Garr, 2010). The percentage of White students in suburbia declined in each of the 25 MSAs, and Latino students, who are now the second largest group of suburban students, fueled much of the suburban growth since 1990. As the number of Latino students in suburbia has grown, so too has their segregation from White students.

Despite this diversity of suburban areas, there remain striking disparities between the racial composition of city schools and suburban schools in almost all metropolitan areas. In other words, while the suburbs are becoming diverse, in almost every MSA, they retain a disproportionately higher percentage of White students than is the case among the city public school enrollment.[5] In 15 metropolitan areas, for example, the percentage of White students in the suburbs is twice (or more) as high as the percentage of White city students. There are also six MSAs where at least three out of every four suburban students were White. Virtually all suburban areas have a lower percentage of Black and Latino students than their corresponding city. In some places, the discrepancies for Black students are vast, most notably in the Midwestern and, to a lesser extent, Northeastern metropolitan areas. Suburban diversity, then, certainly hasn't spread everywhere nor is it as extensive as that in city schools.

Although the racial differences between city and suburban enrollment still exist as described above, the city-suburban disparity in public school enrollment has shrunk since the beginning of the 21st century. Two groups exemplify the changing composition of suburban schools during this time: Whites and Latinos. The changing racial composition of the suburban enrollment has been much steeper than changing composition of the city enrollment, in part because the city enrollment by 1999 was already more diverse than suburban enrollment (see Table 2.A-3 in the Appendix). The proportion of White students in suburbia (66.75% in 1999-00 to 57.5% in 2006-07) has declined more rapidly than in the central cities since 2000, where the proportion of White students declined from 30.7% to 26.3% during the same time period. The percentage of Latino students in suburban schools, by contrast, has increased by almost ten percentage points since 1990, with most of the change occurring since 1999-2000 and fueled by rapid growth in the suburban schools of many Southwestern metropolitan areas. During this time, Latinos surpassed

Black students as the second largest group of students in suburban schools.

The traditional notion of the "well-to-do" suburban neighborhood and school still holds, for the most part, when aggregating the entire suburban enrollment of the largest 25 metropolitan areas, although the number of poor suburban students is increasing.[6] Overall in 2006-07, the percentage of suburban students who were low-income (23.6%) is approximately half the share of low-income city students (47.2%). In each metro, the percentage of suburban students who are poor is less than that of city students.

Despite the increasing number of suburban poor students, poverty rates across all of the largest metropolitan areas remain relatively low. The suburban poverty rate ranges from a low of 11.9% in the Baltimore MSA to high of 36.3% in the Atlanta MSA. In fact, suburban poverty rates are highest in metropolitan areas in the South and West. In contrast to the suburbs, 10 cities have more than have more than half of students from families at or near the poverty line. Most of these are in the Northeast and Midwest.

Implications of Suburban District Boundaries

Taken together, these data show suburban patterns of growth and diversification among public school students varying across and within metropolitan areas. While these data are informative, the political boundaries structuring students into districts within suburbia also influence the demographic composition that students experience in their schools. Historically, school districts were created by states to help them carry out their duty to educate the state's children. Research on segregation has highlighted the increasingly important role district boundary lines contribute to overall segregation (Bischoff, 2008; Clotfelter, 2004; Reardon & Yun, 2005). Despite the fact that such demographic patterns exist—and the role of the government in contributing to segregated development and settlement of metropolitan areas (e.g., Massey & Denton, 1993)—the Supreme Court effectively closed off most cross-district remedies to de jure segregation in its 1974 *Milliken* decision (Ryan, 2010). Both the reluctance of federal courts to address de facto segregation existing between districts and the long history of local control of education is an impediment to many cross-district desegregation efforts. At the same time, the dozen or so such programs that have existed have been extremely popular, and research has found academic and social benefits for city students who attend integrated, suburban schools (e.g., Wells et al., 2009).

In most suburban areas of MSAs, there are dozens, if not hundreds, of school districts. Unlike the central city of a metropolitan area, the "suburbs" are politically fragmented into many distinct municipalities and/or school districts. Suburban areas may encompass many jurisdictions at varying distances from the central city, have varied types of tax bases and demands for social services, and different settlement histories (M. Orfield, 2002). Further, this political fragmentation of suburbia has institutionalized differing characteristics of suburban populations across these jurisdictions (Frankenberg, 2009a; Oliver, 2001; Weiher, 1991). (For example, some suburbs, typically located close to central cities, tend to be largely Black and Latino while others, even nearby, can be overwhelmingly White.) Political fragmentation is particularly high among inner-ring suburbs in the Northeast and Midwest, making it difficult to develop coordinated land use policies. Fragmentation may create competition instead of a shared approach to dealing with the economic challenges facing these inner-ring suburbs as their population ages (Puentes & Warren, 2006). In addition, state funding cuts following the 2008 recession, reduced state funding tied to enrollment declines, and lower tax revenue due to real estate market declines in segregated, high-poverty suburbs are all likely to have significant consequences for schools in inner-ring suburbs. While more affluent districts are also being affected, they may be less reliant on state funding and may be able to either withstand cuts (to a certain extent) better than high-poverty districts or may be able to raise revenue to compendate for cuts. In addition, it is financially inefficient to have may small school districts in close proximity to one another, as it requires each community to support its own administration, infrastructure, and other needs.

The combination of the slight decline in the number of school districts and increasing suburban enrollment trends means that since 1990, the average size of suburban districts in the largest MSAs has increased from 3,500 students to almost 5,000 students while the reverse trend is seen for urban districts. Urban districts have declined from nearly 31,000 in 1999-2000 to less than 28,000 in 2006-07 on average. While urban districts remain larger than suburban ones, on average, these trends have important implications for districts in terms of funding and capacity (e.g., building/closing schools, hiring/laying off teachers, etc.); for example, suburban districts may need to build more schools and hire new teachers as their average size increases. Urban districts, with an average size that is declining, may face even more unpleasant policy alternatives: should they close school(s)? Will their funding be reduced, causing the need to layoff teachers or reduce expenditures in other ways?

The next stage of analysis examined changing composition at the district level of both cities and suburbs of each MSA. Two MSAs, Miami and Tampa, had countywide districts that included both city and suburban regions in one district.[7] Earlier analyses have suggested that larger, countywide districts have higher interracial exposure due, in part, to not having nearby districts as exit options from diverse schools (Frankenberg & Lee, 2002; Logan, Oakley, & Stowell, 2008; G. Orfield 2001).

This analysis illustrates the complexity of understanding racial change and segregation in the 21st century in these large metropolitan areas. In particular, examining the demographic patterns for Black and Latino students demonstrates how these two groups—traditionally concentrated together in urban districts—find their opportunities for middle-class, integrated districts in the suburbs limited. In most instances, Latino growth surpassed that of Blacks in suburban districts.

In most MSAs, the average district-level change in the percentage of White students was less in suburban districts than their corresponding city districts, particularly when examining change since 1990. Exceptions to this trend were in metropolitan areas with different patterns of school district jurisdictions: countywide districts in three of the four MSAs had district level declines in White enrollment that were lower in city districts than in suburban districts. These city districts encompassed some of suburbia, suggesting that countywide districts stabilized city schools relative to metro racial change in metropolitan areas with more fragmented school district boundaries (e.g., many small municipal districts).

The average district-level percentage of White students declined in the suburban areas of each MSA from 1999 to 2006, but this decline differed depending on the proportion of White students in 1999. Across all metros, districts that experienced the most rapid change had between one third and two thirds of students who were White at the beginning of the period examined (Figure 2.1). Districts that were at least 80% White in 1999, however, had a lower decline than average for suburban districts.

Overall, the percentage of Latino students increased by nearly four percentage points, on average, in suburban districts from 1999 to 2006. This was more than three times the increase of Black students (1.2 percentage points on average) during the same time period. In every MSA, in fact, the average Latino percentage has increased since 1999 and in a handful of metropolitan areas—namely, those with countywide suburban districts—not a single suburban district had a decline in the percentage of Latino students from 1999-2006.

The pattern of suburban racial change is different when we examine it by the district-level percentage of Latino students in 1999, namely that White transition appears sensitive to even small percentages of Latino students (Figure 2.2). At very low levels of Latino percentage, there were high levels of White decline, on average, over the time period examined. For example, in a district with just 8% Latino students in 1999, the average decline in the percentage of White students was more than 10 percentage points. This is in sharp contrast to the patterns with White

Source: NCES Common Core of Data, 1999-2000 and 2006-07.
Note: Used five-percentage point moving average of White % in 1999 (*x* axis).

Figure 2.1.   Racial change in suburban school districts by district (White percentage, 1999-2006).

students showing relatively little change for districts with either few White students or in districts where the vast majority of students are White.

The racial change for majority Latino districts was less, on average, particularly for districts that had at least two thirds of students who were Latino. These patterns may well reflect the fact that such districts may have had relatively few White students in 1999 and, therefore, relatively little room for the White percentage to decline.

When further examining district-level racial change over this time period, Latino growth outpaced Black growth in most suburban regions. The one region where this was not true was the Midwest. With the exception of Chicago, the suburban districts in every Midwestern metro had a larger average increase in the percentage of Black students than they did in Latino students. In other words, while Latino students may be driving suburban diversification of school districts in most areas, Black students were increasing more quickly in Midwestern suburban districts. Suburban Detroit, in fact, was an outlier in the percentage increase of Black students (6.5 percentage points). All other MSAs had average increases in Black

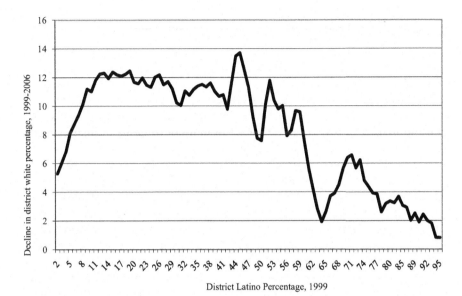

District Latino Percentage, 1999

Source: NCES Common Core of Data, 1999-2000 and 2006-07.
Note: Used five-percentage point moving average of Latino percent in 1999 (x-axis).

Figure 2.2.   Racial change in suburban school districts by District Latino Percentage, 1999-2006.

percentage of three points or less, and several had declines in share of Black students, on average.

Finally, it is also informative to compare district-level racial change in city and suburban areas of each MSA. This analysis shows us that while Latino increases may be driving suburban diversity in most areas, it is actually lagging behind city change in most MSAs. In only seven MSAs—largely in the South and West—did the average district-level increase of Latino students in suburban districts exceed the average increase in city districts. Thus Latino growth in suburban districts is reflective of Latino student growth overall in these large MSAs. By contrast, in 14 MSAs Black student growth in suburban school districts exceeded that of the metro's urban districts, on average. This suggests that Black student growth may be more concentrated in suburban districts; again, however, it's informative to remember that the number of Black students was likely already higher in city than suburban districts.

Racial and Economic Segregation of Districts

While suburbia is undergoing considerable racial transformation as seen above, this has not spread evenly across all districts. It is likely that such patterns of suburban migration may differ across district boundary lines, resulting in racial and economic segregation between school districts. There are several dimensions of segregation (see Massey & Denton, 1988). This analysis considers two: concentration and unevenness. Concentration as measured here denotes the share of students in districts with either 90-100% White students or 90-100% students of color. Unevenness refers to the extent to which groups are evenly distributed across geographic areas. It is typically measured by the Index of Dissimilarity in which 0 denotes perfect integration and 100 is complete segregation.

The *Milliken* decision in 1974 limited the ability to construct cross-district desegregation remedies. As a result, school diversity is constrained, in most cases, by the extent to which district-level segregation exists. There are a few exceptions in the largest MSAs such as St. Louis, Boston, and Minneapolis, which voluntarily operate city-suburban desegregation plans that cross district boundary lines, but even in these MSAs, these plans only pertain to a fraction of the suburban districts. Thus, the extent to which student populations are segregated at the district level will have important implications for the extent to which schools within these districts will be segregated.

In 2006-07, more than one in four suburban school districts had less than 10% students of color, illustrating the fact that the growing diversity of suburbia has not affected all districts. Further, there were six metros, largely in the Rust Belt, where a majority of suburban districts had 90-100% White students: Boston, Cincinnati, Cleveland, Minneapolis, Pittsburgh, and St. Louis. Thus, it is unlikely that most suburban students in these metros attend diverse schools.

By contrast, in two southwestern metros, Phoenix and Los Angeles, a majority of suburban districts are predominantly non-White. These metros, along with Chicago, also have at least one tenth of suburban districts where 90% or more of students are non-White. In contrast to the Rust Belt metros described above, the racial composition of these suburban districts reflects the racial composition of the urban districts in these same metros.

District-level dissimilarity among suburban areas of the largest MSAs reveals a complex racial story. Black students are separated by district boundary lines from White and Asian students in many suburban areas. White-Latino segregation is moderate, but growing. There is much lower district-level segregation for Asian students from either Latinos or Whites in many suburban areas. These patterns play out differently across regions. Although Black-Asian suburban segregation is high in most MSAs, this is not the case in the West, where Blacks are the fourth largest racial group of students. Instead, with growing shares of Latino and Asian students, suburbs in California's MSAs are experiencing increasing Latino-Asian segregation. High segregation exists among districts in the Midwest for Blacks, who are segregated from Whites and Asians. Most metros in the South and border states had moderate segregation—low in some cases—likely due to the predominance of countywide districts.[8]

Economic segregation among districts (measured by the concentration of students below and above the free lunch line[9]) is far lower than racial segregation: in no MSAs were dissimilarity indices greater than 60, and in almost one third, they were low. (This is similar to patterns found by Logan (2003a) in his comparison of racial dissimilarity and economic dissimilarity using the 2000 Census.) There were regional differences in economic dissimilarity, however. The highest dissimilarity—approaching the "high" range—were in the Northeast, specifically Boston and New York, and in Chicago, each of which have hundreds of small suburban school districts. The MSAs with the lowest dissimilarity were all MSAs in the South and border regions (the exceptions to this pattern are the Texas MSAs) and three MSAs in the West.

Teacher Composition and Segregation: Reinforcing Patterns of Student Separation in Suburbia

Since at least the time of the Supreme Court's *Green* decision in 1968, school integration required not simply the desegregation of students, but also that of teachers in order to be judged a thoroughly integrated school district (see Parker, 2009). Research also supports the importance of a diverse teaching staff for both White and non-White students: teachers of color can serve as role models for students of color and through their own experiences can help strengthen family-school relationships and shape schools to be more welcoming and inclusive of students from all backgrounds (Cohen, 1980; Villegas & Lucas, 2002). This inclusivity is perhaps particularly important for White students and teachers who are part of the most isolated racial group in the nation's public schools.

Composition of Suburban Teachers

In all suburban schools, approximately 85% of teachers are White, 5% Latino, 7% Black, 3% Asian, and 0.3% American Indian. This racial composition closely reflects the overall composition of the entire U.S. teaching force.[10] Of course, faculties in suburban schools have a disproportionately higher percentage of White teachers and lower shares of Black and Latino teachers in comparison to schools in the central cities of these same MSAs.

Using the 2007-08 Schools and Staffing Survey, this analysis finds student-teacher demographic gaps to be especially prevalent in suburban schools in the large MSAs.[11] In this sample, the average percentage of White students in suburban schools in large MSAs (e.g., metropolitan areas where the central city had 250,000 or more residents) was 59% while the average percentage of White teachers was 83% (24 percentage point gap). Because suburban schools in smaller MSAs (e.g., MSAs where the city has fewer than 250,000 residents) have a higher share of White students, the gap is not quite as large (18 percentage point gap). (The median suburban school in large MSAs has just over 6% of teachers who are non-White, and schools in smaller MSAs had just 2.6% non-White teachers on the faculty of the median school.) In suburban schools in large MSAs, on average, Black and Latino students each comprised just over 16% of the enrollment while Black teachers were 7% of the faculty and Latino teachers less than 6%.

Among teachers of all racial groups, Asian teachers are disproportionately represented in suburban schools: approximately 40% of all Asian teachers in the SASS sample taught in suburban schools. This was considerably higher than the share of most other groups, with the exception of American Indian teachers who were more likely to teach in rural schools. Just under 30% of White, Black, and Latino teachers, for example, each taught in suburban schools.

Segregation of Students and Teachers

A commonly used measure of segregation is the exposure index, which measures the exposure of the "typical member" of one group to other racial groups. It is essentially a weighted average of each group member's exposure to other students and is particularly useful for understanding the composition of a given school or neighborhood. Traditionally, exposure is measured through exposure of various groups to Whites, because of the historical struggle for non-Whites to gain access to White institutions. This analysis considers the exposure to all groups, among students, among teachers, and between students and teachers to understand fully the integration or segregation of students and faculty in suburban schools.

Not surprisingly, given district-level segregation trends in the suburbs of the largest MSAs described above, segregation at the school level, as measured by exposure, is moderately high. The racial composition of students in this sample is 62.5% White, 15.3% Latino, 15.2% Black, 6% Asian; and 1.1% American Indian (Table 2.1). If schools were perfectly integrated, the exposure of each student would mirror this racial composition. What we find instead is that the exposure for the "typical" student of each race varies substantially from this overall racial composition as well as from one another (Table 2.1). This is indicative of very different daily exposure to students of other races within suburbia's schools.[13]

Several patterns emerge when examining the student exposure indices more closely. Racial isolation for each of the four largest groups (e.g., exposure of one's group to itself) is high. White students, who comprise the largest group in suburban schools, attend schools, on average, where less than one in four students are from another race, which is similar to all public schools (G. Orfield, 2009). Likewise, Black and Latino students have relatively high isolation (44.21% and 44.75%, respectively) given that each accounts for approximately 15% of suburban students. However, their isolation is lower in suburban schools than across all metro schools, which is likely related to their higher isolation in urban schools. Asian and American Indian students have lower isolation, which is not surprising due to their smaller share of suburban students.

Considerable differences exist among suburban students' exposure to White students. As mentioned, the vast majority of students in the school of the typical White suburban student are White. Yet, less than 40% of students in the typical suburban Black or Latino student's school are White—percentages that are much lower than the overall share of White students in suburbia (62.5%). Thus, by this traditional measure of integration, Black and Latino students are substantially separate from White students, even in suburban schools. The smaller groups, Asian and American Indian students, have slightly higher exposure to White students than to Black or Latino students.

Where segregation among students exists, one possibility for interracial exposure is the teaching staff. Within suburban schools, in addition to differences in student exposure, there are substantial gaps in exposure to

Table 2.1.Student-Student Exposure in Suburban Schools, 2007-08

Percent of Students by Race in Student's School	Exposure for Typical Student of Race/Ethnicity:					Racial Composition of Students in Sample
	White	Black	Latino	Asian	American Indian	
White	77.22	37.05	35.40	44.38	52.29	62.51
Black	8.99	44.21	13.98	10.03	10.29	15.18
Latino	8.65	14.07	44.75	12.76	12.47	15.27
Asian	4.25	3.95	5.00	31.91	5.15	5.98
American Indian	0.89	0.72	0.87	0.92	19.80	1.06
Total	100.00	100.00	100.00	100.00	100.00	

Source: NCES Schools and Staffing Survey, 2007-08.

teachers by students of different races. In other words, segregation in suburban schools is evident both among students and also between students and teachers.

White students, who were the least exposed to other-race students, have the lowest exposure to other-race teachers as well. Just 7% of teachers in the typical White suburban student's school were not White, which is considerably lower than the 15% of non-White teachers among the entire suburban teaching force (Table 2.2). Given the lack of student racial diversity, these trends suggest teachers do little to augment diversity for the typical White suburban student. Suburban students of color are also exposed to a disproportionately high share of teachers of their own race, although because the percentages of non-White teachers are smaller, these teachers still comprise only a fraction of the faculty at a typical suburban student's school. For example, 7% of the suburban teaching force is Black, while the typical Black suburban student attends a school where 22% of teachers are African American (Table 2.2).

Black, Latino, and Asian students are all disproportionately underexposed to White teachers. For example, less than 70% of teachers in the typical Asian student's suburban school are White, which is considerably less than the share of White teachers in suburbia (85%). This exposure also differs markedly from that of White students and adds another layer of difference in interracial exposure for suburban White students as compared to suburban students of color.

Finally, when examining segregation among suburban teachers, patterns emerge that are very similar to those of students. The isolation of White teachers is extremely high indicating that the typical White suburban teacher is on a faculty with less than 10% teachers of color (Table 2.3).

Table 2.2. Student-Teacher Exposure, Suburban Schools, 2007-08

Percent of Teachers by Race in Student's School	Exposure for Typical Student of Race/Ethnicity:					Racial Composition of Teachers in Sample
	White	Black	Latino	Asian	American Indian	
White	92.65	71.00	72.63	68.65	89.10	85.09
Black	3.12	22.07	7.85	4.20	3.19	6.82
Latino	2.72	4.59	16.28	3.73	4.38	4.96
Asian	1.25	2.01	2.77	22.70	1.72	2.81
American Indian	0.26	0.34	0.46	0.72	1.61	0.32
Total	100.00	100.01	99.99	100.00	100.00	

Source: NCES Schools and Staffing Survey, 2007-08.

Table 2.3.   Teacher-Teacher Exposure, Suburban Schools, 2007-08

Percent of Teachers by Race in Teacher's School	Exposure for Typical Teacher of Race/Ethnicity:					Racial Composition of Teachers in Sample
	White	Black	Latino	Asian	American Indian	
White	90.95	54.57	52.04	42.47	63.34	85.09
Black	4.37	36.70	8.23	5.67	8.48	6.82
Latino	3.03	5.99	36.83	4.15	8.50	4.96
Asian	1.40	2.34	2.35	47.03	5.87	2.81
American Indian	0.24	0.40	0.55	0.67	13.82	0.32
Total	99.99	100.00	100.00	100.00	100.01	

Source: NCES Schools and Staffing Survey, 2007-08; teacher file.

As was the case with student-teacher exposure, there is also disproportionately high isolation for suburban teachers of color. Asians comprise less than 3% of the suburban teaching force, yet the typical Asian suburban teacher teaches in a school in which 47% of his or her faculty peers are Asian. The high isolation of teachers of color means disproportionately lower exposure to White teachers. While 85% of suburban teachers are White, teachers of color are exposed to a much lower percentage of White teachers on their own faculties, on average. These patterns then reinforce segregation among students and indicate the comprehensive nature of segregation emerging in suburban schools.

Altogether, these patterns show reinforcing patterns of segregation when considering both students and teachers. Although not examined here, the exposure of students and teachers of color to White students and teachers is higher in suburban than urban schools, likely due to the higher shares of White students and teachers in suburban schools. Nonetheless, this analysis does reveal how very different the schooling experiences are for suburban White students and teachers than students and teachers of color in suburbia.

CONCLUSION

The implications of these demographic trends for policy and practice are significant as this analysis contributes to our understanding of how demographic changes are transforming suburban school districts in the largest metropolitan areas in the United States. Suburban districts are rapidly changing, particularly in our largest metropolitan areas. While segregation is not as severe as in central cities, these data reveal concerning patterns of segregation within suburbia despite the diverse, multiracial nature of the enrollment. Segregation (by race and class) is highest in suburban areas with more extensive district fragmentation; that is, those areas with many districts enable different student populations to be institutionalized within different districts. What's more, this analysis reveals that patterns of segregation among students extend to segregation of students from teachers of different races and among teachers as well. Although the composition of students and teachers in suburban schools attended by White students differs substantially from the composition of suburban schools attended by Black and Latino students.

At the same time, there are a number of important empirical questions about suburban school composition and segregation of teachers and students that are difficult to answer by available data. National datasets do not allow us to examine subgroups within student racial groups even though, for example, it is clear that vast differences exist between White Latinos and Black Latinos (Logan, 2003b). Likewise, school-level data for English Learners is not available through these same data sources, and questions exist about the reliability of district-level data across states and years. Further, while the Schools and Staffing Survey allows us to periodically assess the relationship between student and teacher racial composition, this is only a sample of schools that are surveyed every 4 years. Without better data, it is impossible to understand the extent to which suburban diversification may be creating diverse schools or schools that are rapidly transitioning to racially isolated non-White schools—much less understand what kinds of policies to adopt or, just as significantly, enable us to identify and study successful models of suburban integration.

The findings that we may be replicating urban patterns of separation on a wider geographic scale suggest the need for comprehensive policy efforts to help create more diverse schools. The policy implications of these findings for students' experiences are important to consider. For students of color, crossing the suburban boundary line has not automatically granted access them to stable, integrated schools. Despite a prevailing sentiment of race neutrality, these findings suggest a need to consider carefully the stratification of suburbia. This includes developing housing and educational policies that will attract households of color to all segments of suburbia, while ensuring that educational policies do not exacerbate racial transition in the schools or communit. Equally important, given that fragmented metros displayed the highest degree of segregation, local leaders and education policymakers must stress the importance—to suburban residents of all backgrounds—of thinking about issues of equity and diversity on a larger geographic scale. With respect to teachers, there must be attention paid to diversifying the pipeline of teachers as well as to providing all prospective teachers with learning experiences in diverse settings. Especially for White teaching candidates, gaining experience in schools with diverse students and/or teaching staffs may encourage these teachers to choose to begin their teaching career in racially mixed schools. If they are efficacious at teaching in such environments, it may also help stem teacher turnover in diverse schools. Since teachers of color are disproportionately more likely to be in schools with higher shares of students of color, school and teacher accountability systems must account for any school inequities when evaluating teachers so that we do not lose teachers of color at a higher rate simply because of the schools they teach in. Finally, in racially isolated White settings that may still be common in some parts of suburbia, educational leaders should pursue a comprehensive strategy: (1) invest in the recruitment of teachers of color to build a critical mass of the faculty in each building to provide exposure to diverse faculty for students and teachers that is impossible among the student body; and (2) even where diversity does not yet exist, provide teachers and students educational opportunities to learn about, and preferably be in contact with, people from diverse racial/ethnic backgrounds.

As suburbanization continues—and diversification of suburbia as well—understanding the complex, changing diversity of suburban schools is essential for developing appropriate policies to expand opportunity for all students.

ACKNOWLEDGMENTS

This chapter draws on, in part, research supported by the Spencer Foundation (PI: Gary Orfield). All views expressed are those of the author. Thanks to Alison Tyler for her assistance.

NOTES

1. Unlike the Census, which allows for detailed racial/ethnic breakdowns, NCES during the time period examined only had five racial/ethnic categories: American Indian, Asian/Pacific Islander, Black, Hispanic, and White. Likewise, due to questions about the reliability of Common Core of Data counts of English Learners, this chapter does not investigate whether Latino and Asian students who are also nonnative speakers are sorting into suburban districts in ways that may differ from their overall group's patterns.
2. Because of the segregation laws, these regions differ somewhat from Census regions. The following regional definitions were used: South— Miami, Tampa, Dallas, Houston, Atlanta; Border—Baltimore, Washington, DC, St. Louis; Northeast—Boston, New York, Philadelphia, Pittsburgh; Midwest—Detroit, Chicago, Cleveland, Minneapolis, Cincinnati; and

West—San Francisco, San Diego, Los Angeles, Denver, Seattle, Sacramento, Phoenix, Portland.

3. Data for 2010 was not available at the time of analysis.

4. The number of suburban residents at or below the poverty line declined in Cincinnati, Cleveland, Minneapolis, and Pittsburgh during the 1990s.

5. This takes into account charter school enrollment, but not private schools.

6. Note that the latest year of data, 2006-07, was before the recent economic crisis. Yet, even prior to this crisis, the number of students eligible for free or reduced-price lunch had been rising (see G. Orfield, 2009).

7. In the Florida MSAs included here, there are only a few districts that comprise the entirety of the metropolitan region. In Tampa MSA, for example, Hillsborough County contains the city of Tampa and surrounding regions, and Pinellas County contains another principal city in the metro, St. Petersburg, in addition to other parts of the metro. The two other districts are designated as "suburban"; they are less dense, although one has among the fastest growth rates in the country. The Baltimore MSA is also largely comprised of countywide districts (with the exception of Baltimore City, which is a separate district and not part of the county district), while Atlanta and Washington, DC have a mix of county and municipal districts.

8. The results described here are those analyzed without the inclusion of districts that contained only charter schools. However, a separate analysis including charter and noncharter districts found that dissimilarity rates were equal to or higher than rates for the corresponding racial pair in each MSA without charter schools, except in Pittsburgh. In other words, in virtually every MSA, where there is an effect on district-level dissimilarity, charter schools exacerbate these levels.

9. I classify those who are eligible for lowered price meals as "low-income" and those who are not as "middle-class" though there is clearly much variation within these two groups, and it is likely that some who are eligible to be classified as "low-income" may not apply for a variety of reasons (Harwell & LeBeau, 2010).

10. For a discussion of factors influencing the contemporary racial composition of the teaching force, see Frankenberg (2009b).

11. SASS does not specify the metropolitan area of schools in its sample, making it impossible to examine the teachers in the largest 25 metropolitan areas separately.

12. Taking the school-level average faculty composition is somewhat different from assessing the overall composition of teachers since larger schools with more students and teachers tend to have higher shares of students and teachers of color in this sample. The racial composition of all teachers in suburban schools in large MSAs is 85.2% non-Hispanic White; 5.1% Latino; 6.5% Black; 3.7% Asian/Pacific Islander; and 1.6% American Indian. These percentages sum to slightly more than 100% due to multiracial teachers identifying with two or more races/ethnicities.

13. These data report student enrollment at the school level and therefore cannot account for any within-school segregation that may occur, including that via tracking, which may further reduce interracial exposure.

APPENDIX

Table 2.A-1. Suburbanization of Total Population, 1990 to 2010

Metropolitan Area Name	Percent of MSA Population in Suburbs			Change in Suburban Population, 2000-2010
	1990	*2000*	*2010*	
Atlanta-Sandy Springs-Marietta, GA	86.7	89.9	91.8	1,017,350
Baltimore, MD	67.7	73.1	75.8	187,688
Boston-Cambridge-Quincy, MA-NH	74.1	74.5	74.7	128,798
Chicago-Naperville-Joliet, IL-IN-WI	58.1	60.1	63.2	508,500
Cincinnati-Middletown, OH-KY-IN	74.0	77.6	80.5	154,861
Cleveland-Elyria-Mentor, OH	71.3	73.2	76.1	10,685
Dallas-Fort Worth-Arlington, TX	52.0	55.4	59.9	962,012
Denver-Aurora, CO	71.3	73.7	73.4	235,630
Detroit-Warren-Livonia, MI	71.3	74.2	78.9	85,377
Houston-Sugar Land-Baytown, TX	50.4	53.8	61.0	1,085,573
Los Angeles-Long Beach-Riverside, CA	61.4	62.5	64.7	1,269,008
Miami-Fort Lauderdale-Pompano Beach, FL	82.1	84.8	85.1	485,306
Minneapolis-St. Paul, MN-WI	75.1	77.4	79.6	313,150
New York-Northern New Jersey-Long Island, NY-NJ-PA	53.2	53.1	53.6	403,658
Philadelphia-Camden-Wilmington, PA-NJ-DE-MD	67.4	70.1	71.4	269,740
Phoenix-Mesa-Scottsdale, AZ	30.3	36.1	46.1	759,078
Pittsburgh, PA	84.6	85.8	86.6	-45,943
Portland-Vancouver-Beaverton, OR-WA	62.7	64.9	66.4	225,242
Sacramento, CA	72.9	75.0	74.5	253,933
San Diego, CA	50.0	50.9	52.7	197,478
San Francisco-Oakland-Fremont, CA	65.4	67.2	68.1	208,898
Seattle-Tacoma-Bellevue, WA	67.7	69.3	70.9	333,010
St. Louis, MO-IL	76.0	79.1	81.1	143,104
Tampa-St. Petersburg-Clearwater, FL	70.0	72.4	75.3	359,549
Washington-Arlington-Alexandria, DC-VA-MD-WV	80.1	83.1	84.4	726,466
Total	64.1	66.0	68.2	10,278,151

Source: U.S. Census (1990, 2000, 2010).

Table 2.A-2.   Suburban Racial Composition, 1990 and 2010, Largest 25 Metropolitan Areas

Metropolitan Area Name	Suburban Population, 1990				Suburban Population, 2010			
	% White	% Black	% Latino	% Asian	% White	% Black	% Latino	% Asian
Atlanta-Sandy Springs-Marietta, GA	77	19	2	2	52	30	11	5
Baltimore, MD	86	10	1	2	69	18	5	5
Boston-Cambridge-Quincy, MA-NH	94	2	2	2	80	4	8	6
Chicago-Naperville-Joliet, IL-IN-WI	85	6	6	3	64	11	17	6
Cincinnati-Middletown, OH-KY-IN	95	4	1	1	87	7	3	2
Cleveland-Elyria-Mentor, OH	90	8	1	1	81	12	3	2
Dallas-Fort Worth-Arlington, TX	83	6	8	2	59	11	22	6
Denver-Aurora, CO	86	3	9	2	74	2	18	3
Detroit-Warren-Livonia, MI	93	4	2	2	80	11	3	4
Houston-Sugar Land-Baytown, TX	73	9	15	3	47	13	31	7
Los Angeles-Long Beach-Riverside, CA	53	6	31	9	35	5	42	14
Miami-Fort Lauderdale-Pompano Beach, FL	58	15	25	1	36	19	41	2
Minneapolis-St. Paul, MN-WI	96	1	1	2	84	5	4	5
New York-Northern New Jersey-Long Island, NY-NJ-PA	79	9	8	3	62	10	18	8
Philadelphia-Camden-Wilmington, PA-NJ-DE-MD	88	8	2	2	75	13	6	4
Phoenix-Mesa-Scottsdale, AZ	77	2	19	1	63	4	24	4
Pittsburgh, PA	95	4	1	1	90	6	1	1
Portland-Vancouver-Beaverton, OR-WA	93	1	4	3	78	1	11	5
Sacramento	81	4	9	5	61	5	19	10
San Diego, CA	71	4	20	5	51	4	34	7
San Francisco-Oakland-Fremont, CA	67	6	14	13	46	6	23	19
Seattle-Tacoma-Bellevue, WA	89	3	3	5	69	5	9	10
St. Louis, MO-IL	88	10	1	1	79	14	2	2
Tampa-St. Petersburg-Clearwater, FL	89	4	6	1	71	8	16	3
Washington-Arlington-Alexandria, DC-VA-MD-WV	71	19	5	5	50	23	14	10
Total	78	8	10	4	60	11	19	7

Sources: U.S. Census (1990) and Frey (2011).

**Table 2.A-3.   Percentage of Latino and White Students
in Suburban Schools by MSA, 1990 to 2006**

Metropolitan Area Name	Latino Students (%)			White Students (%)		
	1990	1999	2006	1990	1999	2006
Atlanta-Sandy Springs-Marietta, GA	1.75	4.36	10.56	67.12	59.15	45.26
Baltimore-Towson, MD	0.96	1.89	4.23	84.45	79.20	71.78
Boston-Cambridge-Quincy, MA-NH	6.15	8.26	10.79	88.10	81.51	76.13
Chicago-Naperville-Michigan City, IL-IN-WI	8.06	13.41	19.84	77.65	70.31	59.95
Cincinnati-Middletown-Wilmington, OH-KY-IN	0.23	0.60	1.84	93.44	94.56	85.96
Cleveland-Akron-Elyria, OH	2.06	2.28	3.16	82.52	82.12	73.61
Dallas-Fort Worth, TX	9.65	15.55	24.68	79.64	69.75	54.97
Denver-Aurora-Boulder, CO	10.02	13.65	21.08	84.83	79.04	69.34
Detroit-Warren-Flint, MI	0.98	1.50	2.53	89.26	85.54	78.88
Houston-Baytown-Huntsville, TX	18.67	27.58	36.91	66.14	55.93	43.33
Los Angeles-Long Beach-Riverside, CA	35.91	44.73	51.25	47.83	37.04	27.67
Miami-Fort Lauderdale-Miami Beach, FL	10.58	16.56	23.15	60.54	50.96	40.89
Minneapolis-St. Paul-St. Cloud, MN-WI	1.02	2.70	5.80	84.78	81.12	73.89
New York-Newark-Edison, NY-NJ-PA	10.65	14.78	18.94	70.66	64.93	59.96
Philadelphia-Camden-Vineland, PA-NJ-DE-MD	2.28	3.13	5.31	82.02	78.72	72.29
Phoenix-Mesa-Scottsdale, AZ	28.95	29.67	34.81	67.98	60.54	52.52
Pittsburgh-New Castle, PA	0.21	0.33	0.62	92.37	91.24	87.84
Portland-Vancouver-Beaverton, OR-WA	3.07	7.05	12.62	94.13	88.04	76.56
Sacramento--Arden-Arcade--Roseville, CA	11.17	14.76	18.74	73.87	63.91	52.27
San Diego-Carlsbad-San Marcos, CA	26.63	34.66	42.29	60.94	50.08	39.39
San Jose-San Francisco-Oakland, CA	14.31	20.35	26.00	60.82	51.43	41.45
Seattle-Tacoma-Olympia, WA	2.48	4.85	9.18	89.40	79.30	70.32
St. Louis, MO-IL	0.44	0.83	1.81	77.88	75.04	72.10
Tampa-St. Petersburg-Clearwater, FL	3.70	6.34	12.10	89.90	87.64	76.62
Washington-Arlington-Alexandria, DC-VA-MD-WV	4.57	7.64	14.77	61.31	53.37	43.24
Total	10.32	14.74	20.15	73.90	66.75	57.50

Sources: NCES Common Core, 1990-91, 1999-2000, 2006-07.

REFERENCES

Balfanz, R., & Legters, N. (2004). Locating the dropout crisis: Which high schools produce the nation's dropouts. In G. Orfield (Ed.), *Dropouts in America: Confronting the graduation rate crisis* (pp. 57-84). Cambridge, MA: Harvard Education Press.

Berkman, M. B., & Plutzer, E. (2005). *Ten thousand democracies: Politics and public opinion in America's school districts*. Washington, DC: Georgetown University Press.

Bischoff, K. (2008). School district fragmentation and racial residential segregation: How do boundaries matter? *Urban Affairs Review, 44*(2), 182-217.

Bocian, D. G., Li, W., & Ernst, K. S. (2010). *Foreclosures by race and ethnicity: The demographics of a crisis* (CRL research report). Retrieved from Center for Responsible Lending website: http://www.responsiblelending.org/mortgage-lending/research-analysis

Brookings Institution. (2010). *State of metropolitan America: On the front lines of demographic transformation*. Washington, DC: The Brookings Institution Metropolitan Policy Program.

Charles, C. Z. (2005). Can we live together? Racial preferences and neighborhood outcomes. In X. S. Briggs (Ed.), *The geography of opportunity: Race and housing choice in metropolitan America* (pp. 45-80). Washington, DC: The Brookings Institution.

Clotfelter, C. T. (2004). *After* Brown*: The rise and retreat of school desegregation*. Princeton, NJ: Princeton University Press.

Cohen, E. G. (1980). Design and redesign of the desegregated school: Problems of status, power, and conflict. In W. G. Stephan & J. R. Feagin (Eds.), *School desegregation: Past, present, and future* (pp. 251–278). New York, NY: Plenum.

Farrell, C. R. (2008). Bifurcation, fragmentation or integration? The racial and geographic structure of U.S. metropolitan segregation, 1990-2000. *Urban Studies* 45, 467-499.

Frankenberg, E. (2009a). Splintering school districts: Understanding the link between segregation and fragmentation. *Law and Social Inquiry 34*(4), 869-909.

Frankenberg, E. (2009b). The segregation of American teachers. *Education Policy Analysis Archives, 17*(1). Retrieved from http://epaa.asu.edu/ojs/article/view/3

Frankenberg, E., & Lee, C. (2002). *Race in American public schools: Rapidly resegregating school districts*. Cambridge, MA: Civil Rights Project at Harvard University.

Frey, W. H. (2001). *Melting pot suburbs: A Census 2000 study of suburban diversity*. Washington, DC: The Brookings Institution Press.

Frey, W. H. (2011). *Melting pot cities and suburbs: Racial and ethnic change in metro America in the 2000s*. Washington, DC: The Brookings Institution Press.

Galster, G., & Godfrey, E. (2005). By words and deeds: Racial steering by real estate agents in the U.S. in 2000. *Journal of the American Planning Association, 71*(3), 251-268.

Harris, D. J., & McArdle, N. (2004). *More than money: The spatial mismatch between where homeowners of color in metro Boston can afford to live and where they actually reside*. Cambridge, MA: Metro Boston Equity Initiative, Harvard Civil Rights Project.

Harwell, M., & LeBeau, B. (2010). Student eligibility for a free lunch as an SES measure in education research. *Educational Researcher, 39*(2), 120-131.

Kneebone, E., & Garr, E. (2010). *The suburbanization of poverty: Trends in metropolitan America, 2000 to 2008*. Washington, DC: The Brookings Institution.

Linn, R. L., & Welner, K. G. (Eds.). (2007). *Race-conscious policies for assigning students to schools: Social science research and the Supreme Court cases*. Washington, DC: National Academy of Education.

Logan, J. (2003a). Ethnic diversity grows, neighborhood integration lags. In B. Katz & R. E. Lang (Eds.), *Redefining urban and suburban America: Evidence from Census 2000*. Washington, DC: Brookings Institution Press.

Logan, J. R. (2003b). *How race counts for Hispanic Americans*. Albany, NY: American Communities Project. Retrieved May 8, 2012, from at http://mumford1.dyndns.org/cen2000/BlackLatinoReport/BlackLatinoReport.doc

Logan, J., Oakley, D., & Stowell, J. (2008). School segregation in metropolitan regions: The impacts of policy choices on public education. *American Journal of Sociology, 113*, 1116-44.

Massey, D. S., & Denton, N. A. (1988). The dimensions of residential segregation. *Social Forces, 67*(2), 281-315.

Massey, D. S., & Denton, N.A. (1993). *American Apartheid: Segregation and the making of the underclass*. Cambridge, MA: Harvard University Press.

Mickelson, R. A., & Nkomo, M. (2012). Integrated schooling, life course outcomes, and social cohesion in multiethnic democratic societies. *Review of Research in Education 36*, 197-238.

Oliver, J. E. (2001). *Democracy in suburbia*. Princeton, NJ: Princeton University Press.

Orfield, G. (2001). Metropolitan school desegregation. In j. a. powell, G. Kearney, & V. Kay (Eds.), *In pursuit of a dream deferred* (pp. 121-157). New York, NY: Peter Lang.

Orfield, G. (2009). *Reviving the goal of an integrated society: A 21st century challenge*. Los Angeles, CA: Civil Rights Project.

Orfield, G., & Frankenberg, E. (2008, January). *The last have become first: Rural and small town America lead the way on desegregation*. Los Angeles, CA: Civil Rights Project/ Proyecto Derechos Civiles.

Orfield, G., Frankenberg, E., & Garces, L. M. (2008). Statement of American social scientists of research on school desegregation to the U.S. Supreme Court in *Parents v. Seattle School District* and *Meredith v. Jefferson County*. *Urban Review 40*, 96-136.

Orfield, M. (2002). *American metropolitics: The new suburban reality*. Washington, DC: The Brookings Institution.

Orfield, M. & Luce, T. (2009). *Region: Planning the future of the twin cities*. Minneapolis, MN: University of Minnesota Press.

Orfield, M., & Luce, T. (2012). *America's racially diverse suburbs: Opportunities and challenges* (IMO research report). Retrieved November 30, 2012, from University of Minnesota Law School Institute on Metropolitan Opportunity website:

www.law.umn.edu/uploads/e0/65/e065d82a1c1da0bfef7d86172ec5391e/
Diverse_Suburbs_FINAL.pdf

Parker, W. (2009). Desegregating teachers. *Washington University Law Review, 86*(1), 2-53.

Puentes, R., & Warren, D. (2006). *One-fifth of America: A comprehensive guide to America's first suburbs.* Washington, DC: Brookings Institution.

Reardon, S., & Yun, J. T. (2005). Integrating neighborhoods, segregating schools: The retreat from school desegregation in the South, 1990-2000. In. J. C. Boger & G. Orfield (Eds.), *School resegregation: Must the South turn back?* (pp. 51-69). Chapel Hill, NC: University of North Carolina Press.

Rothwell, J., & Massey, D. S. (2009). The effect of density zoning on racial segregation in U.S. urban areas. *Urban Affairs Review, 44*(6), 779-806.

Ryan, J. E. (2010). *Five miles away, a world apart: One city, two schools, and the story of educational opportunity in modern America.* New York, NY: Oxford University Press.

Shapiro, T. (2004). *The hidden cost of being African American: How wealth perpetuates inequality.* New York, NY: Oxford University Press.

Stillman, J. B. (2013, winter). The elephant in the classroom. *EducationNext, 13*(1). Retrieved from www.educationnext.org

Tourkin, S., Thomas, T., Swaim, N., Cox, S., Parmer, R., Jackson, B., Cole, C., & Zhang, B. (2010). *Documentation for the 2007–08 Schools and Staffing Survey* (NCES 2009–318). Washington, DC: National Center for Education Statistics, Institute of Education Sciences, U.S. Department of Education.

U.S. Census Bureau. (n.d.). QuickFacts: Metropolitan statistical area. Retrieved August 27, 2011, from http://quickfacts.census.gov/qfd/meta/long_metro.htm

Villegas, A. M., & Lucas, T. (2002). *Educating culturally responsive teachers: A coherent approach.* Albany, NY: State University of New York Press.

Weiher, G. R. (1991). *The fractured metropolis: Political fragmentation and metropolitan segregation.* Albany, NY: State University of New York Press.

Wells, A. S., Baldridge, B., Duran, J., Lofton, R. Roda, A., Warner, M., ... Grzesikowski, C. (2009). *Why boundaries matter: A study of five separate and unequal Long Island districts.* New York, NY: Teachers College.

CHAPTER 3

EQUITABLE PUBLIC EDUCATION

"Getting Lost in the Shuffle"

Robert G. Croninger and Kathleen Mulvaney Hoyer

What I would like to know is how a student with my talent and intelligence who use to ... not except nothing but the best can be pulled down to such a low level. I could see if I were what is considered a bad student. I don't smoke weed or cigarettes. I don't drink. I am not in any sort of gang, and I rarely go to parties, so give me a reason. It might be too late for me to correct my life but I hope you people can change things so smart person's mind doesn't get lost in the shuffle of life." Former student at Cass Technical High School, Detroit, MI, 1977

In *Milliken v. Bradley* (1977) the Supreme Court affirmed a district court's opinion that the desegregation plan for Detroit Public Schools required additional expenditures by the state of Michigan and the Detroit School Board to address the consequences of racial segregation. In an earlier opinion, the Court ruled against mandating a metropolitan desegregation plan, and, instead, directed the district, state, and lower court to determine an alternative remedy. That remedy focused on improving the educational opportunities afforded elementary and secondary public school students in Detroit, primarily through the enhancement of educational services and programs monitored by the district court, until such a time that public school students in Detroit attained a level of educational

Charting Reform, Achieving Equity in a Diverse Nation
pp. 55–76
Copyright © 2013 by Information Age Publishing

accomplishment that they could conceivably have achieved if racial segregation between the city and surrounding suburbs had not been permitted (Nelson, 2007).

That same year, the Programs for Educational Opportunity, a federally funded Desegregation Assistance Center located at the University of Michigan, conducted a series of surveys with students and faculty at Cass Technical High School, a large college preparatory school in downtown Detroit with a storied history of excellence. The survey was intended to be a pilot of a needs assessment that could be used to help make instructional and program decisions by principals and district administrators. The quote above comes from a former student at Cass Technical High School who heard about the survey. She sent a personal letter to Programs for Educational Opportunity after the surveys had been completed, starting her correspondence with "My mother was supposed to have written this letter but I think I have a better insight to the problem at hand." Although she argued that the "desegregation of Detroit Public Schools is a good idea," she also wondered, "What good is it to bus students from one sorry school to another sorry school." The letter goes on to describe her personally disappointing history of education in the city's schools. She was identified early as talented and a candidate for "double promotion" in kindergarten. She did "excellent work through the fourth grade," until, as she states, "I was finally old enough to notice that I was poorer than most." The remainder of the letter is a narrative of persistence through late elementary school, junior high school and eventual admission to CTHS; it is also, however, a narrative of growing internal doubt, social stigmatization, and dismay. Although Cass Technical High School provided some of the best educational opportunities available in Detroit at the time, she struggled academically and eventually transferred to Northwestern High School, where she felt "she would be lucky just to graduate from one of the lowest rated schools in the city." She argued that her academic struggles were largely because of the educational and social issues born from poverty. "I can't speak for all of the poor people but I know that poverty is the reason that I am not doing as well as I am capable of in school."

Thirty-five years later, as we write this manuscript, we find ourselves wondering whether life chances have substantially changed for such students and, whether, as she asks, our efforts have "change[ed] things so smart person's mind doesn't get lost in the shuffle of life" (or the shuffle of policies meant to promote educational opportunities for students who come from disadvantaged backgrounds). There is plenty of evidence that we have not "changed things" (and some evidence that opportunities are worse). According to the 2010 census, social inequality is greater in Detroit today than it was in the 1980 census. Slightly more than one third of residents (35%) live in poverty, and nearly one quarter (23%) is unemployed. Racial isolation has also increased since 1980: over four fifths (83%) of Detroit residents are African American (U.S. Census Bureau, 2010). In 2009, U.S. Secretary of Education, Arne Duncan, described the reform of public education in Detroit as a "moral obligation" for the federal government, noting especially the high number of dropouts in the city's schools, estimated as somewhere between one half and two thirds of ninth graders (Mrozowski & Wilkinson, 2009.

Such dismal and disappointing statistics are not restricted to Detroit. Nationwide there has been a marked increase in income inequality between 1977 and now. Although family incomes increased between 1977 and 2007, the increase was nearly five times greater for families in the top quintile of earnings (34%) than families in the bottom quintile of earnings (7%) (Duncan & Murnane, 2011). Lower earning families continue to have few options other than to send their children to lower quality schools—schools characterized by high levels of poverty and racial segregation (Orfield & Lee, 2005)—and nearly half of entering ninth-grade Hispanic and African American students fail to graduate in 4 years, the majority eventually dropping out (Rumberger, 2011). Despite 35 years of legislation and litigation, the quality of educational opportunities afforded children remains stubbornly unsatisfactory, especially for students from historically disadvantaged backgrounds. In the face of these disappointing figures, it is important to gain an understanding about the ways in which past policies can inform future judgments. Against a backdrop of inequality, to what extent are future federal and state policy efforts likely to reverse the negative educational trends facing low-income students and ensure that they do not get lost in the shuffle?

In answering this question, we make two claims. First, our policies have increasingly freighted the burden of achieving social equality and fairness in the United States on its public school system. One consequence is that what was once a social contract, a set of beliefs about broader social obligations and responsibilities, has become an educational contract, a set of beliefs that schools bear the primary responsibility (if not exclusive responsibility) for promoting social equality and fairness. Second, as schools are promoted as the primary mediator of life chances and economic success, the civic purpose or collective goods of schooling decrease. Instead, educational opportunities are seen primarily as individual goods, encouraging further stratification of educational opportunities and making it more difficult for courts or any branch of government to claim a compelling interest in creating schools that balance the promotion of desirable civic outcomes with the acquisition of individual goods. The framing of education as an individual good and the subsequent decreased emphasis on the societal outcomes of education serve as impediments to acknowledging a social contract that provides collective assurances *and* collective responsibilities for economic and social prosperity. Although these two claims do not fully explain the limited success federal and state policies have had in achieving equitable public education in the past, they do suggest the need for a broader perspective if we are to make progress in the future.

A SOCIAL CONTRACT PERSPECTIVE

Conceptions of fairness, justice, and equality are socially constructed beliefs formed by the interplay of institutional traditions, social norms, and political power. Although there is continuity in these beliefs, especially when they become codified into law, they still are wont to be dynamic and change over time. Historical conditions identify inconsistencies or contradictions in beliefs and practices, which may promote additional claims for rights and protections, especially among those in society who have experienced persistent economic and social disadvantages. Social institutions may act to further guarantee the current distribution of power and privilege, ignore the social and political pressure for change, or respond with innovative policies that acknowledge perceived injustices (Nonet & Selznick, 2009). These beliefs (and changes to them) are the elements of an evolving, sometimes contested social contract. The history of our beliefs about equitable education is but one example.

Social Contract

The notion of a social contract "refers to the understandings and conventions within a society that help to explain and justify its legal, political, and economic structures" (Paz-Fuchs, 2011, p. 3). Early modern political theorists created the idea of a social contract to discuss the foundations of civil and political society; embedded within these early theories are notions of the tradeoffs that are associated with belonging to society. Philosophers like Locke and Rousseau stressed that under certain conditions it would be advantageous for people to give up some rights and freedoms in order to gain membership in civil society and garner political, economic, and physical security (Locke, 1690/1967; Rousseau, 1762/1954). In other words, individual members of societies should be willing to surrender some degree of their own liberty and grant authority to institutions to govern and distribute public goods as long as they believe that they are being treated justly, fairly, and as possessing equal worth. More contemporary social contract theorists focus on the creation of civil society and subsequent obligations to political rule; they talk about social contracts as seeking to "justify social institutions and policies that reflect justice as the basic virtue in political society," as well as to construct acceptable "rights and responsibilities in the modern welfare state" (Paz-Fuchs, 2011, p. 3). Key in these discussions is the notion of justice and its role as the bedrock standard for social institutions (see, e.g., Rawls 1971; Walzer, 1983).

What is important to note about social contracts is their emphasis on collective responsibility in addition to individual rights; they recognize that rights are accompanied by civic duty and that "rights make common sense only in the context of social, political, and economic relationships" (Ford, 2011, p. 244). Thus, while a social contract perspective of equitable education certainly recognizes the importance of individual rights and protections, it also places a great deal of emphasis on public commitments to shared and just prosperity. Our use of the concept of the social contract reflects this orientation and capitalizes on both classical and contemporary themes. First, we recognize the arguably common-sense notion that there exist tradeoffs between liberty and membership in political and civil societies. An acceptance of these responsibilities and the inherent limiting of liberty provide an opportunity to benefit from society's institutional structures. Second, we acknowledge the importance of justice as a fundamental principle upon which to build and critique societies and their institutions. In other words, justice is a primary standard by which to assess the nature of tradeoffs required of citizens in general and diverse populations in particular within society. Finally, we observe that there is a historical trajectory, at least in democratic societies, for diverse populations to seek changes in institutional structures, redress perceived discriminatory policies, and gain greater access to societal benefits in the pursuit of a more just society (see Pole, 1978, and Minow, 2010, for examples in the history of the United States).

Our ensuing discussion of equitable public education, then, is nested in a social contract perspective that calls for the continued critique and creation of a web of institutions—including but not limited to educational institutions—that will contribute to a just society in which the tradeoffs associated with membership are reasonable and defensible for all of its citizens. We do not see equitable education as an end state, to be achieved and then celebrated, but as an ongoing societal aspiration that requires democratic deliberation and institutional reforms. Although we focus exclusively on education reforms, legislation, and legal decisions in the United States, efforts to expand social, political, and educational opportunities have occurred and continue to occur in other countries throughout the world (see United Nations General Assembly, 1948, and Office of the United Nations High Commissioner for Human Rights, 1966, for global examples). While specific social and political dynamics may vary by country, the call for greater access to societal benefits and educational opportunities by historically disadvantaged groups is commonplace.

The Social Contract in American History

From the early days of United States, members of society set forth competing visions of what constitutes equal opportunities to pursue success and meaningful participation in civic life. Framers of the Constitution and other founders initially set up a series of political contracts designed to protect multiple freedoms and to provide many, though not all, citizens equal access to participation in republican government (Pole, 1978). While the new nation was socially fractured and hierarchical, early understandings of a social contract implied that, given some degree of equality of opportunity in the form of political rights, individuals would be able to forge for themselves the type of lives they wanted within the acceptable norms of society (Pole, 1978). Such political rights were expanded over time to include additional populations who were eventually recognized as not having the same opportunity to participate in democratic deliberations. Policymakers expanded, often begrudgingly, protections for previously excluded populations to participate more fully in the responsibilities and opportunities provided by civic institutions. For example, African Americans received guarantees of equal protection under the law and the right to vote with the Fourteenth and Fifteenth Amendments, respectively, and women eventually won the right to vote with the Nineteenth Amendment. The 1964 Civil Rights Act further underscored these rights when it prohibited major forms of discrimination on the basis of race in voting procedures and forms of discrimination on the basis of "race, color, religion, sex, or national origin" in employment and programs receiving federal funds (Minow, 2010; Salomone, 1986).

With dissent, debate, and dispute, our notions of equality have become more inclusive of diverse populations over time. Nonetheless, they also have become narrower with respect to our understanding of the social institutions most critical to promoting equality and to safeguarding a social contract between members of society and its institutions. Whereas the foundations for the social contract within the United States evolved to include a guarantee of political and economic rights, these institutional spheres have receded into the background as greater and greater emphasis has been placed on guaranteeing educational opportunities as individual rights. Under these conditions, the social contract has been restated or reshaped as an educational contract—as an effort to guarantee that individuals have a reasonable chance to achieve success by obtaining higher levels of education and the economic and social privileges associated with it.

CHANGING PERSPECTIVES

While Americans have long supported education and valued its potential role in creating a more prosperous and desirable society (Hochschild & Scovronick, 2003), the focus on education as *the* central institution for securing a prosperous future for both society and individuals is a post-World War II development. Such a central focus helps to explain the preponderance of litigation and legislation after World War II aimed at defining and guaranteeing equitable education in elementary and secondary schools (Cohen & Moffit, 2009; Rebell, 2009; Salomone, 1986) and in postsecondary institutions (Grubb & Lazerson, 2004). While litigation and legislation have helped to clarify aspects of what constitutes equitable opportunities in education (Minow, 2010), they have also obscured the underlying social contract of which equitable education is only one part. We examine the reshaping of our sense of a social contract, particularly as it pertains to notions of education equity, next.

Decentralized Educational Opportunities

Prior to World War II, American politicians, policymakers, and practitioners promoted a variety of goals for education. While some education philosophers and social observers alluded to the potential for schools to serve as vehicles of social and/or economic betterment (see, for instance, Mann, 1848/2012, or Washington, 1896) these and other thinkers placed greater emphasis on the civic purposes of schooling. Chief among these purposes were citizenship (Jefferson, 1779/2001; Webster, 1790/2001), socialization (Mann, 1848/2012; Webster, 1790/2001) and preparation of workers for engagement in the labor market (Washington, 1896). Despite recognition of the possibility to harness schools to advance the ideal of social and economic equality, early American thinkers suggested more frequently that other collective aims (an informed electorate or a linguistically homogeneous society) should be chief among goals for public schools.

Even though education and political movements attempted to create a centralized system of publically supported common schools during the 19th century (a system that might theoretically be poised to affect citizens' access to equality and public goods on a broad scale), narrower local community interests dominated educational discussions and debates during this time. Even when judicial actors, policymakers and philosophers did discuss the possibility that schools could foster social equality, they did so within an educational context marked by relative decentralization and local control. This context left little room for advancing equality in a systematic manner in educational settings or for seeing educational institutions as a major arena in which to address social inequalities. For instance, more than half of all appellate cases regarding education in the period between 1810 and 1896 fell under the categories of "district debt, securities, and taxation," "government, officers, and district meetings," and "creation, alteration, and dissolution of school districts" (Tyack & Benavot, 1985, p. 353). The prevalence of court cases in these district-focused topics suggests that local and mainly administrative issues took center stage in early American and prewar judicial debates surrounding public education; litigation regarding the actual distribution of public educational resources did not become prominent until the second half of the 20th century. When disputes occurred prior to the 1950s about the equitable distribution of education resources, they were likely to be locally defined and locally resolved (Tyack & Benavot, 1985).

Patterns of educational expenditures also highlight the local nature of education concerns, or at least an absence of broader considerations about how to equitably fund schools. For example, between 1889 and 1896 roughly three quarters of funding for elementary and secondary education came from local sources; little came from the federal government. The local share of expenditures actually increased to a high of 84% in 1925, and then gradually declined to 57% in 1950 (National Center for Education Statistics, 1993). Although the time between World War I and World War II saw the state and, to a much smaller degree, the federal government assuming a greater share of financing for public schools, there were still substantial inequities based on local property wealth, with families from low-income and historically disadvantaged populations bearing a heavier burden for supporting their schools (Hoxby, 1998).

Even when the country faced severe economic threats to the social contract, educational institutions played a minor role in efforts to build trust and address social inequalities. Early 20th century attempts at promoting social equality complemented early American notions of political contracts. For instance, Great Depression era policymakers attacked problems of widespread economic despair and inequality with economic policies that considered the impact of these economic troubles on society as a whole. Largely absent from these policies were attempts to hook educational solutions to social and economic problems. According to Kantor and Lowe (1995, p. 4),

> Although the New Deal initiated several innovative educational programs, during the 1930s education typically was not a conscious tool of federal pol-

icy and was of secondary importance compared to other federal measures to revive the economy and alleviate immediate economic suffering.

Public debate and discussion did not make a connection between economic opportunity and educational opportunity, nor did they link education to social issues surrounding poverty and race. Rather, the focus of these efforts toward equality and stability was job creation, direct and indirect forms of economic assistance, and regulations surrounding minimum wage and pensions (Kantor & Lowe, 1995).

To some extent, the absence of any well-developed set of educational interventions to address the Great Depression might be anticipated given the fragmented nature of public school governance and the relatively weak role of the federal government in determining education policy prior to the 1960s. However, it can also be argued that the absence of a well-constructed set of educational interventions during the 1930s had to do with the relative weakness of educational institutions at the time and their minor role in the life of citizens. In 1940, more than half of the United States population had completed no more than an eighth grade education; only 6% of males and 4% of females had completed 4 years of college (National Center for Education Statistics, 1993). Although educational attainment in the United States was higher than in many European countries at this time, especially at the secondary level and beyond (Hochschild & Scovronick, 2003), the link between educational opportunities and economic opportunities was still tenuous in the popular construction of the nation's social contract (Kantor & Lowe, 1995).

In summary, there is little evidence that early- to mid-20th century efforts to address social ills or promote social equality stemmed from an infusion of resources and energy into public education. Although individuals often saw education as a viable avenue for social mobility and the enhancement of personal life chances, there was not a collective sense of the centrality of education to promoting economic prosperity or addressing social inequality. Public education played a role locally, particularly in large cities, in addressing local concerns about immigration and citizenship, but it did not have a central role in dealing with broader concerns about social inequalities and promoting a sense of justice and fairness in society.

Emerging Education Contract

After World War II and continuing throughout the mid- to late-20th century, reliance on political and social contracts to address issues of inequality began to fade as reliance on an education contract gained

prominence. While policymakers, practitioners, and philosophers continued to espouse varied goals for education during these decades, they
began to discuss more seriously the use of education, particularly the public schools, to address broader problems of social, political, and especially
economic inequality.

During this same period of time, local shares of funding for public education continued to decrease, approaching 50% in the 1960s, just as the
proportion of funding from state and federal revenues increased to
roughly 40% and 9% respectively (National Center for Education Statistics, 1993). Educational attainment also continued to increase, with
approximately 40% of students completing high school and 10% completing 4 years of college by 1960 (National Center for Education Statistics,
1993)—the latter stimulated in part by Roosevelt's signing of the Service-
men's Readjustment Act in 1944, or, as it is more commonly known, the
GI Bill. Although a number of federal legislative acts, such as the Smith-
Hughes Act of 1917, which helped to establish vocational education in
public secondary schools, and the Morrill Act of 1862, which helped to
establish the first land-grant colleges, occurred before the end of World
War II, it was not until much later that the federal government passed legislation that would begin to elevate educational institutions as the institution of choice for ensuring the nation's claim to being the "land of
opportunity."

The Supreme Court's 1954 *Brown v. Board of Education* decision placed
the issue of equality squarely in the domain of the schools. Although *Mendez v. Westminister School* reached a similar conclusion regarding the segregation of Mexican American students in Orange County Public Schools in
1946, *Brown* set a federal precedent and overturned the principle of "separate but equal" endorsed by *Plessy v. Ferguson* in 1896. In framing issues
of racial discrimination as an educational issue, the lawyers of the
National Association for the Advancement of Colored People (NAACP)
believed that they had the best legal strategy by which to dismantle not
only school segregation but social, economic, and political segregation,
particularly in the South (Minow, 2010). The result was a strong rejection
of *Plessy v. Ferguson* and a compelling argument about the central role of
public education in both the life of the country and the development of
the child. In announcing the Court's unanimous decision, Chief Justice
Warren wrote:

> Today, education is perhaps the most important function of state and local
> governments. Compulsory school attendance laws and the great expendi-
> tures for education both demonstrate our recognition of the importance of
> education to our democratic society. It is required in the performance of our
> most basic public responsibilities, even service in the armed forces. It is the
> very foundation of good citizenship. Today it is a principal instrument in

awakening the child to cultural values, in preparing him for later professional training, and in helping him to adjust normally to his environment.
In these days, it is doubtful that any child may reasonably be expected to
succeed in life if he is denied the opportunity of an education.[1]

Although the Court did not identify a remedy until a year later, and
even then only instructed states to desegregate schools "with all deliberate
speed," its decision helped to set a framework for subsequent litigation
and legislation that sought to address broader inequalities through promoting equal education.

Legal scholars and social scientists continue to debate the effects of
Brown, as well as whether the NAACP lawyers made a mistake in challenging school segregation before economic segregation and other inequalities (see Rosenberg, 1994), but there is no denying that the *Brown* case
had a broad wake that influenced other advocates for equality to seek
their causes through litigation and legislation that targeted education policies and practices (Minow, 2010; Salomone, 1986). With the passage of
the Civil Rights Act in 1964, advocates for social equality had two strong
legal principles from which to make their claims: (a) the equal protection
clause provided by the Fourteenth Amendment and (b) the antidiscrimination clause provided by Title VI of the Civil Rights Act. Different populations made different uses of these clauses in their attempts to secure
social equality, with some populations making use of both.

Under the equal protection clause, civil rights activists continued to
press for the desegregation of schools. Equal educational opportunities
meant primarily equal access to schools and the dismantling of the dual
school system. Although states and school boards were reluctant to comply with *Brown*, subsequent court cases in combination with the Civil
Rights Act ratcheted up the pressure on states and school boards to
develop meaningful interventions. By 1964, the Court made it clear in
Griffin v. County School Board of Prince Edward County that school boards
have an affirmative obligation to develop a desegregation plan with a reasonable chance of success and that the time for acting with "mere deliberate speed" was over. However, resistance to busing, particularly in the
North, diminished the effectiveness of the equal protection clause in promoting equal education in schools, let alone using schools to address
broader inequities in society. Since the 1970s, when the reassignment of
pupils was a commonplace component of desegregation plans, the courts
have largely retreated from court-ordered desegregation or even voluntary desegregation. Public schools continue to be racially segregated, in
some regions even more so than prior to *Brown* (Orfield & Lee, 2005).
Despite these trends, the Court has rejected the use of race as an admission factor, ironically, even when the intent is to voluntarily integrate

schools (*Parents Involved in Community Schools v. Seattle School District 1*, 2007).

Although other groups have used the equal protection clause to gain access to educational opportunities previously denied them (e.g., access to prestigious all-male schools for women or access to traditional classrooms for students with disabilities), the antidiscrimination clause of the Civil Rights Act has proved more flexible in acquiring new educational opportunities. Policy responses based on antidiscrimination, however, can conflict with policy responses based on equal protection. While the former leaves open the possibility that different populations may require different educational opportunities to prevent being discriminated against by education policies and practices, the latter seeks to treat individuals equally, providing access to resources they have been denied. This potential conflict between equitable and equal educational opportunities has been framed in terms of a "dilemma of differences" by Minow (1985) and as a conflict between "'bare' opportunities" and "opportunities worth wanting" by Howe (1992).

One of the earliest examples of how these conceptions of equity and equality can conflict can be found in *Keyes v. School District No. 1* (1972). Keyes involved the Denver School District and is considered to be the first court order to desegregate a Northern or non-Southern school district. Although one consideration was the racial segregation of schools that prohibited access to all-White schools in the Denver school system, the other consideration was the desire of Hispanic families to maintain their neighborhood schools, in part to maintain linguistic and cultural connections of their children to their families. Two years later, in *Lau v. Nichols* (1974), the Court further articulated an alternative to access by arguing that public schools must provide students with a "meaningful educational opportunity." The suit, which identified a group of children of Chinese ancestry who did not speak English, argued that being included in a traditional English-instructed classroom without bilingual support discriminated against these children. In other words, to be provided a "meaningful" educational opportunity, non-English-speaking children required *different* educational opportunities than those afforded to English-speaking children; they needed educational opportunities that would help them bridge the divide between what was provided without bilingual support and what might be provided with bilingual support. In *Castaneda v. Pickard* (1978) the requirements for providing a "meaningful educational opportunity" were further defined as providing "effective services" for overcoming language barriers to education, though the court left it to educators to determine what those services might be.

The Elementary and Secondary Education Act (ESEA) of 1965 represented another approach to using the public school system as a means to addressing social inequalities and strengthening the social contract. Prior to this point in time, the federal government had never played a major role in financing public education. Although the federal investment in public education has never been more than 10%, that amount of financial support, when coupled with the Title VI of the Civil Rights Act, gave the federal government substantial leverage to influence state and local education policies and practices (Cohen & Moffitt, 2009).

Subsequent reauthorizations of ESEA have sought to ensure appropriate use of funds, build the capacity of state departments of education to support local school districts, promote effective programs for low-income children, direct greater funding to schools that serve low-income families, and, most recently, hold schools accountable for the achievement level of specific populations of students (Cohen & Moffitt, 2009). The general trend in reauthorizations has been to shift from providing compensatory resources to schools with low-income students to enacting high-stakes standards to ensure "equal" educational outcomes for students, at least at the basic proficiency level established by states.

On the one hand, the most recent authorization of ESEA, No Child Left Behind, which emphasizes holding schools accountable for the differences in achievement between historically advantaged and disadvantaged students, would seem like a major advance in our understanding of equitable education—education in which resources are distributed in such a way that there is no difference in the achievement of students from historically advantaged and disadvantaged backgrounds. On the other hand, the higher stakes associated with schools has been accompanied by a divestment in accountability in other institutions. When Lyndon Johnson passed the ESEA it was part of a broader program of a "War on Poverty." As he explained in his 1964 state of the union address, by providing compensatory resources to schools that served low-income families, *along with* a series of social welfare programs, the Johnson administration sought to end poverty and the social inequalities associated with it (Johnson, 1964). While the Personal Responsibility and Work Opportunity Act of 1996 increased accountability for welfare recipients, it also decreased the accountability of political institutions for addressing broader social inequalities. As Kantor and Lowe (2006, p. 475) argue, this most recent reauthorization of ESEA "has become virtually the only federal social policy meant to address wider social inequities."

EDUCATION AS A PRIVATE GOOD

Education has always been seen as a potential avenue for social mobility, which is one reason it has been targeted during the past half century as the policy lever for addressing social inequalities. The notion of getting ahead by getting a good education has been a central thread in the tapestry of the American Dream since the birth of the nation (Hochschild & Scovronick, 2003; Labaree, 1997). However, prior to World War II, multiple purposes were identified with education—not only was education a way of securing a private good, such as attaining a set of skills that might help in securing a more prosperous economic future, it was also a way of securing public goods, such as helping students become good citizens or transition into adulthood. Moreover, even though education was seen as a potential avenue for social mobility, so too were other social, political, and economic institutions. The lore of the American Dream included stories about individuals starting a business, inventing a new technology, working hard in a job, or achieving promotion in the military. Hard work and good fortune could help one get ahead without high levels of education attainment.

Although these success stories continue, most avenues for social mobility have become intricately intertwined with educational achievement. The tapestry of the American Dream has increasingly become a tapestry where both the warp and weft comprise divergent histories of educational attainment. One explanation for the growing importance of education in determining life chances is the belief in what Grubb and Lazerson (2004) refer to as the "education gospel." The gospel combines a strong desire by individuals to get ahead through education with a belief that education can solve many of the country's economic challenges. Strains of the education gospel can be heard in national calls for school reform (examine any of the reauthorizations of the Elementary and Secondary Education Act since *A Nation at Risk* [National Commission on Excellence in Education, 1983]), in concerns about the growing number of youth failing to graduate from high school on time or even complete high school (Rumberger, 2011) and in the Obama administration's ambition for every American to have at least 1 year of additional education beyond high school (Obama, 2012).

While the education gospel can be critiqued, especially regarding the assumption that the skills currently promoted by educational institutions reflect the skills required in the workplace (Grubb & Lazerson, 2004; Labaree, 1997), there is no denying that education is becoming increasingly more important in predicting individual economic outcomes. Between 1977 and 2007, inflation-adjusted wages for college graduates grew by 25% while inflation-adjusted wages for high school graduates grew by only 1%. For individuals without a high school diploma, inflation-adjusted wages during this period dropped by 13% (Duncan & Murnane, 2011). Whether the relationship between education and wages is due to the acquisition of valuable human capital, the procurement of prestigious credentials or both, educational attainment predicts individual economic outcomes, and disparities in income based on educational attainment have widened over time.

The education gospel has spurred calls for the reform of elementary and secondary schools, as well as expansion in postsecondary enrollments—both outcomes that would seem laudable. Yet it has also promoted education as a private good, a primary determinant of future life chances, a way to get ahead and possibly gain a competitive advantage over others in the workforce (Labaree, 1997). Families and children, Labaree (1997) argues, have become education consumers, seeing schools and teachers as commodities that if acquired can secure the best educational opportunities in the pursuit of personal advantage. When education is seen as primarily a private good rather than a public good there is little incentive to sacrifice some level of personal liberty for a civic outcome. One interpretation of *Parents Involved in Community Schools v. Seattle School District 1* (2007) is that school officials saw educational and social benefits to promoting the integration of schools in the district—a public good. Plaintiffs countered that denying them access to desirable schools to promote racial integration violated their rights—a private good. The more education is seen as a private good, the more difficult it is to promote public goods, including equitable public education.

When education is seen as a private good, there are strong incentives to stratify educational opportunities. Families seek educational opportunities that will distinguish their children from peers and make their children more competitive for more prized educational and economic opportunities. At the elementary and secondary levels, many of these hierarchical structures are built on residential segregation and geography (Logan, Minca, & Adar, 2012; Orfield & Lee, 2005). Racially segregated schools tend to intersect with economically segregated schools. These schools find it difficult to hire and retain quality teachers and principals, implement effective instructional and professional development programs, and address day-to-day issues like truancy, discipline, and crime that are less of a challenge in schools that serve students in advantaged neighborhoods. Even with additional resources, such as those provided by school finance reform or federal legislation like Title I, these schools find it difficult to break a history of failure, particularly because there are so few additional policies that target economic opportunity and safety in their neighborhoods.

At the postsecondary level, where educational opportunities are directly funded through tuition, government subsidies, and endowments, hierarchies also exist. These hierarchies reflect the creation of status distinctions that privilege one set of educational opportunities over another. Higher education is a tiered system, with mostly private but some public universities and colleges at the top. These colleges and universities provide students with the most prestigious credentials and the greatest advantages in gaining valued positions in the workforce. Multiple tiers of schools that include second tier state-sponsored colleges and universities, community colleges and for-profit training institutions follow these more prestigious institutions (Grubb & Lazerson, 2004). Although obtaining a college education may be better than failing to graduate or graduating from high school, not all postsecondary credentials are created equally. As many students have discovered, attaining some level of postsecondary education, even a diploma from a 4-year institution, does not guarantee social mobility or employment.

The stratification of educational opportunities is problematic because it mirrors social inequalities that educational reforms are supposed to address. While the linkage between educational attainment and personal income has become stronger since 1977 (Duncan & Murnane, 2011), so too has economic inequality. In 1977 the difference in inflation-adjusted income between families in the 80th percentile and 20th percentile in earnings was nearly $60,000; by 2008, the difference had grown to roughly $85,000. Differences in expenditures in enrichment activities, such as music lessons, travel, and camps, between the 80th percentile and 20th percentile in earning went from nearly $3,000 to roughly $7,500 during the same time period. When educational opportunities are highly stratified, those with greater wealth have greater access to the most desirable educational opportunities. They can access these opportunities through choices in residence, through additional investments in enrichment activities and through investments that provide their children with access to the most desirable postsecondary institutions.

When education is seen as the primary source of social mobility, it also becomes a highly valued private good. Although education policies meant to promote educational opportunities as a way to address social inequalities might be seen as advancing a public good, this need not be the case. When education becomes the primary policy lever for prosperity—individual and social—the competition for private benefits tend to dominate. The irony is that as education policy has focused more exclusively on a fairer distribution of educational opportunities as the means for addressing social inequalities, these same efforts have increased incentives to stratify educational opportunities during the past half century.

DISCUSSION

How do we keep the next generation of students from being lost in the "policy shuffle" of efforts to achieve equitable public education in this country? The challenge of doing so, we argue, is made more difficult by the narrowing of the civic notion of a social contract to an education contract and policies that emphasize public education as a private good. Moreover, these two trends are mutually reinforcing. The more education is seen as the means for addressing social inequalities, primarily by promoting individual attainment for members of historically disadvantaged groups, the more it is seen as a valuable private good, which in turn increases incentives to stratify educational opportunities in the competition for prestige and economic advantage. And the more education is seen as the central avenue for social mobility, the greater the excuse policy makers have to focus almost exclusively on public education to address persistent social inequalities.

Current conceptions of equitable education are a mix of legal and legislative legacies that attempted to ensure meaningful educational opportunities, particularly through the desegregation of schools, and to respond to the unique educational needs of specific populations of students. Although these legacies established broad principles that continue to inform education policies and practices, they continue to promote a narrow view of how to address social inequality and preserve a highly stratified hierarchy of educational opportunities. Residential segregation remains a significant barrier to achieving equitable public education, but the courts have withdrawn from concerns about "separate but equal" education, even barring attempts to prevent the resegregation of schools by using race as a factor in determining school enrollments (see *Parents Involved in Community Schools v. Seattle School District 1*). There is *no* significant federal or state effort to address residential segregation at this time, though specific communities have sought to do so with some positive effects through low-income housing policies that integrate low-income families into higher income neighborhoods (Schwartz, 2010).[2]

Our current conceptions of equitable public education are based less on ensuring equal access to public schools and more on the intersection between state and federal efforts to reform schools and school finance litigation. The Elementary and Secondary Education Act represents the primary federal policy vehicle for achieving equitable public education. Subsequent reauthorizations have gradually shifted from a compensatory perspective on equitable education, in which the federal government provided additional financial resources to low-income schools to improve programs, to an outcomes perspective on equitable education, in which schools are held accountable for the differences in achievement between historically disadvantaged students and advantaged students. No Child Left Behind, which strengthened sanctions, increased testing requirements, and mandated the disaggregation of testing results by race, gender, eligibility for free and reduced meal services, and disability status, set a goal of 2014 to achieve equitable public schools, defined as all students reaching a level of state-determined proficiency levels in reading and mathematics. While some achievement gains can be attributed to No Child Left Behind, 48% of schools in the nation failed to meet annual yearly progress goals in 2011-2012 (Usher, 2012). Of these schools, the vast majority are racially segregated, low income, or both.

Concurrent with legislative reforms that have emphasized an outcomes conceptualization of educational equity has been the school finance reform movement. Although federal courts refused to consider the wealth or poverty of residents as relevant to considerations of the equitable distribution of educational resources (see *San Antonio Independent School District v. Rodriguez*), state courts have been more receptive to complaints that state education policies are not "wealth neutral" (Rebell, 2009). Because state constitutions include education clauses that require the "the establishment of a free education system" or an "efficient and effective education," state courts have been more willing to consider whether or not state policies distribute education resources equitably. Early court cases that sought to guarantee equal distribution of funding, primarily under the "equal protection clauses" of states, were not especially successful. But a new wave of state litigation, which focuses on whether states provide an "adequate education" for children have been far more effective (Rebell, 2009).

Because states must comply with federal legislation, state legislation meant to comply with school finance reform mimics federal legislation. Although school finance reform has led to greater fiscal investments by states into their public education systems, including low-income schools that had been seriously underfunded compared to other schools in the state, the basic framework calls for establishing a threshold for what constitutes an adequate education, considering the populations of students served and their differential needs, and developing a funding formula that is politically viable and provides some reasonable chance of success. In most states, the courts' rulings have been largely tied to the states' standards-based reform or stimulated the state to develop one in response to the court's concern. Although state school finance reform expands the conceptualization of equitable education to include the fair funding of schools, it still accepts a "minimum standard" for achieving equitable public education, just as federal legislation does (Koski & Reich, 2006). Moreover, judging by the number of schools that failed to make annual yearly progress goals, an outcome-based approach to finance reform may be a necessary but not sufficient condition for achieving equitable public education.

Policy makers are still discussing the contours of a reauthorization of the Elementary and Secondary Education Act, the contours of which will influence not only federal efforts but also state school finance litigation. Race to the Top, which began with funds from the American Recovery and Reinvestment Act of 2009 (U.S. Department of Education, 2012b), may provide some indication of what a reauthorization might include under an Obama administration. The legislation allocated $4 billion in competitive grants to states to develop new standards and assessments that prepare students to succeed in postsecondary education and the workplace; develop statewide data systems that measure student growth and success; recruit and reward effective teachers and principals and focus on turning around the lowest performing schools. Twelve states received awards in the first round of competition. The content of the proposals from these states suggest that a new reauthorization would include, among other initiatives, pay for performance incentive structures for teachers and principals, alternative preparation and credentialing programs for teachers and principals, greater use of charter schools and more sophisticated state monitoring of individual students outcomes, including the possibility of outcomes outside of schools (e.g., use of social services).

Another indication of the contours of a reauthorization could be the Obama administration's Promise Neighborhood program. Inspired by the Harlem Children's Zone (2009), the initiative seeks to lift children and families out of poverty by fostering collaboration among a variety of agencies and organizations in local communities, including businesses, schools, human service providers, and civic leaders (U.S. Department of Education, 2012a). Although the funds allocated to the initiative are much smaller than the funds allocated to the Race to the Top initiative, they do represent a broadening of agencies and institutions that could come to bear on addressing social inequalities. As such, it is more consistent with a social contract perspective that sees equitable education as an important public good that requires civic collaboration. By acknowledging that important contextual factors influence the effectiveness of schools, such as political, social and economic inequality, Promise Neighborhoods, and initiatives like it, establish a broader, civic perspective from which to promote equitable public education (Rothstein, 2004).

Future efforts to achieve equitable public education will undoubtedly be informed by past legacies of litigation and legislation. However, they should also be informed by thoughtful evaluations and assessments of past efforts and current social and economic realities. If subsequent generations of children are not to be lost in the shuffle of life and policies, then we require a broader policy framework from which to understand and improve the educational opportunities afforded to every child. Such a policy framework would recognize the manner in which achieving equitable public education is only one part of a broader social contract, which also requires addressing social and economic inequalities outside of our schools through housing policies, preschool programs, labor market initiatives and investments in neighborhoods. Such a policy framework would acknowledge the private goods that can be derived from public education without sacrificing important public goods, such as promoting racially diverse schools and civic responsibility. During a time of high unemployment and high spending deficits, additional investments in public education and communities may be unthinkable for federal and state governments. Nonetheless, if we are to make greater progress in realizing equitable public education, we need policies that target a broader spectrum of children's lives and promote education as a public good.

NOTES

1. *Brown v. Board of Education*, 1954, p. 494.
2. See also, Schwartz in this volume

REFERENCES

Brown v. Board of Education, 347 U. S. 483 (1954).

Castaneda v. Pickard, 648 F. 2d 989 (5th Cir., 1981).

Cohen, D. K., & Moffitt, S. L. (2009). *The ordeal of equality: Did federal regulation fix the schools?* Cambridge, MA: Harvard University Press.

Duncan, G., & Murnane, R. (Eds.). (2011). Introduction: The American dream, then and now. In *Whither opportunity?* (pp. 3-26). New York, NY: Russell Sage Foundation.

Ford, R. T. (2011). *Rights gone wrong: How law corrupts the struggle for equality.* New York, NY: Farrar, Straus and Giroux.

Griffin v. School Board of Prince Edward County, 377 U. S. 218 (1964).

Grubb, W. N., & Lazerson, M. (2004). *The education gospel: The economic power of schooling.* Cambridge, MA: Harvard University Press.

Harlem Children's Zone. (2009). History. Retrieved from http://www.hcz.org/about-us/history

Hochschild, J. & Scovronick N. (2003). *The American dream and the public schools.* New York, NY: Oxford University Press.

Howe, K. R. (1992). Liberal democracy, equal educational opportunity, and the challenge of multiculturalism. *American Educational Research Journal, 29*(3), 455-470.

Hoxby, C. M. (1998). How much does school spending depend on family income? The historical origins of the current school finance dilemma. *The American Economic Review, 88*(2), 309-314.

Jefferson, T. (2001). A bill for the more general diffusion of knowledge. In J. W. Fraser (Ed.), *The school in the United States: A documentary history* (pp. 19-24). Boston, MA: McGraw Hill. (Original work published 1779)

Johnson, L. B. (1964, January 8). *Annual message to the Congress on the state of the union.* Retrieved from http://legacy.c-span.org/Transcripts/SOTU-1964.aspx

Kantor, H., & Lowe, R. (1995). Class, race, and the emergence of federal education policy: From the New Deal to the Great Society. *Educational Researcher, 24*(3), 4-11, 21.

Kantor, H., & Lowe, R. (2006). From New Deal to no deal: No Child Left Behind and the devolution of responsibility for equal opportunity. *Harvard Educational Review, 76*(4), 474-502.

Keyes v. School District No. 1, 413 U.S. 189 (1973).

Koski, W. S., & Reich, R. (2006). When 'adequate' isn't enough: The retreat from equity in educational law and policy and why it matters. *Emory Law Journal, 56*(3), 555-618.

Labaree, D. F. (1997). Public goods, private goods: The American struggle over educational goals. *American Educational Research Journal, 34*(1), 39-81.

Lau v. Nichols, 414 U. S. 563 (1974).

Locke, J. (1967). *Two treatises of government* (P. Laslett, Ed.). Cambridge, England: Cambridge University Press. (Original work published 1690).

Logan, J., Minca, E., & Adar, S. (2012). The geography of inequality: Why separate means unequal in American public schools. *Sociology of Education, 85*(3), 287-301.

Mann, H. (2012). Twelfth annual report of the Massachusetts school board. In T. W. Johnson & R. F. Reed (Eds.), *Philosophical documents in education* (pp. 89-99). Upper Saddle River, NJ: Pearson Education, Inc. (Original work published 1848)

Mendez v. Westminster School District, 64 F. Supp. 544 (C.D. Cal. 1946).

Milliken v. Bradley, 433 U.S. 2167 (1977).

Minow, M. (1985). Learning to live with the dilemma of difference: Bilingual and special education. *Law and Contemporary Problems, 48*(2) 157-211.

Minow, M. (2010). *In Brown's wake: Legacies of America's educational landmark.* Oxford, England: Oxford University Press.

Mrowowski, J., & Wilkinson, M. (2009 February 14). DPS fails kids, fed school chief says. *Detroit News.* Retrieved from http://www.detroitnews.com/article/20090214/POLITICS/902140377.

National Center for Education Statistics. (1993). *120 years of American education: A statistical portrait.* Washington, DC: U.S. Department of Education

National Commission on Excellence in Education. (1983). *A nation at risk. The imperative for educational reform.* Washington, DC: U.S. Government Printing Office.

Nelson, A. R. (2007). *Rodriguez, Keyes, Lau,* and *Miliken* revisited: The Supreme Court and the meaning of equal educational opportunity, 1973-1974. In C. F. Kaestle & A. E. Lodewick (Eds.), *To educate a nation: Federal and national strategies of school reform* (pp. 202-224). Lawrence, KA: The University Press of Kansas.

Nonet, P., & Selznick, P. (2009). *Law and society in transition. Toward responsive law* (2nd edi.). New Brunswick, NJ: Transaction.

Obama, B. (2012, January 24). *Obama's 2012 state of the union address.* Retrieved from http://www.cbsnews.com/8301-503544_162-57365343-503544/obamas-state-of-the-union-address-full-text/.

Orfield, G., & Lee, C. (2005). *Why segregation matters: Poverty and educational inequality.* Cambridge, MA: Harvard University, The Civil Rights Project.

Parents Involved in Community Schools v. Seattle School Dist. No. 1, 551 U. S. 701 (2007).

Paz-Fuchs, A. (2011). *The social contract revisited: The modern welfare state.* Retrieved from www.fljs.org/uploads/documents/Paz-Fuchs-SummaryReport.pdf.

Plessy v. Ferguson, 163 U. S. 537 (1896).

Pole, J. R. (1978). *The pursuit of equality in American history.* Berkeley, CA: University of California Press.

Rawls, J. (1971). *A theory of justice.* Cambridge, MA: Harvard University Press.

Rebell, M. A. (2009). *Courts and kids: Pursuing educational equity through the state courts.* Chicago, IL: The University of Chicago Press.

Rosenberg, G. N. (1994). Brown is dead! Long Live Brown!: The endless attempt to canonize a case. *Virginia Law Review, 8*(1), 161-171.

Rothstein, R. (2004). *Class and schools: Using social, economic, and educational reform to close the Black-White achievement gap.* Washington DC: Economic Policy Institute.

Rousseau, J. J. (1954). *The social contract* (W. Kendall, Trans.). Chicago, IL: Henry Regnery. (Original work published 1762)

Rumberger, R. W. (2011). *Dropping out: Why students drop out of high school and what can be done about it.* Cambridge, MA: Harvard University Press.

Salomone, R. C. (1986). *Equal education under law: Legal rights and federal policy in the post-Brown era.* New York, NY: St. Martin's Press.

San Antonio Independent School District v. Rodriguez, 411 U. S. 1 (1973).

Schwartz, H. (2010). *Housing policy is school policy: Integrative economic housing promotes academic success in Montgomery County, Maryland.* Washington, DC: Century Foundation.

Tyack, D., & Benavot, A. (1985). Courts and public schools: Educational litigation in historical perspective. *Law and Society Review, 19*(3), 339-380.

United Nations General Assembly. (1948). *Universal declaration of human rights.* Retrieved from http://www.un.org/en/documents/udhr

United Nations High Commissioner for Human Rights. (1966). *International covenant on economic, social and cultural rights.* Retrieved from http://www2.ohchr.org/english/law/cescr.htm

U.S. Census Bureau. (2010). Detroit (city) quick facts from the US Census Bureau. Retrieved from http://quickfacts.census.gov/qfd/states/26/2622000.html

U.S. Department of Education. (2012a). *Promise neighborhoods.* Retrieved from http://www2.ed.gov/programs/promiseneighborhoods/index.html#description

U.S. Department of Education. (2012b). *Race to the top.* Retrieved from http://www2.ed.gov/programs/racetothetop/index.html

Usher, A. (2012). *AYP results for 2010-2011–May 2012 update.* Retrieved from http://www.cep-dc.org/displayDocument.cfm?DocumentID=403

Walzer, M. (1983). *Spheres of justice: A defense of pluralism and equality.* New York, NY: Basic Books.

Washington, B. T. (1896, September). The awakening of the negro. *The Atlantic.* Retrieved from http://www.theatlantic.com/magazine/print/1896/09/the-awakening-of-the-negro/5449/

Webster, N. (2001). On the education of youth in America. In J. W. Fraser (Ed.), *The school in the United States: A documentary history* (pp. 35-46). Boston, MA: McGraw Hill. (Original work published 1790)

PART II

PROMISING STRATEGIES

CHAPTER 4

THE POTENTIAL OF ECONOMIC INTEGRATION TO RAISE ACADEMIC ACHIEVEMENT FOR LOW-INCOME STUDENTS

Heather Schwartz

As Erika Frankenberg describes in this book, an increasing share of low-income and non-White families in the United States live in suburbs and attend suburban public schools. This trend does not uniformly apply to each suburb, but it means that a growing number now confront what has been historically deemed an urban phenomena. Suburban demographic shifts have a profound impact on schools' performance, since the gap in academic achievement between children from low-income and higher income families is large and growing larger. Over the past 55 years, the test score gap between the students from the highest and lowest income families has doubled in size, whereas by contrast the much discussed gap in test scores between Black and White children narrowed by half (Reardon, 2011, in Ladd, 2012).

Given the strong and long-standing correlation between family income and academic achievement in the United States and internationally, it is hard to argue convincingly that a majority of high-poverty schools can attain the same average academic achievement among its students as low-

Charting Reform, Achieving Equity in a Diverse Nation
pp. 79–107

poverty schools (Reardon, 2011, in Ladd, 2012). Of course, this raises the question of what policy responses would be most effective to raise achievement for children from low-income families and to counteract flagging performance levels in high-poverty schools.[1] The number of reforms that have been advocated and attempted are far too many to enumerate here, but common approaches include school-based policies to reduce inefficiencies by adopting various test-based accountability policies (such as those described in Holcombe, Jennings, and Koretz's chapter, this volume) or by extending time spent in school, particularly for young children. Advocates of the so-called "bigger, bolder approach" also suggest greater investments in non-school-based policies, such as expanding access to health care and nutritional programs or investing in out-of-school time programs like summer enrichment (A Bigger Bolder Approach to Education, n.d.).

In this chapter, I describe one type of non-school-based intervention—a housing policy called inclusionary zoning (IZ)—that I argue can raise achievement for students from disadvantaged families. Given the enormity of the challenge to narrow income-based achievement gaps, it is important to stress that the housing policy I describe is not a one-size-fits-all approach that promises to single-handedly narrow the national achievement gap. Instead, it is a policy that a particular type of suburb—and, to a lesser extent, gentrifying cities—have adopted to house relatively small numbers of low-income families within otherwise affluent locations. In so doing, I argue, inclusionary zoning has the potential to not only provide a stable source of affordable housing to some disadvantaged families, but also to further provide those households with access to the many amenities that low-poverty schools and low-poverty neighborhoods typically offer.

Although the intent of IZ policies is to integrate lower income households into higher income neighborhoods, they may not achieve it in practice. The specific elements of each locality's inclusionary zoning program combined with the local housing market conditions determine the extent of exposure to low-poverty places. There is no national dataset to verify the income levels of the neighborhoods where IZ homes are located. However, based on data I collected from 11 geographically dispersed jurisdictions with some of the largest IZ programs nationally, I find that the large majority of these IZ policies do, in fact, place affordable homes in low-poverty neighborhoods. Further, the majority of the IZ homes are residentially assigned to low-poverty and to relatively high-performing schools. The placement of inclusionary zoning homes in low-poverty neighborhoods with residential access to lower poverty schools is a notable outcome since other affordable housing programs intended to promote economic integration have historically struggled to achieve this end (Ellen, O'Regan, & Voicu, 2009; Newman & Schnare, 1997).

The largest IZ program in the United States is in Montgomery County, MD. In a separate study of only that county's IZ program, I find large academic benefits accrue to children living in public housing that is integrated via its IZ program into low-poverty neighborhoods and, by extension, low-poverty schools. Extended exposure to low-poverty schools in particular raised those children's achievement over time and narrowed by half the gap in math test scores between them and their high-achieving, nonpoor district-mates by the end of elementary school.[2]

While most IZ programs are small in scale, the results from Montgomery County suggest that their proliferation within affluent suburbs could offer relatively disadvantaged households and children access to very low poverty places, which could potentially raise those children's academic achievement. To explain how, I first explain inclusionary zoning policies and then describe the characteristics of 11 of the larger IZ programs in the United States. After establishing that these 11 programs generally offer access to low-poverty neighborhoods and schools, I then describe the results of a longitudinal study of children living in public housing that is dispersed via IZ into hundreds of neighborhoods and schools with varying levels of poverty within Montgomery County, Maryland. I conclude with a discussion of what these results do and do not suggest and to which type of suburbs the results might apply.

OVERVIEW OF INCLUSIONARY ZONING

IZ policies are termed "inclusionary" because they either mandate or encourage real estate developers to incorporate into their market-rate developments a proportion of homes that are sold or rented at below-market prices. In exchange, most IZ programs in the U.S. offer ways to cover the financial losses developers incur on the IZ homes, for example, by allowing developers to increase the overall size of a development or by providing other zoning variances (Calavita & Mallach, 2010).

Within the United States, IZ policies are highly localized; individual jurisdictions and, in a few cases, states have opted to create ordinances intended to make it possible for some low- and moderate-income households to live in middle- and upper-income communities.[3] Over the past 40 years since the concept was first developed, IZ policies have spread both in the United States and internationally. The best available estimates indicate that at least nine countries worldwide have IZ policies, while more than 500 localities in the United States have adopted IZ in some form (Calavita & Mallach, 2010). Based on their review of the literature,

Calavita and Mallach (2010) estimate that IZ policies since inception have caused the development of 129,000 to 150,000 affordable units, most of which are in California, New Jersey, Maryland, and the Washington, DC, metropolitan area. Data about IZ programs are generally scarce, but most of the programs are thought to be much smaller, producing dozens to hundreds of IZ homes per jurisdiction (Rusk, personal communication, July, 2009).

IZ ordinances are predicated on two aspects of the local market: (1) there must be sufficient demand to prompt the addition of new market-rate housing and (2) the IZ requirements, which often include incentives to offset costs, must not be so onerous as to render a development unprofitable (Mallach & Calavita, 2010). As a consequence of the first condition, IZ policies tend to be found in high-cost housing markets. It is generally assumed, therefore, that IZ is indeed inclusionary. But IZ may not promote inclusion at all if the production of IZ homes increases market prices or reduces the number of homes built. The evidence on these points, however, suggest mixed, weak effects of IZ policy adoption on housing production and prices (Knapp, Bento, & Lowe, 2008; Schuetz, Meltzer, & Been, 2011).

Nevertheless, the simple existence of an ordinance does not guarantee the creation of IZ homes, let alone the inclusion of below-market-priced homes in affluent neighborhoods. Some localities may have an IZ law on the books for years yet produce no IZ homes. For those that do, a number of features of IZ policies might diminish their ability to meet their goals even for direct beneficiaries. IZ policies may be voluntary; may include opt-out provisions allowing developers to build IZ homes off-site or to contribute land or money in lieu of IZ units; and may serve households above low- or moderate-income ranges. Some IZ policies do not require IZ homes to remain at below-market rates after the first occupants move out. Other program features, such as the proportion of homes in a housing development that must be set aside, whether IZ units are to be rented or owned, and the type and size of developments to which IZ requirements apply, also affect the extent to which IZ programs succeed in increasing the supply of affordable housing and promoting social inclusion.

IZ POLICIES WITHIN 11 JURISDICTIONS

As a first test to understand whether IZ programs promote social inclusion, several RAND researchers and I collected data on IZ programs in 11 jurisdictions dispersed throughout the country. Specifically, we wished to verify some central assumptions about the social inclusiveness of IZ policies: namely, whether they serve lower income families and whether they provide IZ recipients with access to low-poverty neighborhoods and residentially assign them to high-performing schools. Given the limited data from these IZ programs, this study did not match housing records to student transcripts to track the school assignment and academic performance over time of students living in IZ homes (as is done in the Montgomery County IZ study described below). Instead, the study descriptively analyzed whether the placement of IZ homes provided families access to low-poverty neighborhoods and schools.

Methods

One of the key goals of IZ programs is to promote social inclusion, which we interpreted for our study to mean offering low-income households the opportunity of social inclusion by providing affordable homes in low-poverty neighborhoods (i.e., where 10% or fewer of households live in poverty) with access to low-poverty schools where less than 20% of students qualify for free or reduced-price meals and high-performing schools (i.e., schools with average test scores at the 50th percentile or above among schools within the state). We applied these definitions to all jurisdictions in the study to document the potential of the programs as a whole to economically integrate disadvantaged children.

We collected data from 11 jurisdictions that we identified from a list of the 50 largest programs in the United States (Rusk, personal communication, July, 2009). We selected only programs that mandated rather than simply encouraged developers to set aside a minimum proportion of newly constructed or renovated market-rate homes to be made affordable. The programs are relatively large and geographically diverse; at least one program was selected from each of the five regions in the United States. We also sought to include both well-established IZ programs such as those in Montgomery County and Fairfax County and newer programs in urban locations such as Denver and Chicago.

To determine whether IZ programs served low-income populations and provided access to both low-poverty neighborhoods and low-poverty, high-performing schools, we gathered the IZ household-income eligibility requirements from each of the 11 localities listed in Table 4.1 and, where available, incomes of households living in IZ homes. We then identified the geographic coordinates for each IZ address (i.e., geocoded the address) to assess the demographic characteristics of neighborhoods with and without IZ homes in each jurisdiction, as well as the academic performance and demographic characteristics of public schools that, by virtue of

Table 4.1.   IZ Program Locations in the Study

Location	Region	Year Current Version of IZ Policy Enacted	Number of IZ Homes Built (as of 2010)
Boulder, CO	West	2000	364
Burlington, VT	Northeast	1990	~ 200
Cambridge, MA	Northeast	1998	~ 460[a]
Chicago, IL	Midwest	ARO enacted in 2003 and revised substantially in 2007; CPAN enacted in 2001	1,235[a]
Davidson, NC	Southeast	2001	54
Denver, CO	West	2002	77
Fairfax County, VA	Southeast	1990	2,338
Irvine, CA	West	2003	183
Montgomery County, MD	Southeast	1973	13,133[a]
Santa Fe, NM	Southwest	2005	602
Santa Monica, CA	West	1990	862

Sources: Data obtained by authors from local administrators of IZ programs.
Notes: The numbers of homes built are the city or county's best estimates. ARO = Affordable Requirements Ordinance; CPAN = Chicago Partnership for Affordable Neighborhoods. [a]The number of addresses we obtained did not match city estimates. We obtained fewer addresses in cases where the data are incomplete, developments did not get built, or addresses were once IZ units but were converted out of the program by resale. In each case, we queried local officials about the discrepancies.

residential assignment to schools, would serve children living at those addresses.

We obtained a total of 15,659 unique IZ addresses from the 11 localities, of which 15,626 (99.2%) were successfully geocoded. The geographic coordinates for each address allowed us to merge public information from the Census, local school districts, state departments of education, and the federal Department of Education to identify the demographic characteristics of the neighborhoods and schools associated with the addresses.

To identify characteristics such as the poverty level of the neighborhoods with and without IZ homes in each of the 11 jurisdictions, we drew on the most current Census data available at the time, which was the 2005–2009 American Community Survey 5-Year Estimates.[4] Since our primary interest was the neighborhood in the immediate vicinity of an IZ address, we report neighborhood characteristics at the census block group level, which is the smallest geographic area at which key demographics (e.g., income, educational attainment, housing values) are publicly available.

To enable us to identify the specific schools to which IZ units were residentially assigned, the nine school districts with residential school attendance boundaries provided their school attendance zone boundary files.[5] Although we requested historical boundary files for 2000–2008, we could uniformly obtain attendance boundary files only as of school year 2007–2008. We used these files to identify the specific elementary, middle, and high schools to which the IZ units were assigned. We assumed for this study that residential school assignments in each of the 11 districts were constant during school years 2005–2006 through 2009–2010.

Using data from the National Center for Education Statistics Common Core of Data, we then linked schools to the characteristics of the student body, such as the percentage of students who qualify for free or reduced price meals and the racial and ethnic composition in each of school years 2005–2006 (hereafter referenced as 2006) through 2009–2010 (hereafter referenced as 2010). We selected these years to best align with the American Community Survey's rolling, multiyear data-collection calendar of January 2005–December 2009.

Finally, we downloaded from each of the nine state education agency web sites publicly available school performance data to rank each school on statewide standardized tests in math and ELA in each of school years 2006–2010. We then developed a single ranking for each school that averaged its rank over the five school years considered.[6] Although standardized test scores were the best information available about the schools, a single metric like the weighted average of students who score proficient or above on math and ELA tests is a crude yardstick for school quality. Partly for that reason, we separated schools into five categories—bottom quintile up through the top quintile among elementary, middle, and high schools within a given state—to provide a proxy for the general performance of the schools without placing undue weight on a specific percentile rank.

The Integrative Potential of IZ Policies

Although the 11 programs studied varied considerably in design, we found that, on the whole, the IZ homes *serve low-income people*. Six of the programs exclusively serve households making 80% or less of the Area Median Income, which is the income criteria for federally subsidized public housing, and three target households earning as little as 30% of the Area Median Income for rental units (of which, Montgomery County is one). The other five reserve a portion of the IZ homes for households earning up to 100 or 120% of the Area Median Income.

In most cases, IZ homes are delegated on a first-come, first-serve basis. Often, they are administered by property managers, which means that a household wishing for an IZ home must apply directly to the property manager rather than to a central municipal office. However, a lack of clear procedures for data collection and reporting by property managers to municipalities about the IZ units stymies the collection of data about IZ recipients and applicants, so our information about each programs' eligibility verification and selection process is incomplete.

The IZ policies also *predominately serve owners rather than renters.* Seventy-eight percent of the IZ homes in this study were for sale, and only one of the IZ programs exclusively operated a rental program. The vast majority of the for-sale homes were sold to low-income households that would otherwise qualify for federally subsidized rental housing on the basis of income. The predominance of ownership is primarily due to many IZ programs' requirement that the IZ units share the tenure of the market-rate homes within the same subdivision.

As in Montgomery County, we found that IZ homes are *widely dispersed throughout the jurisdictions.* This is important, since one concern about the provision of affordable housing is the clustering of low-income families in what can thereby become high-poverty neighborhoods zoned into high-poverty schools. In contrast to other supply-side affordable housing programs that tend to concentrate the homes within a few neighborhoods in a municipality (e.g., public housing projects), IZ units were located in one out of every ten census block groups in the 11 localities and one out of every five census tracts as of 2005–2009. IZ homes were residentially assigned to one in four elementary schools in the neighborhoods.

More importantly, a large majority of IZ homes are *located in low-poverty neighborhoods* where 0-10% of households have incomes below the federal poverty line. Across the 11 localities, the typical IZ unit is located in a census block group (or tract) where 7% of households lived in poverty as of 2005–2009. This is lower than the average poverty rate among the block groups without IZ homes in the same jurisdictions (16%) and the typical U.S. census block group nationally for the same years (14%). Further, 75% of the IZ units in this study are located in a low-poverty census block group or tract, which we define as having 10% or less of households in poverty. However, as shown in Figure 4.1, the percentage of IZ homes in low-poverty neighborhoods substantially varied across the 11 localities.

In Davidson, Fairfax County, Irvine, and Montgomery County, the majority of IZ units were in low-poverty neighborhoods, while in several other cities such as Cambridge, Santa Fe, and Santa Monica, a large share of the IZ units were located in neighborhoods with moderate poverty rates (i.e., 10 to 30%).

As expected, very few IZ homes (2.5%) were in *high-poverty* neighborhoods where 30% or more of the households were in poverty. This is notable since 17% of the block groups across the 11 jurisdictions were high-

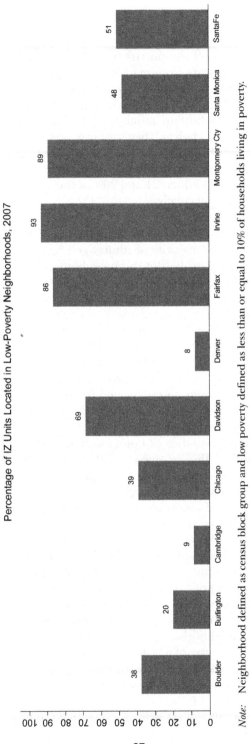

Note: Neighborhood defined as census block group and low poverty defined as less than or equal to 10% of households living in poverty.

Figure 4.1. Percentage of IZ units located in low-poverty neighborhoods, 2005–2009.

poverty neighborhoods. The jurisdictions with IZ homes in high-poverty neighborhoods also had off-site provisions, meaning that IZ homes could be located in places separate from market-rate developments. Half of the IZ homes in high-poverty neighborhoods homes were in Chicago, one quarter were in Boulder, and the rest were spread across five other jurisdictions. Although the absolute number of IZ homes in high-poverty neighborhoods was small, their relative proportion was sometimes high in jurisdictions with small IZ programs. For example, in Denver, 31% of the 77 IZ homes were located in high-poverty neighborhoods as of 2007, while in Burlington and Boulder, 21 and 26% of the IZ units were in high-poverty block groups, respectively.

Looking beyond poverty, the typical IZ unit is located in a neighborhood where, as of 2005–2009, the vast majority of adults of working age were employed (94%), the majority of adults aged 25 and older had a college degree, and more than half of the neighborhood population (57%) was White. Table 4.2 confirms that within all 11 jurisdictions, the household income and rates of college-educated households in the neighborhoods where IZ units were located exceeded national averages.[7] The second row of Table 4.2 shows that in some locations, IZ units were clustered within a small number of neighborhoods (in cases where few developments had IZ units), while in other locations, IZ units were found in hundreds of neighborhoods. In the relatively new IZ programs in Denver, Irvine, and Chicago, IZ homes were located in less than 5% of neighborhoods, while in the majority of the programs, one quarter to one half of the neighborhoods housed at least one IZ unit.

To test systematically whether IZ homes were placed in the less-advantaged neighborhoods within a given jurisdiction—a phenomenon that would lessen potential social inclusion—we performed statistical tests of whether the demographics of IZ neighborhoods differed from those of non-IZ neighborhoods.[8] In most instances, IZ neighborhoods did not differ from their non-IZ counterparts in terms of income, education levels, or race. However, there is evidence that the populations within IZ neighborhoods were less advantaged than those in non-IZ neighborhoods in Burlington, Fairfax County, Montgomery County, and Santa Monica, since the median household income in IZ neighborhoods in these locations was lower than that in non-IZ neighborhoods. Chicago was the only city in which we found that IZ neighborhoods had *more* markers of advantage than non-IZ neighborhoods—an indication that new residential development within the city (of which IZ units were a small share) was typically marketed to attract new households with higher incomes.

Looking then at the schools to which IZ homes are residentially assigned, we found that *44% of IZ homes are residentially assigned to low-poverty schools* where 0-20% of schoolmates qualified for a free or reduced-

Table 4.2. Characteristics of Neighborhoods With IZ Units (2005–2009)

	Boulder	Burlington	Cambridge	Chicago	Davidson	Denver	Fairfax	Irvine	Montgomery County	Santa Fe	Santa Monica
Number of IZ units	364	199	385	1,225	54	77	2,318	183	9,286	575	860
Neighborhoods with 1+ IZ unit	19	15	20	107	5	6	81	3	167	44	40
Percentage of all neighborhoods with 1+ IZ unit	29	56	25	4	100	1	15	3	30	49	50
Median household income ($)	71,197 (27,923)	54,994 (19,582)	78,304 (20,645)	75,438 (47,313)	132,430 (45,578)	45,548 (13,933)	122,201 (42,065)	109,862 (6,277)	126,342 (41,905)	67,647 (21,583)	63,414 (32,031)
Percentage of heads of households with a BA or higher degree	54 (17)	45 (12)	62 (13)	50 (28)	72 (14)	46 (12)	62 (13)	60 (2)	56 (15)	34 (18)	54 (19)
Percentage of household heads who were white	88 (6)	92 (4)	69 (16)	46 (30)	89 (13)	81 (6)	57 (13)	46 (9)	54 (17)	76 (7)	70 (14)
Percentage of household heads who were black	1 (1)	2 (3)	10 (13)	35 (37)	8 (14)	10 (9)	11 (8)	0 (1)	20 (14)	1 (1)	6 (6)
Percentage of household heads who were Hispanic	19 (15)	2 (1)	8 (4)	15 (19)	2 (2)	23 (25)	10 (9)	22 (6)	12 (10)	61 (20)	20 (17)
Racial heterogeneity of households	0.28 (0.12)	0.14 (0.7)	0.46 (0.10)	0.41 (0.23)	0.18 (0.16)	0.38 (0.11)	0.58 (0.10)	0.64 (0.06)	0.59 (0.13)	0.40 (0.06)	0.48 (0.19)
Percentage of households employed (tract)	96 (2)	95 (2)	95 (3)	85 (17)	95 (71)	94 (2)	97 (2)	93 (1)	95 (2)	93 (2)	93 (2)
Percentage foreign-born (tract)	15 (7)	10 (2)	28 (6)	14 (11)	6 (1)	13 (7)	30 (6)	43 (3)	30 (9)	18 (11)	27 (4)

Source: Authors' computations using IZ address data matched to 2005–2009 ACS 5-Year Estimates at the census-block-group level unless otherwise noted. Tract-level data are shown for areas where measures were not available at the block-group level. Standard deviations are shown in parentheses. Averages are weighted by IZ unit locations to represent the average neighborhood characteristics of a typical IZ occupant.

price meal. Across all 11 jurisdictions, the typical IZ unit was located within an elementary school catchment area that had lower proportions of students who qualified for free or reduced-price meals than elementary schools with no residentially assigned IZ homes (44 versus 64%) in school years 2006–2010. This also compares favorably to the average elementary school nationally, where one out of every two students (49%) qualified over school years 2005–2006 to 2009–2010.

Figure 4.2 shows that the elementary school poverty rates in IZ schools closely tracked those in non-IZ elementary schools within the same jurisdiction. This finding comports with the neighborhood demographic comparisons described above, which generally revealed parity among IZ and non-IZ neighborhoods. Nevertheless, there are differences within some of the 11 localities. In Santa Monica and Boulder, for example, IZ units were located in neighborhoods having schools with statistically significantly higher poverty rates. In Denver and Montgomery County, by contrast, IZ schools had slightly lower (but not statistically significantly different) poverty rates than non-IZ schools.

To test whether IZ homes provided children access to high-performing (and not just low-poverty) schools, we also examined the ranking of each school within its state on standardized math and ELA tests. We found that IZ homes also were assigned to *schools performing slightly above average within their state*. On average, IZ units were located in attendance zones of public schools performing in the third quintile, or the 40th to 60th percentile in their state. This was slightly better than the average performance of schools to which no IZ units were assigned; non-IZ schools performed at an average of the 20th to 40th percentile within their state.

Again, we found substantial variation among the 11 localities but much less variation within jurisdictions across IZ and non-IZ schools, as shown in Figure 4.3. In Chicago, IZ elementary schools (like most non-IZ elementary schools) were below average among Illinois elementary schools. This is not surprising, since school poverty highly correlates with school performance, and the large majority of students in any given year in Chicago qualify for free or reduced-price meals (e.g., 85% of students in 2007–2008, compared with 38% in the average public school in the rest of the state). In Irvine and Davidson, both of which are affluent, the IZ schools were in the top quintile within their states.

RAISING ACADEMIC ACHIEVEMENT THROUGH ECONOMIC INTEGRATION IN MONTGOMERY COUNTY

Looking in depth at the largest of the 11 IZ programs reveals that disadvantaged children benefited academically from the economic integration

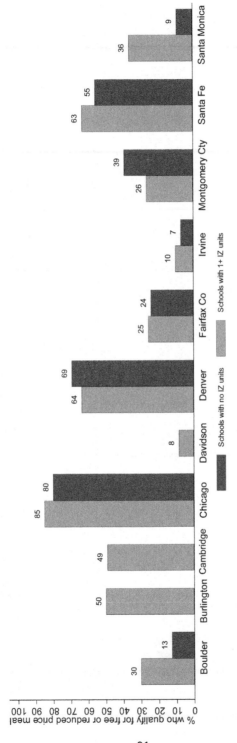

Note: Note that Cambridge and Burlington have citywide controlled choice plans so IZ and non-IZ rates are the same. In Davidson, IZ units are zoned into the one elementary school (additional charter school excluded).

Figure 4.2. Poverty rates in elementary schools with and without IZ Units (2006–2010).

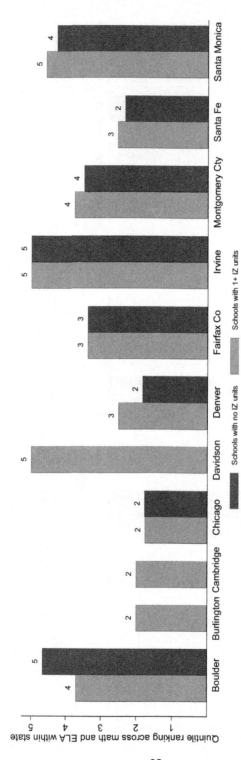

Note: Note that Cambridge and Burlington have citywide controlled choice plans and Montgomery County has choice for middle schools, so IZ and non-IZ rates are the same.

Figure 4.3. Rankings of elementary schools to which IZ units were and were not zoned.

achieved through IZ. The results from elementary-age children living in public housing in Montgomery County, Maryland suggest there are large returns to attending low-poverty schools for students' math scores. However, the effects took years to accrue; by the end of elementary school, the initial, large achievement gaps between the children in public housing and their nonpoor, high-performing district-mates who attended the most advantage schools substantially narrowed.

The Context

Montgomery County is a particularly affluent, inner-ring suburb abutting Washington, DC that became a job center decades before most other suburbs. As early as 1970, a majority of its residents both lived and worked there. Since its inception in the 1950s, the county has ranked among the top 10 wealthiest counties as measured by median household income. According to the most recent statistics available, the median household income in Montgomery County from 2006-2010 was $93,373, which was almost double the national level of $51,914 (U.S. Census Bureau, n.d.). While the aggregate statistics establish the community's affluence and privilege, they gloss over the area's substantial heterogeneity; the County is best understood as a large region (almost 500 square miles) that contains urban, suburban, and rural communities.

With a highly skilled R&D employment base, the County in the early 1970s struggled to meet the attendant demand for lower-skill and lower-wage workers who were steadily priced out of the jurisdiction. The number of reverse commuters and suburb-to-suburb commuters to the County rapidly increased during this period, and the challenge of attracting commuters was most acute for the lowest-paid segment of the workforce.[9] By the mid-1970s, the shortage of blue-collar workers in the county was so severe that some employers in the suburb arranged for their transportation by private van service.[10] As further proof of the detrimental effects of an affordable housing shortage in Montgomery County, IBM announced in 1969 its decision to locate a new plant in neighboring Prince George's County because it was where its workers could afford to live.[11]

With a rapid rise in housing costs and a shortage of lower paid workers in the county, fair housing advocates' and business owners' interests sufficiently aligned to create in 1974 one of the first inclusionary zoning (IZ) policies in the United States.[12] As the oldest and largest continuously operating IZ policy in the United States, the Moderately Priced Dwelling Unit (MPDU) program stipulates that housing developments of a certain size must set aside between 12-15% of the homes built to be sold or rented at below market prices. In exchange, the county grants developers a density bonus allowing them to build more square feet per acre than otherwise allowed under the zoning stipulations, and thus recover financial losses on the below-market IZ homes. In essence, the MPDU program introduces small numbers of affordable homes into market-rate developments, inducing some degree of economic integration into otherwise nonpoor settings. In total, the policy has caused the development of more than 13,000 MPDUs, both rental and for-sale, that are dispersed into hundreds of neighborhoods.

The public housing authority has the right to purchase up to one third of inclusionary zoning homes in any given subdivision. (For example, if 15 homes in a 100-unit subdivision must be set aside for IZ, the housing authority may elect to purchase 5 of the 15 IZ homes.) To date, the housing authority has acquired about 1,500 IZ homes in total, of which it operates a little over 700 as public housing rental homes.[13] Since the IZ homes generally match the rest of the development, they can be single family structures, townhomes, duplexes, or situated within low- or high-rise buildings.

The public housing authority in Montgomery County operates a total of 992 public housing family apartments (some clustered in small public housing developments) that are located in hundreds of neighborhoods throughout the county and are zoned into 114 of the school district's 131 elementary schools.[14] Tenants of Montgomery County's family public housing had an average income of $22,460 as of 2007, making them among the poorest households in the county. The homes are leased at a fraction of the normal market rates: whereas the average monthly rent for a two-bedroom apartment in Montgomery County in 2006 was $1,267, public housing tenants' average rent contribution was $371 (equal to one third of their income, per federal regulation) in the same year.

Random Assignment to Public Housing

The public housing authority randomly assigns applicants to the public housing apartments. Since almost all of the county's elementary schools have neighborhood-based attendance zones, children in public housing thus are assigned randomly to their elementary schools via the public housing placement process.[15] To qualify for public housing during the years examined in my study (2001-2007), a household first had to sign up on a waiting list and, if selected, pass a criminal background check and provide proof of income eligibility. Income-eligible households only could get onto the waiting list by submitting an application to the housing authority during a 14-day window every other year. Several thousand households did so each time (applicants must resubmit each time the waiting list is reopened), so any given applicant had approximately a 2% chance of being selected via rolling computerized lotteries.[16] The lottery selection of applicants is without respect to seniority.

As public housing apartments become available, the housing authority offers to each randomly selected household up to two size-appropriate public housing apartments of the housing authority's own choosing. During a 6-month period in 2008, which is when the only count of rejections is available, approximately 93% of public housing households selected the first offer, and they typically did not know the location of the second unit at the time the first offer was made. Households who rejected both offers were removed from the waiting list.[17] The initial random assignment of families to apartments persisted due to tight restrictions by the housing authority on internal transfers and to low turnover among public housing families with children; 96% of children in public housing remained enrolled in Montgomery County public schools during the study period, and 90% of the children in public housing in the sample remained in the original elementary school to which they were assigned during 2001-2007.

Study Design

Taking advantage of this natural experiment, the study compares the math and reading test scores of elementary-age children in public housing within the most advantaged half of schools to the balance of the elementary-age children in public housing zoned into the county's more disadvantaged schools. I first compare student achievement across low- and moderate-poverty schools, defining low poverty as 0-20% of schoolmates qualifying for a free or reduced-price meal and moderate poverty as approximately 20-60% free and reduced-price meals (FARM) (a more detailed discussion of these definitions is below).

While eligibility for or receipt of free and reduced price meals are the most widely used metric to measure income levels of students in schools,[18] the Montgomery County school district also created in 2000 its own measure of school need, designating 60 of 131 elementary schools as being in a "red zone." This term arose out of the district's decision to more heavily invest in its most impacted elementary schools after a county commission in the late 1990s found that students' demographic characteristics and academic performance in third grade could perfectly predict their subsequent level of participation in Advanced Placement and honors courses in high school.[19] As of 2006, no single school statistic cleanly divided green from red zone schools. For example, the red zone schools had subsidized meal rates ranging from 17% to 72%, while White and

African American students accounted for 0% to 50% and 10% to 74%, respectively, of any given red zone school's population. During the years examined in this study (2001 to 2007) the district directed approximately $2,000 additional dollars per student in 1999 dollars to red zone schools (Childress, Doyle, & Thomas, 1999) so that they could extend kindergarten from half to full day, reduce class sizes from 25 to 17 in kindergarten and first grade, provide 100 hours of additional professional development to red zone teachers, and introduce a literacy curriculum intended to bring disadvantaged students up to level by third grade. Today, about one half of the district's elementary age students attend red zone schools, while the other half attend "green zone" schools.

In brief, I find that over a period of 5 to 7 years, children in public housing who attended the school district's most-advantaged schools (as measured by either subsidized lunch status or the district's own criteria to designate additional resources to so-called red zone schools) outperformed in math and reading those children in public housing who attended the district's least-advantaged elementary schools.

Students in the Study and the Characteristics of Their Schools

A total of 877 out of 1,019 children living in public housing met the three sample restrictions: (a) enrollment in any grades K–6 for at least two consecutive years within the 2001–07 school-year period, (b) possession of at least one test score, and (c) nonqualification for special education services of more than 14 hours per week.[20] Of these 877 children, a total of 2% of the sample (19 children) exited between 2001-2007, leaving a total of 858 children for the analysis. The characteristics of these 858 children are shown in Table 4.3. The 19 children that met the sample criteria and that exited the district were not systematically higher or lower performing than their peers, nor did they first attend public schools that were poorer or wealthier on the whole than their peers.[21]

Data regarding the characteristics of children and families living in public housing reveal no discernible pattern of sorting among public housing children across the poverty levels in the elementary schools they attended. Examining 17 observed characteristics about children and their families including family annual income, annual assets, employment status, household size, and children's race, ethnicity, gender, special education status, and initial test scores, there were two statistically significant differences among the families whose children were placed into the lowest poverty (i.e., where 0-20% of grademates qualified for a free or reduced-

Table 4.3. Characteristics of Children and Families in the Study

Race/Ethnicity of Children Living in Public Housing	
African American (%)	72
Hispanic (%)	16
White (%)	6
Asian (%)	6
Family Characteristics	
Average family income (2006 dollars)[a]	21,047
Average family assets (2006 dollars)[a]	775
Female headed household (%)	87
Average length of tenancy (years)	8.4

Sources: Housing Opportunity Commission and Montgomery County Public Schools.
Notes: $N = 858$ students with a total of 2,226 reading scores and 2,302 math scores.
[a]Since the housing authority collects annual recertification data for every household, income and assets figures were first converted into 2006 real dollars, then averaged within each household across up to 7 years of data (2001–07), and then that figure was averaged across the sample.

price meal) relative to the highest poverty elementary schools (i.e., where 40-85% of grademates qualified for a free or reduced-price meal).[22]

In broad strokes, about one half of the 858 students living in public housing attended elementary schools I define as low-poverty where 0-20% of their schoolmates qualified for a free or reduced-price meal. The other half attended elementary schools I define as moderate-poverty where 20 to approximately 60% of students qualified for a free or reduced-price meal.[23] As anticipated, the lowest poverty elementary schools in the county had characteristics correlated with better student performance such as higher proportions of students deemed gifted and talented, who were White, and fewer student absences per year.

Estimating the Effects of Attending Low-Poverty Schools

To estimate the effects of attending a low-poverty relative to a moderate-poverty school, I fit a multilevel regression model where the outcome of interest is public housing student i's test score Y (level 1), which are nested within student i (level 2A) who is, in turn, nested within a school (level 3) and separately nested within a neighborhood (level 2B). Since neighborhoods as defined in this study (that is, census block groups) are unaligned with school boundaries, the fitted model has both a nested and nonnested structure.

In a base model described in Appendix 4 of Schwartz (2012), each test score Y for student i at time t is modeled as a linear function of: a mean for the student i who produced the score; the contribution of school s in which student i was enrolled at time t; the contribution of neighborhood j in which student i lived at time t; the poverty level of the school student i attended in the year $t - 1$; and student i's ESL status at time t (which is included in the model since there was a statistically significant difference in mean ESL rates for public housing children across low- and moderate-poverty schools), year fixed effects, and a residual term that represents the unexplained difference between the student i's test score at time t and the sum of the fitted model predictors.

To test when effects of attending low-poverty schools occur, I expanded the base model by introducing six additional predictors: the interactions of three time-related predictors—time (in days) elapsed since student i first entered the school district and time t of the test score, time elapsed squared, and time elapsed cubed—with each of the two dichotomous indicators for whether the school is a low- or a moderate-poverty school. The interaction terms are included to see if the effects of poverty differ according to the number of years the child has been enrolled in the district.

Effects of Attending Low-Poverty Schools

Examining the longitudinal school performance from 2001 to 2007 of the 858 students in public housing who attended elementary schools and lived in neighborhoods that fell along a spectrum of low-poverty to moderate-poverty rates, I find the following:

There was a large, positive effect on math scores from attending a low-poverty school throughout the elementary grades. After 2 years in the district, which is when a sufficient number of students in the sample began to take standardized tests since the earliest grade levels were not tested, children in public housing performed equally on standardized math tests regardless of the poverty level of the school they attended. By the fifth year in the district, statistically significant differences ($p < 0.05$) emerged between the average performance of children in public housing in low-poverty schools compared to those in moderate-poverty schools. By the seventh year in the district, children in public housing in low-poverty schools performed an average of 8 normal curve equivalent (NCE) points higher than children in public housing in higher-poverty schools. This difference is equal to 0.4 of a standard deviation in math scores.

More importantly, public housing students in the least-poor schools were catching up to their average nonpoor district-mates over the course of elementary school. The average child in public housing started out performing about 17 points (NCE score of 33) below the typical Montgomery County student (NCE score of 50) in math—0.8 of a standard deviation, which comports with the national income achievement gap. Over time, however, children in public housing in the district's low-poverty schools began to catch up to their nonpoor district-mates in math; by the end of elementary school, the math achievement gap halved from an initial disparity of 17 points to 8 points. In contrast, the achievement gap between the children's average (nonpoor) district-mate and the average child in public housing in the district's poorest elementary schools held constant.

These improvements occurred despite within-school sorting such that children living in public housing tended to enroll in lower-level math classes where the other most disadvantaged students within the school clustered. Each elementary school in the district provided differentiated math offerings starting in the second grade, by which point a student could have tested into either accelerated or standard math. By third grade, a child could place into one of three levels of math, and by sixth grade the offerings split into a total of four levels. Within low-poverty schools, the math classmates of children in public housing scored an average of 9 points lower than their grademates as a whole. Likewise, the proportion of their math classmates who were gifted and talented was 14 percentage points lower than the rate among their grademates. By contrast, the math classmates of children in public housing who attended moderate-poverty schools were more similar to that of their grademates and schoolmates as a whole.

There are smaller, suggestive positive effects on reading scores from attending a low-poverty school relative to one that is moderate poverty. By the end of elementary school, the children in public housing in the lowest poverty elementary schools performed an average of 5 points higher in reading (0.2 of a standard deviation, $p < 0.20$) than children in public housing attending moderate-poverty schools. As in math, they started out far behind their district-mates in their reading achievement. Those enrolled in low-poverty schools made modest gains relative to their district-mates, such that the achievement gap narrowed from 17 to 13 NCE points.

Benefits of attending low-poverty schools diminished as school poverty levels rose. The typical student in public housing in a school with a poverty rate as high as 35% performed no better in math than the typical student in public housing in an elementary school with 35% to 85% poverty. For reading scores, it was only at the low school poverty rate of 20% or less that children in public housing outperformed their peers in public housing attending schools with greater poverty rates.

It is important to note that the comparison largely excludes high-poverty schools since less than 5% of schools in Montgomery County had poverty rates in excess of 60%. Given the lack of high-poverty schools within this study, this finding does *not* suggest that 35% school poverty is a tipping point, after which low-income students no longer benefit from socioeconomic integration. We cannot know from this study, for example, how students in 35% to 60% low-income schools perform compared with students in 60% to 100% low-income schools. In fact, national trends suggest that it is in high-poverty schools that students perform least well (Aud et al., 2010).

Students in advantaged school outperformed students in disadvantaged schools in spite of a district policy to direct greater resources to its disadvantaged schools. Comparing the test scores of children living public housing by whether they attended a red or green zone school reveals larger impacts of school advantage on the performance of children in public housing over time. As shown in Figure 4.4, the cumulative positive effect on math scores of attending a green zone school by the end of elementary school (9 NCE points, $p < 0.12$) was about the same as that of attending the low-poverty elementary schools (8 NCE points, $p < 0.05$). However, in reading, the cumulative effect of attending a green zone school (8 points, $p < 0.12$ level) was larger than attending the lowest poverty schools (5 points, $p < 0.20$ level).

The larger effect from the green/red zone comparison relative to the low/moderate poverty school comparison was attributable to the erosion in average math and reading test scores toward the end of elementary school among children in public housing who attended red zone schools. One possible explanation for the negative turn was that the fourth and fifth grades did not receive the same level of intensive investments within red zone schools, which was a policy that primarily focused its resources on getting children on level by grade three.

In other words, the extra attention paid to grades K–3 could have caused the scores of children in public housing attending red zone schools to improve, as shown in years two through five in Figure 4.4. But the positive effect faded and even reversed after the extra investments stopped, as shown in the scores of children in public housing from fifth and sixth grade (that is, years six and seven in the left and right hand pane of Figure 4.4). If true, this trend would not necessarily have emerged in the comparison of school poverty levels shown in Figure 4.4, since both green and red zone schools comprised the set of schools with 20% to 85% of school children qualifying for a free or reduced-price meal. Children in public housing enrolled in red zone schools not only did not keep pace with their green zone peers in public housing, but by the end of elementary school they fell even further behind their average district-mate (who

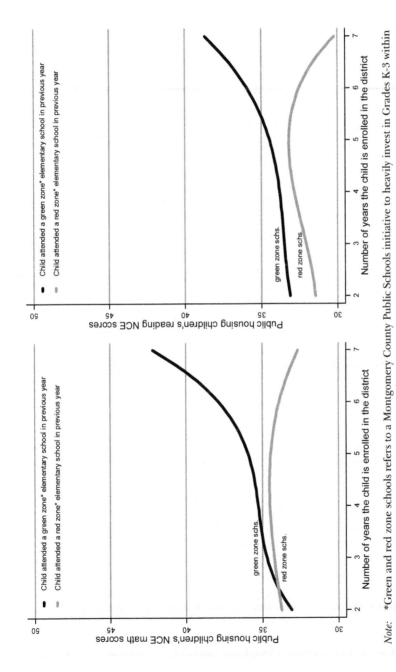

Note: *Green and red zone schools refers to a Montgomery County Public Schools initiative to heavily invest in Grades K-3 within in its 60 highest need (i.e., red zone) elementary schools.

Figure 4.4. The effects of attending green zone and red zone schools on public housing students' math and reading scores.

earned a score of 50 in any given year) than when they first entered school in the district.

This trend is especially distributing given the evidence that red zone investments modestly raised campuswide achievement that persisted through fifth grade. Comparing Montgomery County's red zone elementary schools with demographically similar elementary schools throughout Maryland, the school district's investments in the red zone schools was associated with a statistically significant 4.9-point increase and a 3.3-point increase in the percentage of fifth grade students in the school who scored "advanced" on the Maryland State Assessment in reading and math, respectively. This finding is consistent with the school district's explicit goal that students achieve at the advanced level on the reading state standardized test by Grade 3, which the district stipulated was one of seven "keys" to college readiness (Our Call to Action, 1999).

CONCLUSION

Our findings indicate that, overall, the IZ policies studied provide access to low-poverty schools and neighborhoods—something other affordable housing policies have struggled to achieve (Deng, 2007; Newman & Schnare, 1997; Pfeiffer, 2009). In providing that access, the IZ policies offer the potential, if not the promise, of social inclusion of it recipients.

Not surprisingly, the most urban of IZ programs offered a lower degree of access to low-poverty neighborhoods and schools than their suburban counterparts. While not each IZ program matches Montgomery County's remarkable degree of inclusion of IZ recipients in low-poverty neighborhoods and school attendance zones, they approach and, in some cases, meet the same high degree of inclusion in low-poverty places. This is especially significant in consideration of the rising levels of economic and racial segregation across suburbs that Frankenberg describes elsewhere in this book.

Certainly, inclusionary zoning pertains to that subgroup of suburbs and cities where high demand for newly constructed or rehabilitated homes exceeds the regulatory barriers that additional zoning imposes. And, in serving primarily low-income homeowners, the zoning policy does not currently target the most disadvantaged of households as the federal public housing and housing voucher programs do. The outcomes found for children from low-income families living in Montgomery County would likely best generalize to other low-income families with a tolerance or a preference for living in suburban, low-poverty locations. The most directly correlative populations might be low-income families who have selected low-poverty places through private, unsubsidized choices;

through federally subsidized housing vouchers or other affordable housing vehicles, such as low-income housing tax credit projects; or through the more than one hundred other inclusionary zoning programs that operate in the United States. Consequently, the inclusion of affordable housing within higher performing schools' attendance zones is but one of many examples that are needed of nonschool policies—a so-called bigger, bolder approach—that can substantively improve disadvantaged children's academic performance.

ACKNOWLEDGMENT

The research described in this chapter was first published in Schwartz (2012), Schwartz, Ecola, Leuschner, and Kofner (2012) and Schwartz (2009).

NOTES

1. See Aud et al. (2010) for national analyses that compare average test score performance in low- and high-poverty schools.
2. In brief, I hypothesize that the improvements to low-income students' achievement is likely due to effects from the school—where low-poverty schools generally reap stability-conferring benefits from lower rates of student, teacher, and administrator attrition, from higher rates of parental stewardship of schools, from better qualified teachers who tend to apply to and remain at lower poverty schools for longer periods of time, and from students who arrive at schools better prepared to learn—and to effects from the neighborhood—where heightened poverty rates tend to increase stress, lower academic expectations, and encourage antisocial behaviors. See Schwartz (2009) for an extended discussion of the mechanisms by which economic integration might benefit children from low-income families.
3. Thirteen states explicitly or implicitly authorize the use of IZ by local governments (Hollister, McKeen, & McGrath, 2007). Two states, Texas and Oregon, prohibit IZ. The remaining states offer no guidance to localities regarding the legality of IZ, although IZ programs exist in at least eight states (Hollister et al.).
4. The 5-year estimates represent the average characteristics of households in a given census block group in 2005–2009. Since these data are multiyear estimates rather than point-in-time estimates, they do not capture rapid changes in neighborhood characteristics; rather, they reflect longer term trends within an area (U.S. Census Bureau, 2008).
5. The Cambridge, Burlington, and Montgomery County school districts use systems of parental choice rather than residential assignment for a certain

number of their schools. Since home addresses do not determine school assignment in these cases, we used districtwide school characteristics for the grade levels (i.e., elementary, middle, and high) at which school choice applies.

6. To develop these rankings, we first derived the weighted average of the percentage of all students who scored proficient or above in math and the percentage scoring proficient or above in ELA. (Unequal numbers of students may take the math and ELA tests within the same school, thus necessitating a weighted average.) These ranks are specific to each state and to each year. Within each state and school year, we separately ranked elementary, middle, and high schools, since we often found systematic discrepancies in proficiency rates across these school levels. For schools that include grades at multiple levels (e.g., K–8 or K–12 schools), we averaged the elementary, middle, and high school ranking as applicable to come up with a single ranking.

7. As of 2005-2009, in the average neighborhood nationally, 92% of adults 16 and older were employed, and 25% of adults 25 and older had a college degree.

8. In our statistical tests, we made 40 comparisons. Therefore, we adjusted the level of statistical significance using the Benjamin Hochberg step-up method to control at 0.05 the proportion of false positives identified among the total set of statistically significant differences.

9. Staff writer, "Job, Housing Rise Spurred by Beltway" *The Washington Post* (18 January 1968), B6.

10. Donnel Nunes, "Blue-Collar Workers Needed in Fairfax and Montgomery" *The Washington Post* (18 March 1974), C1. Note that the connection to the regional subway system would not come for another decade.

11. Jared Stout, "A New Idea for Old Suburbia" *The Washington Post* (2 January 1969), E1.

12. Zina Greene, Phone Interview, 1 April 2005. Ms. Greene was a consultant to the county and one of the authors the MPDU legislation. She negotiated drafts of the policy with builders, developers, the business community, and County Council for about a year before its passage.

13. The public housing authority subsidizes the balance through other combinations of federal, state, or local funds.

14. All but one elementary school in the county had residential attendance zones during the time of the study. Elementary schools are K-5 in Montgomery County.

15. This assumes only a small minority of children living in public housing attend private schools, which the housing authority anecdotally confirms.

16. The precise likelihood varied by household since households must be not only income-eligible but also size-eligible for the given home that has become vacant and is to be leased. For example, if a 3-bedroom public housing unit becomes available, only a household with 3-6 persons on the waiting list are eligible to prevent under- or over-housing stipulations. Further complicating the eligibility, the age and gender of children in the household determines whether a shared bedroom(s) for the children is

acceptable per federal regulation and further restricts the likelihood of a 3-6 person household obtaining the 3-bedroom apartment.

17.   Although the housing authority does not collect information about rejection rates, but it estimates that about 5-10% of households (including elderly and families) turn down a first offered unit, and slightly lower rate turn down both offered units. The elderly, which only qualify for a separate supply of public housing that is in addition to the 992 family public housing apartments considered in this study, tend to reject offers at a higher rate because the shortage of elderly-only housing is less than for families with children (larger-size public housing units are the most in demand). Based on a hand count of 6-months' worth of public housing offers made by the housing authority in 2008 (that the housing authority performed at my request), 4 out of 57 elderly or family households (7%) turned down either the first or second unit offered. The household may sign up again when the waiting list re-opens, which is generally biannual. To the extent that there is self-selection, the staff who run admissions indicate that the most common reason families (as opposed to the elderly) cite for turning down a unit is they hope to obtain a scattered site apartment as opposed to a public housing apartment in one of the county's five multi-family public housing properties. However, this designation does not segregate higher- from lower-performing or higher- from lower-poverty schools within the district. See Appendix C of Schwartz (2009) for a detailed description of the random selection process.

18.   To qualify for a free or reduced-price meal, a family must earn no more than 130% or 185% of the poverty level respectively.

19.   *Our Call to Action* (1999). Rockville, MD: Montgomery County Public Schools.

20.   Children receiving more than 14 hours of services per week are frequently enrolled in Learning and Academic Disabilities classrooms that are often smaller in size and are designed to provide more intensive services to children that are deemed to have a disability that "significantly impacts" academic achievement. Children receiving more than 30 hours per week of special education services generally are removed from their home school and enrolled in one of the district's special education schools. These special education schools are excluded from this analysis. Those students receiving 1 to 14 hours of special education services were retained in the sample. Over half of public housing students receiving such services are classified with a speech or language disability.

21.   A total of 1,198 children lived in public housing and enrolled in any one grade in K–6 in Montgomery County Public Schools during 2001–07. Of this entire set, 4% exited the district during 2001–07 before reaching seventh grade. (When children rise into seventh grade, they drop from the sample.) The 48 exiting children (4% of 1,198) were no different in aggregate from their remaining peers in public housing in terms of family income, initial test scores, or initial school poverty levels. Putting this in a regression framework, students whose first test score was above the average of their peers in public housing and whose first school had moderately

high poverty (that is, more than 20% of students qualified for FARM) were no more likely to exit the sample than their peers in public housing who also first scored above average but were enrolled in the district's lowest poverty schools.

22. For public housing children in the lowest and the highest poverty schools, the two differences were 9 versus 16% of public housing children were classified as English as Second Language in their first year within the district, and the average age of the head of household was 40 versus 39. See Appendix 2 of Schwartz (2012) for the statistics. A separate analysis on the subset of public housing families who moved in less than 12 months prior to their child's first year in the public school district shows no statistically significant differences in the 17 demographic indicators except for one: more White public housing children enrolled in 20-40% FARM schools than did White children in 0-20% FARM schools.

23. The highest poverty rate among the 114 elementary schools that a public housing child attended in any year from 2001 to 2007 was 85%. But only 1 in 114 elementary schools had a poverty rate in excess of 80%, and up to 3 schools in any given year had a poverty rate of 70% to 80%. The vast majority of the 114 schools had poverty rates of 0-65%.

REFERENCES

Aud, S., Hussar, W., Planty, M., Snyder, T., Bianco, K., Fox, M., ... Drake, L. (2010). *The Condition of Education 2010, NCES 2010-028*. Washington, DC: National Center for Education Statistics.

A Bigger, Bolder Approach to Education. (n.d.). Mission statement. Retrieved from http://www.epi.org/files/2011/bold_approach_full_statement-3.pdf

Harris, D. R. (1999). *All suburbs are not created equal: A new look at racial differences in suburban location* (Report No. 99-440). Michigan: Population Studies Center at University of Michigan. Retrieved from http://www.psc.isr.umich.edu/pubs/pdf/rr99-440.pdf

Calavita, N., & Mallach, A. (2010). *Inclusionary housing in international perspective: Affordable housing, social inclusion, and land value recapture*. Cambridge, MA: Lincoln Institute of Land Policy.

Childress, S, Doyle, D., & Thomas, D. (2009). *Leading for equity: The pursuit of excellence in Montgomery County Public Schools*. Cambridge, MA: Harvard Education Press.

Deng, L. (2007). Comparing the effects of housing vouchers and low-income housing tax credits on neighborhood integration and school quality. *Journal of Planning Education and Research, 27*(1), 20–35.

Ellen, I. G., O'Regan, K. M., & Voicu, I. (2009). Siting, spillovers, and segregation: A reexamination of the Low Income Housing Tax Credit program. In E. L. Glaeser & J. M. Quigley (Eds.), *Housing markets and the economy* (pp. 233-267). Cambridge, MA: Lincoln Institute of Land Policy.

Hollister, T. S., McKeen, A. M., & McGrath, D. G. (2007). National Survey of Statutory Authority and Practical Considerations for the Implementation of

Inclusionary Zoning Ordinances. Washington, DC: National Association of Home Builders.

Knapp, G., Bento, A., & Lowe, S. (2008). *Housing market impacts of inclusionary zoning.* College Park, MD: National Center for Smart Growth Research and Education. Retrieved May 11, 2012, from http://smartgrowth.umd.edu/assets/documents/research/knaapbentolowe_2008.pdf

Ladd, H. F. (2012). Education and poverty: Confronting the evidence. *Journal of Policy Analysis and Management, 31*(2), 203-227.

Newman, S., & Schnare. A. (1997). '... And a suitable living environment': The failure of housing programs to deliver on neighborhood quality. *Housing Policy Debate, 8*(4), 703-741.

Our Call to Action. (1999). Rockville, MD: Montgomery County Public Schools.

Pfeiffer, D. (2009). *The opportunity illusion: Subsidized housing and failing schools in California.* Los Angeles, CA: The Civil Rights Project, University of California, Los Angeles.

Reardon, S. (2011). The widening achievement gap between the rich and the poor: New evidence and possible explanations. In G. J Duncan & R. J. Murnane (Eds.), *Whither opportunity? Rising inequality, schools and children's life chances* (pp. 91-116). New York, NY: Russell Sage.

Schuetz, J., Meltzer, R., & Been, V. (2011). Silver bullet or Trojan horse? The effects of inclusionary zoning on local housing markets in the United States. *Urban Studies, 48*(2), 297-329.

Schwartz, H. (2009). Do poor children benefit academically from economic integration in schools and neighborhoods? Evidence from an affluent suburb's affordable housing lotteries (PhD dissertation). Columbia University, New York, NY.

Schwartz, H. (2012). Housing policy is school policy. In R. Kahlenberg (Ed.) *The future of school integration: Socioeconomic diversity as an education reform strategy.* New York, NY: Century Foundation.

Schwartz, H., Ecola, L., Leuschner, K., & Kofner, A. (2012). *Is inclusionary zoning inclusionary? A guide for* practitioners (TR-1231-MCF). Santa Monica, CA: RAND.

U.S. Census Bureau. (n.d.). 2006-2010 American Community Survey. State and County QuickFacts. Data derived from Population Estimates, American Community Survey, Census of Population and Housing, State and County Housing Unit Estimates, County Business Patterns, Nonemployer Statistics, Economic Census, Survey of Business Owners, Building Permits, Consolidated Federal Funds Report. Retrieved June 3, 2012 from http://quickfacts.census.gov/qfd/states/00000.html

U.S. Census Bureau. (2008). *A compass for understanding and using American community survey data: What general data users need to know.* Washington, DC: U.S. Government Printing Office.

CHAPTER 5

ADVANCING EQUITY IN AN INTEGRATED, SUBURBAN COMMUNITY

Gail L. Sunderman

One of the more perplexing issues in education is the persistence of the racial achievement gap in suburban schools and communities, particularly those that are relatively affluent and have maintained a level of integration in both housing and schooling. When racial and socioeconomic achievement gaps persist in integrated, suburban communities it is often the result of less obvious ways in which advantage and disadvantage is maintain by structural, institutional, and symbolic mechanisms (Diamond, 2006). According to Diamond, "because they live in a racialized society, African American and White students, even in the same schools and communities, navigate a racialized educational terrain" (Diamond, 2006, p. 498). In this racialized educational terrain, multiple forms of disadvantage, both inside and outside the schools shape the experience and access to learning opportunities of students, and these are likely to be played out very differently for Black and White students. Diamond identifies these disadvantages as (1) structural inequalities outside the schools that limit access to resources that can support and enhance learning; (2) institutional patterns inside schools that shape students' experiences and access to learning opportunities in schools and classrooms; and (3) sym-

Charting Reform, Achieving Equity in a Diverse Nation
pp. 109–132
Copyright © 2013 by Information Age Publishing
All rights of reproduction in any form reserved.

bolic, or ideological patterns in schools and society about what constitutes intellectual and cultural capabilities (Diamond, 2006).

Even as suburbs have become more diverse, only a few studies investigate the experiences of minority students in suburban schools (Diamond, 2006; Diamond, Lewis, & Gordon, 2007; Ferguson, Ludwig, & Rich, 2001; Morris, 2009; Wells & Crain, 1997; Wells et al., 2009). Not much scholarship, however, focuses on how educational, social, economic, and other issues structure educational opportunity in suburban communities with diverse populations. This chapter examines how institutional and structural factors influence access to learning opportunities in the Village of Oak Park, an integrated suburb west of Chicago. A tradition of support for diversity, a history of integrated housing policies, and a relatively affluent and well educated population, and yet a community where the achievement gap between Black and White students persists, makes Oak Park an ideal case for examining the challenges of diverse communities.

Oak Park today, and its schools, has greatly benefited from the policies put in place in the 1960s and 1970s to promote integrated housing. These policies created the foundation for integrated schools and a belief system among the Village residents that valued diversity. While Oak Park has maintained integrated schools, the racial achievement gap has been a persistent issue in Oak Park. Federal policy requirements under the No Child Left Behind Act of 2001 (NCLB) brought the achievement gap into sharp focus and heightened public awareness as never before. However, addressing the achievement gap encountered built-in tensions between a commitment to equity, limited resources, and individual priorities focused on achieving the very best education for one's own children. These tensions where heightened by structural, institutional, and ideological patterns that disadvantage minority students. Structural inequalities outside of the schools were reflected in persistent income disparities and efforts to maintain integrated housing in the face of growing income inequality between Black and White residents, rising housing costs, and a diminishing number of affordable housing units. Institutional practices within the schools that affected the opportunities and experiences available to students were highly resistant to change and vulnerable to community and faculty pushback. From an ideological perspective, a new generation of residents held a very different view of diversity than what had emerged in the 1960s and 1970s, thereby increasing the tension between a commitment to equity and academic excellence.

This study draws from case study data, collected in 2008 and 2009, on the Village of Oak Park and its schools. The data includes interviews with school and district administrators as well as prominent community members and representatives from Village organizations, and document analysis. The following section describes the enrollment and demographic characteristics of the two Oak Park school districts and discuses how the community conceptualizes the race-related challenges facing the schools. It then examines how structural inequalities, institutional patterns, and symbolical patterns structure educational opportunity in Oak Park. The chapter concludes with a discussion of the implications of these patterns and the challenges they pose for supporting the success of minority students in diverse suburban communities.

THE OAK PARK SCHOOL DISTRICTS

Two school districts—the Oak Park Elementary District 97 and the Oak Park-River Forest High School District 200 (OPRF)—serve the residents of Oak Park. The elementary district enrolls over 5,000 students in eight K-5 schools and two middle schools, Grades 6-8. In 2009, when this study was conducted, the elementary school district enrollment was 56.9% White, 25.8% Black, 3.8% Latino, 4.3% Asian, and 9.2% multiracial; poverty was 19.1%. In the mid-1970s, the district converted its ten K-8 schools to eight K-6 schools and two 7-8 schools. At that time, the district located the Grade 7-8 schools so that the student population was fairly racially balanced. In 1999, a referendum passed to build two new middle schools (on the same location as the previous schools), resulting in the current middle school configuration (Elementary Administrator 1, November 17, 2009). The high school, founded in 1873, also serves residents of River Forest, an affluent community adjacent to Oak Park, and enrolls over 3,200 students. It is a comprehensive public high school where about 90% of graduates pursue postsecondary education. The student demographics are similar to those of the elementary district, with 59.1% White, 26.7% Black, 5.6% Latino, 2.8% Asian, and 5.6% multiracial; poverty is 17.4% (Table 5.1).

Student enrollment and demographic characteristics for the Oak Park elementary district by school for 2009 are presented in Table 5.1. While most of the schools reflect the district averages, a few schools are outliers. Two schools with the highest percentages of minority students—Irving and Longfellow—also have the highest percentages of low-income students. Irving Elementary is the only minority-majority school in the district, with 58.5% minority students and 41.5% White students. It has the highest percentage of low-income students at 26.2%. Longfellow Elementary has the second highest percentage of minority students at 47.7% and the second highest poverty at 18.8%. Longfellow is also the largest elementary school with 527 students in 2009. Mann Elementary has the highest proportion of White students at 78.7% and the lowest poverty rate at 3.1%. Lincoln Elementary has the second highest proportion of White

**Table 5.1.   Student Enrollment and Demographics,
Oak Park Elementary District 97, Oak Park and River Forest
High School District 200, and Illinois State, 2009**

School	Enroll	Asian %	Black %	Latino %	White %	Multi-racial %	FRL %	Class Size Grade 1/6*	Class Size Grade 3/8**
Beye	396	4.3	25.5	3.0	58.1	9.1	18.4	18.3	17.8
Hatch	303	3.0	27.1	2.0	56.8	11.2	14.2	23.7	19.5
Holmes	452	6.6	21.5	4.4	54.4	13.1	16.6	15.2	19.8
Irving	381	5.2	32.0	6.3	41.5	15.0	26.2	18.3	16.0
Lincoln	527	7.8	17.1	5.9	61.7	7.6	11.2	16.0	19.4
Longfellow	581	5.0	29.3	3.8	52.3	9.6	18.9	16.8	18.8
Mann	479	1.9	10.2	2.3	78.7	6.9	3.1	22.3	20.5
Whittier	435	2.8	23.7	2.5	59.5	11.5	17.0	20.9	18.2
Brooks MS	827	4.1	31.8	2.6	53.0	7.5	19.5	14.6*	15.4**
Julian MS	866	3.1	32.0	3.5	55.0	6.2	21.8	19.7*	17.9**
Elementary District	5,247	4.3	25.8	3.8	56.9	9.2	17.1	18.8 17.0*	18.7 16.5**
High School District	3,076	2.8	26.7	5.6	59.1	5.6	17.4	n/a	n/a
Illinois State	2.7 million	4.1	19.1	20.8	53.3	2.5	42.9	20.9 22.0*	21.8 21.4**

Source: Illinois State Board of Education (n.d.-b).
Note: *Grade 6. **Grade 8.

students at 61.7% and second lowest poverty rate at 11.2%. The distribution of race and poverty is similar to the district average across the other schools.

The Persistence of the Racial Achievement Gap

The primary equity issue in the schools—in both the elementary and high school districts—was defined as the achievement gap, primarily between Black and White students. While the Oak Park elementary district had made progress since 2001 in narrowing the achievement gap, the magnitude of the gap varied by grade and subject (Table 5.2). In the elementary grades, the achievement gaps were larger in reading than

**Table 5.2.   Black/White Achievement Gap
by Subject and Grade, Oak Park Elementary
and Oak Park High School, 2001-2011**

Subject/Grade	2001	2011	Difference
Reading/3rd	35	23	−12
Math/3rd	25	17	−8
Reading/5th	37	26	−11
Math/5th	47	14	−33
Reading/8th	33	22	−11
Math/8th	49	22	−27
Reading/11th	47	48	+1
Math/11th	58	56	+2

Source: Illinois State Board of Education (n.d.-b).
Note: For Grades 3, 5, and 8, results are from the Illinois Standards Assessment Test (ISAT); for Grade 11, from the Prairie State Achievement Examination (PSAE).

math in Grades 3 and 5. In the eighth grade, the gap was 22 points in both reading and math in 2011, but the math gap narrowed (from 49 to 22) more than the reading gap (from 33 to 22) between 2001 and 2011. In the high school district, the Black/White achievement gap was large in both reading (48 points in 2011) and math (56 points in 2011), and there was virtually no change in either the math or reading gap between 2001 and 2011. While the achievement gap was evident in the elementary grades, it was magnified in high school where the gaps were 2 to 3 times larger than in the elementary grades in 2011.

Many Oak Park educators acknowledged that the achievement gap had existed for years, but it was the disaggregated data, required under the federal NCLB law, that clearly focused attention on this issue. According to one elementary district administrator, "When you publish the scores broken down by race and income and a few other things by subgroups, it gets a little bit harder to say everyone is at about the same place" (Elementary Administrator 1, November 17, 2009).

Failing to make Adequate Yearly Progress (AYP) toward proficiency goals for all subgroups, as required under NCLB, created a sense of urgency for the high school district to look more closely at the achievement gap. According to the high school superintendent, Attila Weninger,

The thing that drove the board to this sense of urgency about the achievement gap was because it was a very public set of numbers. Although in this community, people identified an achievement gap I think, 10, 15, 20 years ago. But this made it much more urgent because there were public reports. (Weninger, November 19, 2009)

The district and community awareness of the achievement gap at the high school level was documented as early as 1977 in an internal district report (The African American Achievement Study Team, 2003, May). Over the next 3 decades, the district formed ad hoc committees, commissioned reports, and implemented a range of interventions to study and address the gap (Hollis, 1998; Oak Park and River Forest High School, 1991; The African American Achievement Study Team, 2003, May). Many of these initiatives included focus groups or forums to solicit input from a variety of stakeholders. The current board took a similar approach, reflecting the community's openness to talk about these issues if not to change them. For example, in 2009-10, it hosted a series of workshops on race and started a "Courageous Conversations" (Singleton & Linton, 2006) group to talk about personal experiences with race and racism.

Because OPRF high school had not made AYP under NCLB, the district focused its reform efforts on differences in achievement among racial groups of students. In a letter to the high school board of education outlining a plan to address the achievement gap, Superintendent Weninger acknowledged the widening of the gap during high school: "minority students who enter OPRF HS academically achieve at a lesser rate than their Caucasian counterparts, and that gap grows through their high school years. We didn't start this achievement gap; however, because we know it exists as students enter OPRF and continues, then we have an obligation to address it" (Weninger, 2007).

The ability of the high school to serve *all* students also surfaced as an issue in Oak Park. Many pointed out that the high school worked very well for some students, but not for all. One community respondent described it this way:

> It still runs the same way it did when I went there. I grew up here, moved away and came back, and it's set up very similarly. It's about three or four different schools within the school. I think it serves the very bright, very dedicated kind of student extremely well and I think it generally fails the rest.... Those kids that don't respond in class as well, they're doing the whole teenage thing and until they get into deep trouble the teachers don't seem real interested in reaching out to them. There is no one there to really connect with them. It's a huge place. (Community Respondent 1, June 24, 2010)

Similarly, a high school administrator commented on the ability of the high school to address diversity within the African American student body:

We fail to recognize the diversity within the African American community itself.... There is a divide between African American students whose parents have done very well economically and have positions of authority where they work ... and then we have a set of African American students whose parents have not done as well economically in terms of position ... [and] their own schooling. And we have not been successful in trying to address the needs of those students as much as we would like. (High School Administrator 1, November 20, 2009)

This respondent and another noted the failure on the part of many in the community to recognize economic diversity within the African American community. "Some of us have graduated from high school, and even from college. And not all of us have snuck over the Austin line to get a better education" (Community Respondent 2, 6-24-2010). This respondent was critical of the assumption that if the community did not address economic diversity it would lose racial diversity because this assumption assumed "that the African America voice is one voice. And it's the assumption that that voice ... [is one] that is angry, that is confrontational as opposed to African Americans who are middle class and who don't come with that level of anger" (Community Respondent 2, June 24, 2010).

In the elementary district, the administration identified an increase in the number of students who struggled with basic reading and math, something that was unique to Oak Park, as an issue. Because most Oak Park residents were professionals, performance at school had been taken for granted, and to a large extent, it still was. According to one administrator (Elementary Administrator 2, November 17, 2009), the disaggregation requirements of NCLB, coupled with new leadership at the district level,[1] highlighted the achievement gap between Black and White students. Commenting on the gap, he said, "I have a feeling there were always gaps, but we've really started tracking that since about 2003" (Elementary Administrator 2, November 17, 2009). Nonetheless, he acknowledged that this awareness of differences in performance among students was not completely accepted by the community. To address these performance differences and the increases in struggling students, the district had to rethink how it delivered instruction. In the past, students entered the system well prepared so the focus was on accelerated learning and differentiation and not on the kind of support programs designed to support struggling students.

This public exposure of an achievement gap did not translated into a consensus on why the gap existed or what to do about it. To some, particularly African Americans, it was viewed as a lack of responsiveness on the part of the schools to the needs of Black students, particularly Black males. Others attributed the gap to a subset of students—those who were minority (i.e., Black) and/or low-income—and emphasized the character-istics or traits of the students or their families. This "observer's perspec-tive" (Steele, 2010) saw the achievement gap resulting from a lack of parental engagement on the part of the parents of these lower achieving students.[2] These parents were seen as not capable or uninterested in helping their child succeed academically. Another prevalent view was the belief that much of the achievement gap could be attributed to people moving into Oak Park to attend the high school. John Rigas, village pres-ident of River Forest (i.e., mayor) and former OPRF board member described it this way: "They may be coming from the city (Chicago), they may be coming from districts that are different from an academic stand-point and they come in significantly behind their peers that have lived here their whole life" (J. Rigas, personal communication, 2010). A variant of this view was the perception that there were significant numbers of nonresidents who "sneak" into the system from Chicago, primarily along the eastern border.[3] Among those who attributed the gap to a subset of students was a concern that resources would be diverted from the needs of "my child" to this other child who was not achieving, and who may not be legitimately enrolled. Finally, there was the view that the achievement gap didn't matter much—that Oak Park was an elite school system and test scores were not a true reflection of the quality of the schools. This view also tended to discount the usefulness of the focus on using standardized test scores as a sole measure of the districts' quality.

Structural Inequalities Outside the Schools

The legacy of the integration strategies adopted in the 1970s has miti-gated the effects of residential segregation, and have helped to keep both the neighborhoods and schools diverse. Oak Park is among the most inte-grated municipalities with populations over 25,000 in Illinois (Village of Oak Park, 2009). In 2000, the village's dissimilarity index for White and Black residents was 45.1 and it ranked 65th out of 79 communities in terms of diversity (Village of Oak Park, 2009). Between 1990 and 2000, the Village became less segregated as some census blocks had growing proportions of Black residents and others, primarily along the eastern border, became less concentrated by race (Table 5.3). Even so, some cen-sus tracks were more integrated than others with more Black residents concentrated along the eastern border adjacent to some of the poorest neighborhoods in Chicago (pp. 25-26).

Structural inequalities outside of the schools were reflected in persis-tent income inequalities and efforts to maintain integrated housing in the face of rising housing costs and a diminishing number of affordable hous-

**Table 5.3.   Indices of Dissimilarity,
Oak Park, 1980, 1990, 2000, Black to White**

1980	1990	2000
58.2	49.5	45.1

Source: Lewis, Maly, Kleppner, and Tobias (2002).
Note: Zero = perfect integration; 1 or 100% = perfect segregation

**Table 5.4.   Median Household Income and Poverty Rates
by Race/Ethnicity, Village of Oak Park, 2000-2007**

	2000		2007		
	Median Household Income	Poverty Rate	Median Household Income	Poverty Rate	% Gain/Loss 2000-2007
Village	$59,183	5.6%	$74,614	4.9%	26.1%
Whites	$65,932	3.5%	$89.075	3.8%	35.1%
Blacks	$43,828	10.9%	$41,657	8.3%	−4.95%
Asians	$55,929	9.0%	$94,815	n/a	69.5%
Hispanics	$42,563	10.5%	$54,375	n/a	27.8%

Source: Village of Oak Park (2010). Data sources included, U.S. Census Bureau, Census 2000, (SF 3-P53, P152A, P152B, P152D, P152H, P87, P159A, P159B, P159D, P159H); 2005-2007 American Community Survey Three-Year Estimates (B19013A, B19013B, B19013D, B19013I, C17001, C17001A, C17001B).

ing units. While incomes in Oak Park were high and poverty was low, there were substantial differences by race in income and poverty levels. As shown in Table 5.4, in 2007 median family income for White and Asian families was more than double that of Black families and the poverty rate for Black households was double that of White households. Moreover, medium household income for Blacks declined between 2000 and 2007— the only racial group to experience a decline—widening the income gap between Black and other residents.

Rising income inequality has been linked to an increase in the achievement gap between high- and low-income families (Reardon, 2011). While research continues to document a relationship between race and achievement, recent research suggests that the achievement gap between children from high- and low-income families has grown substantially in recent decades, and that the income gap is considerably larger than the Black-White gap (Reardon, 2011).

These income inequalities were likely to have implications for Black residents in Oak Park, given their declining income relative to others residents, since income and poverty disparities were related to parental investments in their children's cognitive development. Research suggests that this investment has increased over the last half century, particularly for higher income and college-educated families (Kornrich & Frurstenberg, 2010; Reardon, 2011). Spending increases among higher income families with preschool children were particularly notable, as were increases in preschool enrollment among 3- and 4-year-olds (Bainbridge, Meyers, Tanaka, & Waldfogel, 2005). Spending among lower income families also increased. While all income groups spent more, those at the top of the income distribution increased spending more than other groups. However, given the decline in income, those in the lowest income quartile spent a greater share of their income on their children. These trends give those at the top a greater advantage because they can more easily absorb the growing costs of education, particularly those for child care and preschool.

Recognizing that race and class segregate early childhood care in Oak Park—there were many premier preschool programs for parents with means, but few for working or low-income families—Oak Park's governmental agencies joined together in 2003 to establish a public-private partnership, Collaboration for Early Childhood Care and Education. This partnership provides a quality preschool program, among other services, for low-income families. In addition, the elementary district implemented full-day kindergarten beginning in the 2008-09 school year.

Efforts to maintain integrated housing in Oak Park were challenged by rising housing costs and a diminishing number of affordable housing units. Housing in Oak Park was expensive, with the decade of the 2000s registering large increases in the value of housing. The median housing value increased more than 77% since 1990, after adjusting for inflation. The average sales price of single-family houses increased by an inflation-adjusted 46.8% between 2000-2007 and the average sales price of condos/townhouses increased by an inflation adjusted 89.9% (Village of Oak Park, 2010, January 19). The effect of the 2007 economic downturn on bringing housing prices down was small. Prices of single family houses declined by 7.8% and condos declined by 13% between 2007 and 2008 (Village of Oak Park, 2010, January 19). In addition, Oak Park lost a substantial number (over 3,300) of affordable rental units since 2000, either through condo conversion or increasing rents (Village of Oak Park, 2010, January 19).

High housing prices can be a deterrent to minorities moving to Oak Park and home ownership. Between 2000 and 2007, the Village (Village of Oak Park, 2010, January 19) reported that home ownership for Blacks and Latinos declined while White and Asian home ownership continued to increase. Home ownership among Whites increased from 64.3% in 2000 to over 70% in 2007. Among Blacks, homeownership declined, from

35.8% in 2000 to about 32% in 2007 (Village of Oak Park, 2010, January 19).[4] The decline in the median household income of Black families between 2000 and 2007 put these families at a disadvantage in a housing market with increasing prices. Taken together, these indicators suggest that Black families may be struggling in Oak Park.

Institutional Patterns Within the Schools

As important as integration strategies are to avoiding racially identifiable schools and communities, it does not necessarily, by itself, reduce achievement gaps. Internal, institutional processes that influence how race and income affect access to educational resources and learning opportunities within the school are also related to disparities in student outcomes. Sources of institutional inequity have been documented in tracking and grouping practices (Oakes, Muir, & Joseph, 2000), access to and support with a rigorous curriculum (Darling-Hammond, 2010), physical resources (U.S. Government Accountability Office, 1996), school funding (Baker & Welner, 2010; Odden, 2003), special education placement (Artiles, Klingner, & Tate, 2006; Losen & Orfield, 2002; Skiba et al., 2008), and discipline policies and practices (Fabelo et al., 2011; Gregory, Skiba, & Noguera, 2010). These practices reinforce and perpetuate racial and socioeconomic disadvantage by limiting the educational opportunities available to Black students. While there are a range of factors that can affect student access to learning opportunities (see Sunderman, Hawley, Brown, Hicks, & Kirton, 2011), this analysis examined access to academic programs, the differentiation of students in athletic programs, and disparities in discipline referrals and outcomes.

One of the more common ways that students experience different levels of academic rigor is that they are tracked and grouped by ability. Black and White students' classrooms often become more differentiated as they move through the elementary grades and into high school (Diamond, 2006). The OPRF high school has a long-standing policy that groups students according to their past performance in specific subject areas into one of three tracks: basic/transitional courses for students whose past performance indicated a need for instructional support; regular/college prep; and accelerated/honors (Oak Park River Forest High School, 2011). Placement was based on standardized test scores, teacher or counselor recommendations, past achievement in relevant subject areas, reading ability, and personal factors. Students were urged to "follow the advice of their counselor and the recommendation of their current teacher of that subject" but the policy did provide for parents to override these recommendations (Oak Park River Forest High School, 2011). While data was not provided to the researcher on enrollment across groups, respondents indicated a pattern of more Black students in the lower tracks and more White students in the higher tracks. Dr. Ralph Lee, an African American board member, raised the issue of ability grouping before the board, a practice he believed had been in place for at least 30 years (Oak Park River Forest High School, December 13, 2007). While there was an awareness of the practice among district administrators and the board, the policy remained intact.

Access to a range of extra or cocurriculum programming and activities can support academic performance and behavior by enhancing student connectedness to school (Weiss, Cunningham, Lewis, & Clark, 2005). Students who feel connected to the school are more likely to attend school regularly, stay in school, and have higher school grades and test scores (McNeely, Noonemaker, & Blium, 2002; U. S. Department of Health and Human Services Division of Adolescent and School Health, 2009). Involvement in extracurricular activities provides opportunities for the development of leadership and social skills, and can help to reduce discipline problems. One measure of participation in extracurricular activities is enrollment in athletic programs. As shown in Table 5.5, participation of Black students in athletic programs was the lowest among all subgroups of students. For example, while 61.2% of all White students participated in athletic programs, just 36.4% of Black students participated.

Disciplinary practices in schools affect both the social and academic environment of schools, and when applied disproportionally to racial/ethnic minorities deny them access to instruction and learning opportuni-

Table 5.5.   Enrollment in Athletic Programs, Oak Park River Forest High School, 2008-09

	White	Black	Asian	Hispanic	Multi	Total
Enrollment	1,850	818	93	160	173	3,094
% of enrollment	59.7%	26.4%	3.0%	5.0%	5.6%	
Enrollment in athletic programs	1,144	298	42	77	85	1,650
% of total athletic programs	69.3%	18.1%	2.6%	4.7%	5.2%	53.3%
% of subgroup	61.8%	36.4%	45.2%	48.1%	49.9%	n/a
Risk ratio	n/a	0.59:1.00	0.73:1.00	0.79:1.00	0.81:1.00	

Source: For enrollment data, Illinois State Board of Education (n.d.-b). For athletic program data: Oak Park River Forest District #200, internal document.
Note: Reference group for risk ratio is to White students.

Table 5.6.   Total Discipline Events & Consequences, by Race, Oak Park River Forest High School, 2010-11

	White	Black	Asian	Hispanic	Multi	Total
Enrollment	1,886	894	100	175	181	3,242
% enrollment	58.2	27.6	3.1	5.4	5.6	
# of discipline events	2,014	5,349	107	497	618	8,585
% of total discipline	23.5	62.3	1.2	5.7	7.2	
% of subgroup	106.8	598.3	107.0	284.0	341.4	
Risk ratio	n/a	5.60	1.00	2.66	3.20	
# of consequences	1,550	4,599	103	408	501	7,162
% of total consequences	21.6	64.2	1.4	5.7	7.0	
% of subgroup	82.2	514.4	103.0	233.1	276.8	
Risk ratio	n/a	6.26	1.25	2.84	3.37	

Source: Oak Park and River Forest High School District 200, 2010-2011 Student Discipline Report (August 25, 2011), available at http://www.oprfhs.org/export/sites/oprf/about_us/board_of_ed/board_meetings/Regular_Meetings/Packets/2011-12/August_2011.pdf
Note: Reference group for risk ratio is to White students.

ties, especially when a student is removed from class (Skiba, Michael, Nardo, & Peterson, 2002). Table 5.6 presents data on the number of discipline events and consequences received by high school students, disaggregated by race. This shows that Black students accounted for 62.3% of all discipline referrals, compared to 23.5% for White students. Black students were 5.6 times as likely as White students to be referred for discipline and 6.25 times as likely to receive a discipline consequence.

District Initiatives to Address the Achievement Gap in OPRF

Actions taken by administrators in both districts suggest that they were aware of and attempting to address many of the institutional sources of inequities. But because education policy is made within a political environment where administrators are subject to the demands of faculty and parents and the influence of national educational priorities and trends, there were compromises and accommodations.

The OPRF district, under the leadership of Superintendent Weninger, introduced a number of initiatives to reduce disparities in disciplinary practices, address students' academic proficiencies, and increase student participation in cocurricular activities. However, these initiatives encountered serious opposition from the faculty, who saw their autonomy and influence threatened, and from a board, split along racial lines, that was responding to community concerns. At the time of the study, the high school board included three African American and four White members. Research suggests that African American membership on the school board is associated with more equitable educational policies (Meier & England, 1984; Meier, Stewart Jr., & England, 1989). Black representatives can make policy decisions consistent with the preferences of those they represent and put pressure on the school system to address issues that disadvantage Black students.

Following a protracted hiring process, the OPRF school board hired Superintendent Weninger in 2007 and charged him with addressing the achievement gap. Hired without the full support of the board, Weninger launched several initiatives to improve the district's discipline system and counseling program, provide focused academic programs in reading and math, increase cocurricular participation, and extend parent outreach (Weninger, November 19, 2009). Key to Weninger's initiatives was the reorganization of the faculty deans and counselors into four Pupil Support Services teams: academic, curricular, cocurricular, and discipline.[5] These teams, an attempt to address the fragmentation in responsibilities between the deans and counselors, were highly controversial and resisted by the faculty.

Weninger undertook other reforms to reorganize the division chairs. Traditionally, the division chair focused almost exclusively on departmental matters and retained considerable power over faculty hires and subject matter issues. The superintendent wanted the division chairs to assume a larger role as an administrative leader within the school rather than act primarily as an advocate for the division (Weninger, November 19, 2009). In addition, division heads were instrumental in the hiring process of new faculty. The district found that this process often resulted in a candidate pool that was not very diverse, so to recruit more minority faculty, the district changed its internal recruitment process by reducing the authority of the division chairs to screen out potential candidates early in the process.

While efforts to address the achievement gap were supported in principle by the faculty, reforms were difficult to implement. Weninger noted: "I think there is a want on the part of everybody to solve the achievement gap. I think there is real disagreement about how to go about doing it, who's responsible for doing it, and the accountability measures for it." He conceded that there was faculty opposition, claiming that some "can't see the links because I think their world is so focused in the classroom when there is a much broader perspective" (Weninger, November 19, 2009).

District Initiatives to Address
the Achievement Gap in the Elementary Schools

The elementary district's efforts to address the achievement gap were informed by three factors: the equal distribution of recourses across schools, instructional and programmatic initiatives, and parental expectations. The elementary district allocated resources equally across schools based on enrollment. For example, distribution of technology and textbooks was based on student enrollment; average class size for each school was between 19.5 and 21.5; and teachers were assigned to schools based on the average number of years of teaching experience for the school. Because of past complaints to the Office for Civil Rights on student placement, the district used a blind selection process to assign students to classes within schools. District wide initiatives to improve teaching and learning included differentiated instruction, heterogeneous grouping, increasing instructional time in core subjects, using data to evaluate the effectiveness of academic programs, increasing opportunities for student leadership, among other initiatives (Oak Park Elementary Schools, 2009.

A challenge for the district was to balance the expansion of programs to support struggling students with a focus on accelerating instruction for academically strong students. To support struggling students, the district implemented full-day kindergarten, provided reading/language arts specialists in all of the schools to work with small groups of students, and purchased supplemental reading programs designed to enhance reading skills (Elementary Administrator 2, 10-6-2010). The elementary schools provided "double dose instruction" where students that were struggling were targeted for extra instruction in math and/or reading and to better prepare students for state testing. Students were placed in small groups and worked with the classroom teacher. This was expanded to the middle schools where students received extra instruction during an elective period, before, or after school so as not to cut into student's academic program.

The focus on the achievement gap and parental pressure pushed the elementary district in the direction of increased tracking, particularly in math. The district practice was not to track, but beginning with the 2008-09 school year, the district established two different math levels in the middle schools—a regular grade level math and an accelerated math. The goal was to increase the number of students completing algebra I by the end of eighth grade. There was also a push from the parents of gifted students to provide more gifted services. The district's preference was to use differentiated instruction, where all students, including gifted students, received appropriate instruction in the classroom. But in an effort to address parental concerns, the district established academic pullout programs in reading, language arts, writing and science and placed gifted resource teachers in each building (Elementary Administrator 3, 11-17-2009).

Symbolic/Ideological Patterns: Changing Perceptions of Diversity

Most Oak Parkers hold a perception of Oak Park as a "diverse" community.[6] Yet how diversity was conceptualized has evolved since the 1970s, with two concepts, not entirely complementary, competing for dominance. One of these perceptions reflects an image of Oak Park that emerged in the 1970s when major changes in the racial composition of the Village took place. The other is more recent and reflects a view of Oak Park that places an emphasis on individual, as opposed to community, goals (Demerath, 2009). One respondent characterized the first perspective as the Oak Park Way: "They have a phrase called the 'Oak Park Way.' It really started in the early seventies when they made a strong commitment to welcome diversity in the community and to make sure that no one felt like they couldn't live in any neighborhood in the community" (Elementary Administrator 2, November 17, 2009). But whether people still think that way, he said:

> They talk of it that way, but it tends to be thrown out like everyone accepts it and I think that, frankly ... there has been a turnover of that attitude. I think more people are concerned more about their own child rather than someone else's children. I know when we have parent groups together, the people who are long time residents are always talking about, is it fair to other children. The newer people to the community talk about, I want this for my child. That's a little different view of things. (Elementary Administrator 2, November 17, 2009)

Some attributed this change in attitude to the people moving into Oak Park. One common perception was that the kind of people moving to Oak Park had changed. While earlier residents were committed to social diversity, more recent residents came to Oak Park for its amenities—including the schools—and its favorable property values. One respondent put it this way:

> On the social capital end, I think that when the real estate went in the direction where this was a great community to invest in because you bought a piece of property here and a couple of years later you could sell it for money. It changed the motivation of why people were moving to Oak Park. They would be moving to Oak Park because it was a great community, had

all the stuff, but the people that were moving in weren't necessarily contributing to it other than paying their taxes.

He went on to contrast the social ethos of an earlier generation of Oak Parkers:

> There was a generation ... where people were moving in [to Oak Park] by choice because they wanted to live in the diverse community, they were committed to the social change and the social stands that were being made at the time. That generation, that guard has moved on and there really hasn't been a generation to replace it at this point. (Community Respondent 3, June 24, 2010)

The notion of the Oak Park Way fostered a belief that Oak Park was unique. Respondents portrayed this as both positive and negative. For some, the Oak Park Way conveyed a strong sense of pride in the community and its history, particularly as a leader during the 1960s in promoting nondiscriminatory housing. For others, it reflected arrogance and often meant that Oak Park had little to learn from those outside the community. One respondent believed that, while there was a spirit of inclusion in Oak Park, there was little appreciation for diversity of thought. That is, "there is only one way and it's our way because we're special, we know how to do it, we're smart" (Community Respondent 2, June 24, 2010).

Several respondents pointed out that community structures that would attract African Americans to Oak Park were not there. For example, there were no integrated churches or African American churches in Oak Park: "One of the interesting things about the Oak Park community, despite its efforts to be supportive of racial diversity for the community, there is not an African American church in the community" (High School Administrator 1, November 20, 2009). In addition, minorities were underrepresented on appointed citizen boards and commissions (Village of Oak Park, 2010, January 19). For example, the 2010 Village Board of Trustees included four White males (including the Village president), one Black male, and three White females. The racial composition of the board of one prominent community organization, which was primarily White, did not change until an African American became chief executive officer and began to recruit a more diverse membership.

These two competing perceptions of Oak Park underscore the tensions between a commitment to the idea of equity and the pressures of obtaining the very best for one's own children. This was illustrated in the opposition to a proposal to implement a full-day kindergarten program in the Oak Park elementary district. Initially, many Oak Park parents viewed full-day kindergarten as free childcare for some groups of students (i.e., low income and/or racial minorities) and as a tradeoff among programs and services. Since property taxes are the primary source of funds for the schools, residents believed that full-day kindergarten would result in the district cutting funding for other favored programs to pay for it. However, the opposition ended when it became clear that the cost would be paid for in full by state funds linked to a change in the state funding formula (Elementary Administrator 1, November 17, 2009).

The conflict at the high school level over the superintendents' contract illustrates the inability of the community to come together around a common agenda. Renewal of Superintendent Weninger's contract was a protracted and divisive issue. Contract negotiations broke down in October 2009 when the board voted 3-4 not to renew the contact and Weninger subsequently announced his retirement. The board's three African American members—John Allen, Ralph Lee, and Jacques Conway—supported renewing the contract (Dean, 2009c).[7] In November 2009, the board reversed itself and reopened contract negotiations. This was made possible when the idea of a 1-year contract extension resurfaced and was supported by a fourth board member—Amy McCormack—and the idea received Dr. Weninger's support. Internal board politics on how this was handled added to the divisiveness and led to the resignation of Dietra Millard as Board president (Dean, 2009b). However, by December contract negotiations ended when the board voted 3-4 to cut the superintendent's salary and Weninger submitted his resignation (personal communication).

The contention over the contract stemmed from divisions over the agenda that Weninger laid out for the district and the changes he made. Those on the board supporting Weninger cited his efforts to address the achievement gap, particularly for Black males, as well as his efforts on student discipline and changing the school's data system by creating a position to oversee that department. Board member Allen maintained that Weninger "made tough decisions that weren't always supported by some stakeholder groups" (Dean, 2009c). Those opposed to retaining Weninger stressed his inability to work with all stakeholders. Board president Dietra Millard noted that "some groups didn't always feel they were listened to" (Dean, 2009c). Many of the issues that Weninger addressed, particularly changes in the dean and counseling program and restructuring the division heads, were very contentious because they changed operating procedures that had been in place for years and challenged the influence of the faculty (Dean, 2009a; Haley, 2009). It should be noted that the board president, Millard, had opposed hiring Weninger, and that the faculty did not support renewing his contract. In addition, the faculty union supported two board members (McCormick and Finnegan) who came on the board in 2009 and voted against renewing his contract.

Implications for Achieving Equity in Oak Park Schools

The experiences of Oak Park illustrate the complexity of providing an equitable education for all students and are particularly noteworthy because of the community's long-standing commitment to diversity. From a structural perspective, the community has sustained highly diverse schools that have avoided resegregating. This is in part related to decisions made in the 1960s and 1970s to adopt housing policies that fostered integrated housing, drawing school boundaries and locating middle schools so that schools were fairly racially balanced, and having one high school that served all students. It was also due to the Village programs, policies, and services still in place that promote and sustain integrated housing. However, other structural inequities were harder to address, in part because they were driven by national economic conditions and policies. Rising housing costs and a diminishing number of affordable housing units may make it harder to maintain integrated housing, and growing disparities in wealth and income between Black and White households may contribute to perpetuating unequal access to resources and learning opportunities outside of the school.

School administrators, board members, and community advocates were acutely aware of the challenges to reducing the achievement gap and were committed to providing an education that was both academically challenging and equitable. Elementary district administrators identified many school level sources of inequities and implemented or attempted to implement reforms and introduce practices designed to address the internal, institutional processes that influence how race and income affects access to educational resources and learning opportunities. The success of these efforts was evident in the progress the elementary district made in narrowing achievement gaps on the ISAT, particularly in math (see Table 5.4).

At the high school level there was a convergence of factors that might have facilitated the district's ability to address equity issues and the achievement gap, at least in the short term: three members of the school board were African American, one of whom was a former high school teacher who specifically came on the board to address issues related to the education of Black students, a superintendent hired to address the achievement gap and committed to that charge, combined with the increased awareness of the achievement gap brought on by NCLB. While this combination of factors did create considerable attention to race-related education issues, it was highly contentious and short lived. The superintendent left the district at the end of the 2009-10 school year, by 2011 there was only one African American on the board, and the federal government removed the pressure of subgroup accountability beginning in 2011 by granting states waivers to these NCLB requirements.[8]

Institutional and systemic changes at the high school level were extremely difficult to make because of organizational structures that were decentralized into academic departments and the commitment of division chairs and faculty to their own subjects and departments. Attempts by Superintendent Weninger to change these organizational structures were resisted by the faculty and some board members. The lack of support from the faculty coupled with the union's ability to elect two sympathetic board members, ultimately contributed to the ouster of the superintendent.

In a community with relatively affluent and well-educated parents, there was an expectation for academically challenging schools and a commitment in principle to the idea of equity. But there was less commitment to accepting the deeper changes that would be necessary for achieving equity when those goals were seen as competing with the provision of a demanding and rigorous education. This was evident in the pushback on adopting a full-day kindergarten program, which was viewed as using limited resources to benefit some students at the expense of providing the other academically challenging programs and services that parents believed were needed to develop the talents of their children. The conflict between these two goals also explains the actions of the high school board over many years to conduct studies on the achievement gap and promote conversations around equity, but its failure to adopt policies that would change practices.

The waning of the community-oriented commitment to diversity that emerged in the 1960s and 1970s and the rise of a more individualist orientation made achieving equity more challenging. A more equitable system will require strong and committed district leadership acting in partnership with community leaders and policy actors from outside the school system. On this, Oak Park has considerable civic capacity, including a tradition of collaboration between the schools and community organizations and a structure in place that brings Village governmental leaders together. This structure could provide the impetus for broader institutional changes. But the Village has not yet developed effective political coalitions that would commit community resources to a concrete policy agenda. Certainly, the turmoil and turnover in the districts' leadership[9] stemming from district level initiatives suggests that gaining consensus on an equity policy agenda for the schools will require generating the type of broad-based coalition that was successful in stabilizing the housing market in the 1960s.

What does the Oak Park experience suggest for other, rapidly diversifying suburban school districts? First, it points to the importance of housing policies that support and sustain integrated housing. Without those policies, communities are likely to replicate patterns of racial and economic segregation found in some of the nation's central cities, making it more difficult to accommodate increasing diversity in the schools. Second, to make informed policies and educational decisions requires having good information on enrollment and demographic patterns, particularly when communities are rapidly changing. Third, to develop and implement polices that support equity and confront issues of demographic and social change will depend on the ability of districts to build coalitions and alliances that cut across business, government, nonprofit, and community sectors. Without a broad based political coalition, communities are likely to adopt strategies and policies aimed at maintaining the stability and equilibrium of the system rather than make the difficult decisions necessary to promote equity.

ACKNOWLEDGMENT

This research reported here was supported by a grant from The Spencer Foundation to the Civil Rights Project/Proyecto Derechos Civiles at UCLA. The opinions presented here are those of the author and do not represent the views of The Spencer Foundation or the Civil Rights Project.

NOTES

1. Superintendent Constance Collins and Assistant Superintendent Kevin Anderson came to Oak Park in 2005. Superintendent Collins resigned at the end of the 2009-2010 school year.
2. The "observer's perspective" tends to emphasize the characteristics of the actor because the circumstances to which he/she is responding are less visible (Steele, 2010).
3. The eastern border divides Oak Park and the western neighborhoods of Chicago, which are among the poorest in Chicago.
4. The rates are contained in a figure; exact percentages for all groups and years are not given.
5. Each student is assigned a dean and counselor when entering high school. The deans are responsible for monitoring attendance and behavior and the counselors advise students on personal, academic and college planning (Oak Park River Forest High School Faculty Handbook, 2009).
6. For most Oak Parkers, diversity was defined as Black/White diversity. While the proportion of Latinos and Asians is much smaller than the Black population, there was little recognition of diversity as encompassing these groups.

7. Those opposed included Dietra Millard, Amy Leafe McCormack, Sharon Patchak-Layman, and Terry Finnegan.
8. The U.S. Department of Education approved Illinois' Elementary and Secondary Education Flexibility request in February 2012 (go to http://www.ed.gov/esea/flexibility/requests)
9. The elementary district superintendent was replaced in the 2010-11 school year. The OPRF board was comprised of one African American and six White members in the 2011-12 school year.

REFERENCES

Artiles, A. J., Klingner, J. K., & Tate, W. F. (2006). Representation of minority students in special education: Complicating traditional explanations. *Educational Researcher, 35*(6), 3-5.

Bainbridge, J., Meyers, M. K., Tanaka, S., & Waldfogel, J. (2005). Who gets an early education? Family income and the enrollment of three- to five-year-olds from 1968 to 2000. *Social Science Quarterly, 86*(3), 724-745.

Baker, B. D., & Welner, K. G. (2010). Premature celebrations: The persistence of inter-district funding disparities. *Education Policy Analysis Archives, 18*(9). Retrieved from http://epaa.asu.edu/ojs/article/view/718

Darling-Hammond, L. (2010). *The flat world and education: How America's commitment to equity will determine our future.* New York: Teachers College Press.

Dean, T. (2009a, October 20). Nub of the debate: How chairs get chosen. *Wednesday Journal.* Retrieved October 17, 2010, from http://www.wednesdayjournalonline.com/main.asp?Search=1&ArticleID=15799&SectionID= 1&SubSectionID=1&S=1

Dean, T. (2009b, November 24). OPRF finds 4th vote to keep Weninger: Hard feelings over how discussion of one-year extension surfaced. *Wednesday Journal.* Retrieved December 6, 2009, from http://www.wednesdayjournalonline.com/main.asp?Search=1&ArticleID=16058&SectionID =1&SubSectionID=1&S=1

Dean, T. (2009c, October 20). Why Weninger chose retirement: Split OPRF board saw superintendent as strong leader or as polarizing force. *Wednesday Journal.* Retrieved January 15, 2010, from http://www.wednesdayjournalonline.com/main.asp?Search=1&ArticleID=15785&SectionID=1&SubSectionID =1&S=1

Demerath, P. (2009). *Producing success: The culture of personal advancement in an American high school.* Chicago, IL: The University of Chicago Press.

Diamond, J. B. (2006). Still separate and unequal: Examining race, opportunity, and school achievement in "integrated" suburbs. *Journal of Negro Education, 75*(3), 495-505.

Diamond, J. B., Lewis, A. E., & Gordon, L. (2007). Race, culture, and achievement disparities in a desegregated suburb: Reconsidering the oppositional culture explanation. *International Journal of Qualitative Studies in Education, 20*(6), 655-680.

Fabelo, T., Thompson, M. D., Plotkin, M., Carmichael, D., Marchbanks, M. P. III, & Booth, E. A. (2011). *Breaking schools' rules: A statewide study of how school discipline relates to students' success and juvenile justice involvement.* New York, NY: Council of State Governments Justice Center.

Ferguson, R. F., Ludwig, J., & Rich, W. (2001). A diagnostic analysis of Black-White GPA disparities in Shaker Heights, Ohio. *Brookings Papers on Education Policy, 4,* 347-414.

Gregory, A., Skiba, R. J., & Noguera, P. (2010). The achievement gap and the discipline gap: Two sides of the same coin? *Educational Researcher, 38*(1), 59-68.

Haley, D. (2009, October 20). Weninger's battle with 'the building'. *Wednesday Journal.* Retrieved October 17, 2010, from http://www.wednesdayjournalonline.com/main.asp?Search=1&ArticleID=15786&SectionID=1&SubSectionID=11&S=1

Hollis, M. J. (1998). *Final report: Building a more hospitable learning community: A community wide dialogue of Oak Park and River Forest high school district 200.* Oak Park, IL: Oak Park and River Forest High School District 200.

Illinois State Board of Education. (n.d.-a). *Interactive Illinois Report Card.* Retrieved May 8, 2012 from http://iirc.niu.edu

Illinois State Board of Education. (n.d.-b). *Interactive Illinois Report Card.* Retrieved September 12, 2010 from http://iirc.niu.edu/Default.aspx

Kornrich, S., & Frurstenberg, F. (2010). *Investing in children: Changes in parental spending on children, 1972 to 2007.* United States Studies Centre at the University of Sydney, Australia.

Lewis, J., Maly, M., Kleppner, P., & Tobias, R. A. (2002). *Race and residence in the Chicago metropolitan area: 1980 to 2000.* Chicago, IL: Institute for Metropolitan Affairs, Roosevelt University and Office for Social Policy Research, Northern Illinois University.

Losen, D. J., & Orfield, G. (Eds.). (2002). *Racial inequality in special education.* New York, NY: The Century Foundation.

McNeely, C. A., Noonemaker, J. M., & Blium, R. M. (2002). Promoting school connectedness: Evidence from a longitudinal study of adolescent health. *Journal of School Health, 72,* 139-146.

Meier, K. J., & England, R. E. (1984). Black representation and educational policy: Are they related? *The American Political Science Review, 78*(2), 392-403.

Meier, K. J., Stewart, J. Jr., & England, R. E. (1989). *Race, class, and education: The politics of second-generation discrimination.* Madison, WI: The University of Wisconsin Press.

Morris, J. E. (2009). *Troubling the waters: Fulfilling the promise of quality public schooling for Black children.* New York, NY: Teachers College Press.

Oak Park and River Forest High School. (1991). *Report of the African-American achievement committee.* Oak Park, IL: Author.

Oak Park River Forest High School. (2011). *Academic catalog 2011-2012.* Oak Park, IL: Author.

Oak Park River Forest High School. (2007, December 13). *Minutes of an instruction committee of the whole board.* Retrieved August 8, 2012. from http://www.oprfhs.org/board-of-education/2007-8-Archive.cfm#.UC0FFhw_0sk

Oakes, J., Muir, K., & Joseph, R. (2000, May, 2000). *Course taking and achievement in math and science: Inequalities that endure change.* Paper presented at the National Institute for Science Education Conference, Detroit, MI.

Odden, A. (2003). Equity and adequacy in school finance today. *Phi Delta Kappan, 85*(2), 120-125.

Reardon, S. F. (2011). The widening academic achievement gap between the rich and the poor: New evidence and possible explanations. In G. J. Duncan & R. J. Murnane (Eds.), *Whither opportunity? Rising inequality, schools, and children's life chances.* New York, NY: Russell Sage Foundation.

Singleton, G. E., & Linton, C. (2006). *Courageous conversations: A field guide for achieving equity in schools.* Thousand Oaks, CA: Corwin.

Skiba, R. J., Michael, R. S., Nardo, A. C., & Peterson, R. (2002). The color of discipline: Sources of racial and gender disproportionality in school punishment. *Urban Review, 34,* 317-342.

Skiba, R. J., Simmons, A. B., Ritter, S., Gibb, A. C., Rausch, M. K., Curadrado, J., et al. (2008). Achieving equity in special education: History, status, and current challenges. *Council for Exceptional Children, 74*(3), 264-288.

Steele, C. M. (2010). *Whistling Vivaldi: How stereotypes affect us and what we can do.* New York, NY: W. W. Norton & Company.

Sunderman, G. L., Hawley, W. D., Brown, J., Hicks, B., & Kirton, E. (2011). *Beyond equity assessment: Developing a research based tool for equity planning in schools and districts.* Paper presented at the American Education Research Association, New Orleans, LA.

The African American Achievement Study Team. (2003, May). *The learning community performance gap: Oak Park and River Forest high school.* Oak Park, IL: Oak Park and River Forest High School District 200.

U.S. Department of Health and Human Services Division of Adolescent and School Health. (2009). *Fostering school connectedness.* Washington, DC: Author.

U.S. Government Accountability Office. (1996). *School facilities: America's schools report differing conditions* (No. HEHS-96-103). Washington, DC: Author.

Village of Oak Park. (2009, October 12). *Anaylsis of impediments to fair housing choice: Draft for public review.* Oak Park, IL: Author.

Village of Oak Park. (2010, January 19). *Anaylsis of impediments to fair housing choice.* Oak Park, IL: Author.

Weiss, C. L. A., Cunningham, D. L., Lewis, C. P., & Clark, M. G. (2005). *Enhancing student connectedness.* Baltimore, MD: Center for School Mental Health Analysis and Action, Department of Psychiatry, University of Maryland School of Medicine.

Wells, A. S., Baldridge, B., Duran, J., Lofton, R., Roda, A., Warner, M., et al. (2009). *Why boundaries matter: A study of five separate and unequal Long Island school districts.* New York, NY: Teachers College.

Wells, A. S., & Crain, R. L. (1997). *Stepping over the color line: African-American students in White suburban schools.* New Haven, CT: Yale University Press.

Weninger, A. J. (2007, October 22). Memo to board of education: A plan to raise student achievement. Oak Park, IL: Author.

CHAPTER 6

FORD FOUNDATION'S EFFORTS TO ACHIEVE EDUCATIONAL EQUITY

Measurable Reform or Quixotic Tilting?

Marian A. Bott

This chapter describes the Ford Foundation (Ford)'s education reform activities, which were designed to decrease the funding differences between high-income and low-income communities. Specifically, the chapter describes Ford's long-term, and successful, strategy to use litigation and public engagement to address inequities in K-12 education funding through initiating and advocating changes to state fiscal policies. It addresses two related research questions. First, is there evidence that state policymakers, advocates and grantmakers have improved educational funding equity in the United States? Second, if there is such evidence, what duration can these improvements be expected to have?

From 1966 to 1980, Ford showed that school finance equity could be measurably improved through strategic grantmaking. At that time, Ford was led by McGeorge Bundy, former National Security Advisor under Presidents John F. Kennedy and Lyndon B. Johnson, all of whom had aggressive civil rights agendas. Under Bundy, Ford focused its grantmak-

Charting Reform, Achieving Equity in a Diverse Nation
pp. 133–160
Copyright © 2013 by Information Age Publishing
133

ing on school finance equalization by encouraging states to reduce inter-district school spending disparities and intervening in some hard-fought school finance equity battles (Bott, 2012). Because of Ford grants and reform efforts, certain key school finance metrics improved between 1969-70 and 1979-80. Shifting the school finance burden from local property taxes to broader based, higher state taxes was one strategy of early reformers, and with Ford grants, they ultimately persuaded many legislatures to enact such shifts.

Maintaining K-12 school finance equity, however defined, has been deemed by two highly regarded education policy experts as difficult at the least, possibly naïve, and perhaps quixotic. Henry M. Levin analyzed political constituencies in 1974; Kenneth K. Wong focused on intergovernmental policy incoherence in 1994. Their theories, explained in this chapter's first section, pessimistically suggest that tilting by school finance reform advocates is ultimately doomed to defeat by formidable windmills of local control and special interest groups. The chapter's second section analyzes the key challenges that Ford faced from 1966 to 1980, when its school finance equalization grantmaking began. With strategic grantmaking, Ford achieved a measure of financial equity in an era of a nationwide civil rights movement focused, in part, on ending segregated schools. The third section reviews Ford's school finance grantmaking from 1980 forward, primarily using New York State and two of its school districts as a case study of the impact of Ford's multiple strategies including litigation, public engagement, and support of academic research. The chapter concludes with observations, based on the success of its prior strategies, about how Ford's future school finance grantmaking might be aligned more tightly with its ongoing civil rights mission.

TWO THEORIES OF PERSISTENT INEQUITY IN U.S. SCHOOL FINANCE

Levin (1974a) posits that a romantic notion—schools can remake society—persisted in the early 1970s. The notion that "school reform can effect change in the sponsoring society is an improbable and unsupported one" (Levin, 1974a, p. 305). School reform, he argued, is highly unlikely. As society supports inequities in political, economic, and social status, it will also support educational inequity because of the principle of correspondence (p. 306), meaning that the hierarchical work organizations that characterize modern societies are mirrored in the diversity of school settings: some are boring, leaving students alienated but forced to conform to the required setting, whereas some students are involved in intense competition as a part of their school setting (p. 312). Levin predicts that "compensatory education," as mandated by *Brown v. Board* (1954), will not "succeed in reducing the competitive edge of the advantaged in the race for income and status" (p. 315).

Levin (1974b) also analyzed local constituencies that influence the allocation of state or federal funding (see Table 6.1). He predicted that school finance reform efforts would increase teacher salaries and reduce class size in a mechanistic fashion through collective bargaining, without focusing on student needs and responses to them. Levin's model asserts that differing goals, amounts of power, and use of coalitions influence the outcome of reform efforts. Low-power constituencies do not gain from school finance reforms, but constituencies with moderate or high power, including school boards, teachers' unions, and administrators, are able to allocate increased revenues garnered from the state or federal government. More recently, wealthy private sector financiers and federal government policymakers, both advocating for prioritizing charter schools, have become high-power constituencies, challenging the traditional power of teachers' unions (H. Levin, personal communication, June 2012).

Kenneth Wong (1994) similarly observed that "educational opportunities are socially structured" (p. 257). He blames the governance structure, explaining that "inequity in educational resources has been perpetuated by the design and practice of our governing system" (p. 257). Even though governmental resources are theoretically allocated to address

Table 6.1. Local Constituencies and the Decision for Allocating Increased Revenues From State or Federal Government

Constituency	Goal	Power	Coalition	Outcome
1. Local taxpayer	Minimize local burden	Moderate	With 4	Substitution of outside money for local
2. Disadvantaged parent	Improve educational outcomes for disadvantaged children	Low	No	No change
3. Disadvantaged student	Improve educational environment	Low	No	No change
4. School board	Minimize conflict	High	With 1 and 6	Low conflict
5. Teachers	Increase employment and job benefits	High	With 6	More employment
6. Administrators	Increase employment and minimize conflict	High	With 4 and 5	More employment low conflict

Source: Levin (1974, p. 183).

social inequity in schools (those with concentrations of high poverty and racial minority students), *territorial inequity* in fiscal capacities, and *distributive inequity* within districts (i.e., failure to distribute quality instructors equitably), they in fact fail to increase equity. While the federal government focuses on socially redistributive policies, and state governments on reducing interdistrict disparities, Wong asserts that at the local level, districts "allow resources to follow the instructional staff instead of paying greater attention to the diverse needs of students in different neighborhoods" (p. 260). He calls for greater "policy coherence."

These models suggest that a two-pronged approach is needed in order to achieve some measure of financial equity. From Levin's model, a school finance strategy needs to empower low power constituents in order to raise the visibility of their needs. Wong's model suggests that achieving financial equity requires a strategy for reducing both interdistrict and within district disparities. Facing these challenges, the case of the Ford Foundation suggests that an external entity with proactive thinking and committed resources can make a difference in reducing financial inequities.

FORD'S SCHOOL FINANCE ACTIVISM BETWEEN 1966 AND 1981

One driving force of the civil rights movement of the 1960s was the failure of school districts nationwide to implement the school desegregation order of the U.S. Supreme Court under Chief Justice Earl Warren in *Brown v. Board* (1954) and the fact that, despite the passage of the Civil Rights Act in 1964, racist policies and practices persisted. Community violence followed desegregation orders that were being enforced by President Johnson's Commissioner of Education, Harold "Doc" Howe II. Johnson's withholding of federal education funding polarized communities, prompting presidential candidate Richard M. Nixon in 1968 to pledge to "fire Doc Howe" (Goldberg, 2000, p. 161). Subsequent suburban flight escalated school finance inequities; increased suburban property values exacerbated spending differences.

Beginning in 1967, prompted by incidents of urban rioting in Detroit, Michigan, and Newark, New Jersey, Ford made grants to both start-up and existing entities that wished to form coalitions to connect the affected communities and businesses with the protesting racial minority groups. The contrasts between the physical conditions and funding in urban and suburban schools were highly contentious issues. Yet, the challenges forecast by Levin's model of differential constituency power were evident as families who could afford to live in the suburbs paid property tax to support new and better schools. Urban schools became a default choice for poorer families. Detroit, Newark, New York City, Los Angeles, and San Francisco were among the urban areas located in states that then exemplified extreme school spending differences (Wise, 1967).

In the late 1960s and 1970s, Ford's $3 billion in assets made it by far the largest U.S. foundation (Ford Annual Report, 1968). It saw an opportunity to address with substantial grantmaking both the concerns of minority groups and those of local business leaders, who saw a threat to work force readiness as well as employee safety. The following discussion traces Ford's use of a strategy to empower urban minority students and their families. Ford gave substantial and continual grants to the National Urban Coalition (NUC) to enable it to advocate for reducing funding inequities between urban and suburban schools. However, one seemingly logical strategy for the NUC, lobbying elected officials, was curtailed early on in Ford's relationship with the NUC because of constraints placed on foundations by the Internal Revenue Service.

Ford's Involvement With the National Urban Coalition (NUC)

John W. Gardner, who headed the Department of Health, Education and Welfare under President Lyndon B. Johnson, was tapped in 1968 to lead the NUC. Its mission was to establish coalitions in large, troubled cities and mediate minority and business concerns. Gardner asked Ford for a large grant, and opened branches in New Jersey, California, Michigan, and other states with large urban areas. NUC branches coordinated with other community organizations and provided subgrants to minority groups to give them a greater voice in school budget allocations. NUC also filed *amicus curiae* briefs supporting school finance litigation which, in the early 1970s, argued that federal Fourteenth Amendment equal protection and due process clauses were being violated. One such case was *McInnis v. Ogilvie* (1969), concerning four school districts in Cook County, Illinois (three in Chicago), where spending was substantially less per student than in surrounding districts. Gardner also garnered Ford support to lobby Congress for economic improvements in major cities to benefit minority populations. By supporting NUC actions, Ford was acting to reduce both social and territorial inequities (Wong, 1994) and increase the constituency power of urban students and their parents (Levin, 1974b). As early as 1969, the NUC used Ford grants to support social scientists' research documenting inequities in public school spending in Michigan (Guthrie, Kleindorfer, Levin, & Stout, 1971). Gardner and his staff met with Congressional leaders to plead the case of urban poor families, and while the lobbying was effective, it also bore some risk, as will be described next.

Impact of Tax Reforms

The November 1968 presidential election placed Richard M. Nixon, who opposed forced desegregation by busing, in the White House. "Doc" Howe joined Ford as head of its Education and Research Division. At the end of 1969, after years of hearings about foundation abuses, and wary of the liberal and wealthy Ford's civil rights agenda, Congress enacted the Tax Reform Act of 1969, defining "private" foundations, forbidding their lobbying of elected officials, and restricting their grantees' lobbying rights. Thereafter, Ford had to ensure that its grantees adhered to lobbying restrictions, while nevertheless attempting to persuade policymakers to alter school finance budget allocation formulas.

Gardner resigned from NUC in 1969 and founded Common Cause, an advocacy organization lobbying for better government. The NUC, with new leadership and staff, continued to receive substantial Ford grants to support its activist public engagement in school finance reform, though, as noted above, it could no longer lobby.

Ford Recruits Kelly

Ford recognized the importance of a knowledgeable program officer with top credentials in U.S. school finance policies. By 1970, Bundy and Howe had recruited James A. Kelly, who had been the NUC's education policy officer and had orchestrated the organization's 1968 social science research and lobbying initiatives supporting school finance equalization. Kelly was hired to design Ford's school finance equalization grantmaking program. His strategy emphasized academic research, paired frequently with litigation, to improve U.S. school finance equity. Education researchers at universities including Syracuse, Stanford, Columbia, and New York were generously funded by Ford.[1] Their school finance policy research was used to support plaintiff claims in the early school finance litigation, and to provide expert testimony to legislatures. These studies focused on identifying inequities in the distribution of resources across social and racial groups, and identifying between and within district financial inequities.

Kelly recognized the need to debate multiple definitions of equity and inequity, but also to measure, document, publicize, and, when necessary, litigate school finance inequities. Thus, Ford focused on inequitable and inferior school financing arrangements nationwide, attending to the concerns of Blacks and Mexican Americans, but also listening to suburban superintendents, who worried that equalization meant diminishing the quality of their schools (Ford Archives, 719-0064). While not promulgating any one remedy for the existing inequities, Kelly's grants encouraged legal activism: litigation combined with public engagement. However, Kelly's were not Ford's only school finance activities; some had preceded Kelly's arrival, and they were not well coordinated with his efforts in the State of Texas. Ford's work in Texas illustrates the risks and challenges of relying on a combination of social science research, public engagement/empowerment, and litigation as a strategy for advocating school finance equalization, in light of high-power forces of local and, in this instance, state control that resisted reform efforts.

Ford's Grant to MALDEF

In Texas, Ford used litigation on behalf of low-power constituents to challenge school segregation as well as school finance inequities. In 1968 Ford's National Affairs Division granted $2.2 million (about $15 million in 2012 dollars) to create the Mexican American Legal Defense and Education Fund (MALDEF), based in San Antonio. Widespread discrimination was endemic in Texas education, housing, and employment. Separate schools had been established for Mexican American students (U.S. Commission on Civil Rights, 1972). MALDEF's legal strategy aimed at Texas' school segregation as well as its school finance inequities. *Rodriguez v. San Antonio* (1968) had recently been filed in federal district court by a local attorney, Arthur Gochman, alleging that the state's school finance system violated federal and state equal protection rights, and citing conditions in the Edgewood section of San Antonio, which had multiple school districts. Gochman sought MALDEF's support; the organization declined, preferring to maintain strategic control and advising Gochman that litigation based on equal protection grounds would not succeed (P. Sracic, personal communication, January 2011).

Nonetheless, in January 1969 MALDEF filed its own equal protection school finance lawsuit, *Guerra v. Smith*, also focused on the educational needs of students in Edgewood. *Guerra* alleged that Mexican American children's needs were not considered, and that a state-funded teacher pay supplement program that compensated only school districts that could afford to hire teachers with higher degrees was discriminatory. The protracted case was brought before a single judge in the U.S. District Court, Western District, and finally dismissed in 1973. By supporting litigation and identifying civil rights violations, Ford's National Affairs Division contributed to identifying inequities that Texas ultimately addressed in the 1980s, but initially fought to maintain.

Kelly's Work on *Rodriguez*

In 1972, separately, in Ford's Education and Research Division, Kelly focused his Texas school finance reform efforts on *Rodriguez v. San Antonio*, which on appeal became the landmark *San Antonio v. Rodriguez* (1973) U.S. Supreme Court case (hereinafter *Rodriguez*). A three-judge federal district panel was to hear the case; at that time, such cases challenging state constitutions and heard by such panels were automatically appealable to the U.S. Supreme Court. Kelly sent experienced education litigators to help prepare Gochman to appear before the U.S. Supreme Court. Kelly believed, following Levin, that disadvantaged families would have less power in litigation than the State of Texas, and wanted to provide intellectual counterweight by also funding social science research.

Kelly knew that social science evidence documenting Texas school finance inequities already existed. While he was at the NUC, the Syracuse University Research Corporation (SURC) had used a Ford school finance-related grant to conduct quantitative research on the impact of President Johnson's landmark initiative, the 1966 Elementary and Secondary Education Act, which was meant to address social inequities (students in poverty) as suggested by Wong's (1994) model. Kelly believed that SURC's work on disparities in school spending and differences in property wealth and personal income could be built upon to support plaintiffs in *Rodriguez v. San Antonio*. If plaintiffs were to prevail, the State of Texas would be ordered to address interdistrict disparities, most likely through legislation to amend distribution of, or increase, state school aid. In 1972, SURC further analyzed school districts near and within San Antonio. Metrics such as equalized tax rate, property value per student, local and state funding levels per student, median per capita income, and student demographics such as race and family income were considered. In Bexar County, there were multiple independent school districts. Seven of them enrolled 93% of the public school students in the county; all were in the metropolitan San Antonio area. One of them, the Edgewood Independent School District, was characterized by a 90% concentration of poor Mexican American students (*Rodriguez*, 1973). The housing pattern had been abetted by state-enforced deed restrictions (*Rodriguez*, Brief for Appellees) that barred Mexican Americans from any but the poorest neighborhoods until after World War II (*Shelley v. Kraemer*, 344 U.S. 1, 1947) and the passage of the Fair Housing Act of 1968 (Title 42, U.S.C. §3601, et seq.). Edgewood had $5,429 of property value per student; neighboring Alamo Heights, with only 18% Mexican Americans, had $45,095 per student.

The statistics were persuasive in the Texas federal district court. Plaintiffs won their case (*Rodriguez v. San Antonio*, 1971) because the three empanelled judges agreed that, on balance, the evidence supported the plaintiffs' claims. However, in April 1972, Texas appealed to the U.S. Supreme Court, which heard the case in the fall of 1972. SURC statistics remained crucial when the case was heard by the U.S. Supreme Court.

In the U.S. Supreme Court, a portion of SURC's data was used to refute the validity of the plaintiffs' claims because in the second lowest and middle quintiles of median property values, median family income showed an aberration: a nonlinear relationship indicating that the lower the equalized property value, the higher the family income. A law clerk for U.S. Supreme Court Judge Lewis F. Powell, Jr., Larry Hammond, whose own Texas school district was poor but who travelled to a wealthier district for high school (Sracic, 2006, p. 69), seized on SURC's nonlinear data pattern. Hammond's analysis, together with Connecticut school funding statistics prepared by Yale University graduate students (Yale Note, 1972), strengthened Justice Powell's assertion that district wealth and family wealth were not necessarily correlated. Apparently Hammond did not believe that Texas' school finance system had jeopardized his education, and reasoned it would not jeopardize the education of Texas' Mexican American students.

Rodriguez: Outcome and Impact

Perhaps the most widely cited school finance equity litigation in U.S. history, *Rodriguez* (1973) was decided 5-4 in Texas's favor in March 1973. The Rehnquist court, with several new Nixon appointees, overturned the Texas district court's decision, over objections by Justice Thurgood Marshall and three other Justices. It determined that education was not a fundamental right under the U.S. Constitution, and Texas's legislature had a rational basis for its school finance policy. This decision changed the course of school finance litigation; future cases were based on state constitutions, retreating from federal equal protection arguments. The outcome of the case turned on whether variations in family wealth were highly correlated with district spending on education. Levin (1974a) not only predicted that such variations were inevitable in U.S. society, but that efforts to reduce such variations would meet with powerful forces of resistance (1974b). Wong (1994) predicted that states would try to reduce territorial inequity, but in *Rodriguez*, the State of Texas instead prevailed in maintaining it. Texans were not prepared for racial diversity within their schools, specifically the integration of Mexican American students, nor were they prepared for equalizing expenditures to the degree sought by the plaintiffs. The decision was a setback for Ford's advocacy efforts.

After re-energizing reformers at a Ford-sponsored 1974 national conference, Ford's funding of state level school finance litigation resumed, as did its public engagement efforts. There were 29 states (see Figure 6.1) where Ford's grantmaking played some role in school finance reform; the foundation funded over 100 entities, including the Lawyers' Committee for Civil Rights Under Law, the National Urban Coalition, the University of California at Berkeley, and the U.S. League of Women Voters Education Fund. Support for 35 school finance equity lawsuits was derived from Ford grants to 57 different entities. Until 1980, Ford continued to host conferences, networking educators, economists, and legal scholars and their graduate students.

A Decade of Progress: Ford's School Finance Equalization Grants in the 1970s

When Kelly (1980) evaluated Ford's $30 million school finance equalization program, he highlighted measures of overall increases in national, state, and local spending, and substantial shifts in the sources of revenue from local to state. Nationally, between 1969-70 and 1978-79, while public elementary and secondary school enrollment declined about 6%, from

USA REGIONS

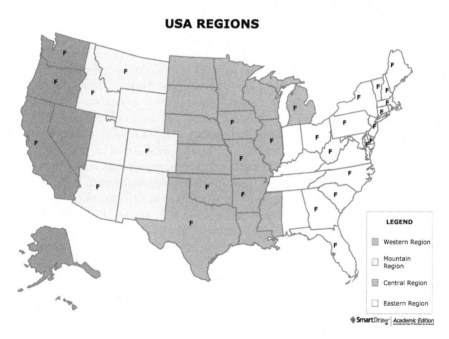

Figure 6.1.   States undergoing school finance reform 1970-82 while Ford Grants were in place.

44,719,200 to 42,149,420, annual school expenditures increased from $34.2 billion to $75.6 billion, a 121% increase before inflation adjustment, or a 24.6% increase after inflation adjustment (Kelly, 1980).

Between the 1969-70 and 1979-80 fiscal years, school revenues from local sources increased from $21 billion to $40.5 billion, an unadjusted increase of 93%, but after inflation adjustment local source revenues declined by 3.1%. Conversely, between 1969-70 and 1979-80, school revenues from state sources grew from $16 billion to $46.2 billion, an increase of 288% before inflation, and an increase after inflation adjustment of 44.4% (Kelly, 1980).

At the same time, the burden on localities declined proportionately vis-à-vis gross national product (GNP). Local revenues for schools had been 2.24% of GNP in 1969-70, but were only 1.73% of GNP in 1979-80. Conversely, state revenues for schools had been 1.72% of GNP in 1969-70, but rose to 1.97% of GNP in 1979-80. This funding source shift was coupled with a decreased reliance on property taxes. Property tax revenues in 1980 constituted about 15% of total state-local revenues, down from 26% 15 years prior (Kelly, 1980). Kelly cited major reforms in California, New Jersey, Florida, Maine, Kansas, and Michigan, and "a dozen other states," constitut[ing] a major step forward toward improved equity and adequacy in school financing (p. 9).

Ford grantees' reform strategies and outcomes varied by state. Whereas in New Jersey, litigation (*Robinson v. Cahill*, 1972-1973) required multiple returns to court, South Carolina implemented reform measures without the need for court action. As one League of Women Voters participant in the South Carolina reform campaign in the 1970s remarked, the existence of fewer county-level political subdivisions made it easier to form a broad coalition for change without litigation (A. Kinkead, personal communication, January 2011). The Connecticut reform movement, which did entail litigation (*Horton v. Meskill*, 1977), benefited from research performed by a Teachers College doctoral student team (S. Fuhrman, personal communication, July 2010) under the leadership of political economist and Ford grant recipient Donna Shalala, who also worked with League of Women Voters members in South Carolina. These groups called on state policymakers to present data showing district-by-district budget options, thereby improving the odds that reforms would be enacted.

In California, school finance litigation succeeded in 1971 (*Serrano I*), then again in 1976 (*Serrano II*), facilitated by continued efforts of Ford-funded litigators based at the University of California at Berkeley. However, by 1978, property owners who were concerned about potential tax increases that they feared would result from compliance with the *Serrano II* order had successfully lobbied for Proposition 13, which blocked

increased school spending by local governments in California and ultimately suppressed support for the state's public schools (Kirst, 1980).
Ford grants provided to the California League of Women Voters to coun-
ter Proposition 13 were too little and came too late to make a difference
(Ford Archives, PA 730-0555). The decimation of the California public
school system after 1978, as wealthier taxpayers increasingly abandoned
it for private schools (Albada, 2010), provides a cautionary lesson for
other states where policies discourage taxpayer support for public
schools.

In summary, despite several setbacks, the push by Bundy, Howe, and
Kelly was the golden age of Ford's national school finance reform efforts,
characterized by a strong civil rights mission and consistent organizational leadership. Ford combined litigation, academic research and public
engagement to ensure the program's abiding impact. Forty-one states
began litigation or public engagement leading to school finance reforms
between 1970 and 1982. Under Bundy's successor, Franklin Thomas,
Ford cut back on the program. Kelly's 1981 departure weakened the
national network of reformers after annual Ford-sponsored conferences
were curtailed, but the groundwork was laid, and new program officers
soon renewed Ford's efforts (Petrovich, 2008).

FORD'S SCHOOL FINANCE GRANTMAKING SINCE 1980

Since about 1980, in state litigations, the plaintiffs' legal argument has no
longer been "equitable" funding under state constitutions' equal protection clauses, but rather "adequate" funding under state education clauses.
To ensure that policymakers feel compelled to provide adequately for students, Ford funds universities and independent entities such as the Center for American Progress to conduct and publicize studies (Ford, 2012).
The Education Law Center, founded by Ford in the 1970s to focus solely
on litigation and advocacy for equal educational opportunity (Education
Law Center, 2012), has continually litigated New Jersey school finance
arrangements, and provided research and technical support for state litigation nationwide. Ford continues its work in Texas, largely through its
support of MALDEF. Texas achieved reform legislation after extensive
school finance litigation from 1984 to 2006 (Kauffman, 2008). Ford is one
of only a few private foundations articulating problems with school funding equity in the 21st century and its voice is still needed, because spending disparities tend to widen over time, even after years of litigation.
Many states have this problem.[2] Because of this author's work in the state,
this section profiles New York as an example of postlitigation increases in
interdistrict spending disparities.[3] Ford remains concerned about New

York, and often cofunds New York projects with other foundations in an initiative known as the Donors' Education Collaborative (New York Community Trust, 2012).

Ford's Role in New York State

In 2010, Stanford University's political economist Michael W. Kirst explained that in the 1970s, as a Ford consultant, he assessed the potential efficacy of state and local grants by weighing the likelihood that state economics, demographics, and politics would enable school finance reforms to occur (Bott, 2012). Although Kirst deemed New York State unlikely to embrace measures solely benefiting minority and poor students, since the 1970s Ford has supported New York State school finance reform.

In 1978, a group of concerned parents on Long Island attempted reform through *Levittown v. Nyquist* (1982), litigation which sought to show that the state's system of financing education violated its constitution's education clause (N.Y. Const. art. XI, § 1). Decided in the state's favor in 1982, the case failed to produce the intended financial reforms partially because it diluted its plaintiff poverty argument by adding New York City (possessed of substantial property wealth) and other large urban school districts to its plaintiff list. In addition, terms such as "inequity" and "municipal overburden" were ill-defined in the lawsuit and deemed nonjusticiable (incapable of being settled by applying principles of law).

Fifteen years later, in 1993, concerned parents in New York City initiated litigation, this time based on adequacy language (in New York a "sound basic" education is mandated by the state constitution's education clause) (Rebell, 1999). In this case, the *Campaign for Fiscal Equity v. State of New York* (*CFE I*, 1995; *II*, 2003; *and III*, 2006), Ford funded litigants as well as civic organizations (New York Community Trust, 2012; Petrovich, 2008) to press the case for declaring the state's school finance system unconstitutional. This effort spanned 13 years, from 1993 to 2006; plaintiffs argued that the state provided inadequate funding to meet the state's educational standards (N.Y. Const. art. XI, § 1) for "high needs" students (those in poverty, with special educational needs, and English language learners) in New York City.

In 1995, in *CFE I*, the state's highest court, the Court of Appeals, established definitions of a "sound basic education" and set the stage for a protracted battle to define an adequate education rather than an equitable one. The case was remanded to the lower court, and subsequently progressed slowly as attorneys developed evidence. George Pataki, the State's governor from 1995 to 2006, opposed the aims of *CFE*, despite approving substantial increases in elementary and secondary education spending.

Under the direction of Pataki's attorney general, Elliot Spitzer, taxpayer resources were controversially expended for a Georgia-based law firm to defend New York against claims that its K-12 public school finance system was unconstitutional (Feiden, 2001; Rebell, 1999). As for social science evidence, the State knew that the most logical in-state university-based school finance specialists, including two former Ford school finance grant recipient institutions, Syracuse University and New York University, were unlikely to produce a cost analysis jeopardizing the *CFE* plaintiffs. Indeed, their social science evidence supported the plaintiffs' contention that "high needs" students required additional weighting in an equitable state funding policy (Berne, 2004; Duncombe & Yinger, 2004). Standard and Poor's Corporation, then a new entry in the public school finance consulting field, was hired by a state-appointed study commission (Zarb, 2004) to provide a range of increased spending level alternatives for the state to consider. Plaintiffs, in turn, hired two out-of-state consulting firms, American Institutes for Research (AIR) and Management Analysis and Planning (MAP), and a Texas university-based researcher, Lori Taylor (collectively known as AIR/MAP) (Chambers, 2004), a team with strong credentials in school finance research, to do an extensive costing-out study. Ford, the Atlantic Philanthropies, and the then newly formed Bill and Melinda Gates Foundation, provided financial support for this research. Annual Yearly Progress guidelines in the 2001 federal No Child Left Behind Act (Chambers et al., 2004), requiring disclosure of progress toward meeting standards broken down by racial classifications, strengthened the plaintiffs' case.

Data provided by the state's witnesses and experts recommended financial remedy measures that were modest in comparison with the AIR/MAP study's cost estimates. These data left the Court of Appeals in an unwanted position: mediating expert witnesses' cost increase recommendations. In 2003, it issued a compromise decision, granting some of the relief requested by the New York City plaintiffs, but state lawmakers failed to act until 2006.[4]

After 2003, the evolving composition of the powerful Court of Appeals was a matter of interest and concern to observers of the protracted *CFE* case. Pataki adamantly opposed the aims of the *CFE* plaintiffs, and he was open with his view that activist litigators had inappropriately challenged the state's constitution. His court appointees were aware that he believed it was the legislature's task to set school finance policy and, by 2006, five of the seven Court of Appeals judges were Pataki appointments, the result of retirements and departures from the court during his 12 years as governor. Not surprisingly then, in 2006, in *CFE III*, the Pataki-dominated court disallowed inflation-driven upward cost adjustments to *CFE II*. These inflation adjustments would have reduced interdistrict disparities between high- and low-needs districts more quickly.

School Budgeting Policies Counterbalancing Ford's Work in New York State

During *CFE*, powerful political constituencies aligned against the plaintiffs, including wealthy school districts, key legislative committee members (including the head of the Senate Education Committee), and other Senators who feared Robin Hood remedies would harm their constituents. In addition, the New York State Business Council opposed any tax increases. Winning in court in 2003 may have been a legal victory, but it held no promise to reduce disparities in interdistrict spending. In 2007 the legislature began to phase in a $5.5 billion increase to basic classroom operating aid over 4 years, with 70% of the increase allocated to high-needs districts and 30% allocated to appease powerful constituencies (Alliance for Quality Education, 2011). However, the phase-in was never completed; it stalled then reversed, reducing operating foundation aid to districts in both school fiscal years ending 2011 and 2012, and very slightly increasing it for 2013 (see Figure 6.2) (Alliance for Quality Education, 2012).

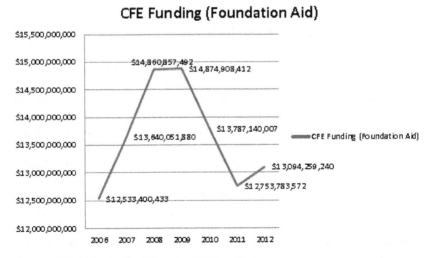

CFE Funding (Foundation Aid)

Source: Alliance for Quality Education (2012, p. 6).

Figure 6.2.   Changes in New York State Foundation Aid 2007-2012.

While Ford, together with other smaller private foundations like the Schott Foundation, supported statewide public engagement efforts and litigation research during the *CFE* lawsuit, after 2006, in the remedy phase, Ford's advocacy was far less effective. One major challenge for any advocacy effort in New York State is that there are large differences in local income and property wealth among the nearly 700 school districts. Some school districts are not granted any more than 4-5% of their budget from the State; these are the "low needs/high resource" districts. When substantial budget cuts are required in an economic downturn, those cuts by necessity reduce aid largely to the high needs/low resource districts because they depend the most upon state aid. State budget cuts since the 2007 economic recession have largely reversed the financial remedy order in *CFE II* (New York State Regents, 2012). State legislators instituted a Gap Elimination Adjustment, intended to eliminate the state's "budget gap"; it resulted in reducing state education aid to all districts including high-needs districts as defined by the New York State Education Department (NYSED) (2010-2011). This adjustment had the most dramatic effect on New York City, the target of the *CFE II* 2003 remedy, but also on many other districts classified as low resource, high needs. Starting in 2009-10, over $2 billion of reductions to the state school aid budget helped balance the state budget, leaving wealthier school districts in a relatively better position and decreasing territorial distribution equity of school aid. New York's policy of maintaining many separate school districts has the effect of tolerating greater interdistrict spending disparities despite a state equalization formula.

In addition, New York lawmakers usually allow interdistrict inequities to persist by (1) holding districts "harmless" from year to year in budget decision making (no less aid than previous year) thereby avoiding politically difficult redistribution decisions; and (2) reimbursing for capital expenditures through a building aid formula that favors those districts that gain voter approval for debt financing and often driving large capital reimbursements to wealthy districts. Starting in 2012-13, despite opposition by the teachers' union, other professional educators' groups, and the Alliance for Quality Education (2012), a new competitive grant program was included to offer aid to districts that intend to employ innovative practices, but the distribution has been stalled because of its teacher evaluation plan requirement. Even if implemented, those grants would not necessarily be targeted to high-needs districts. For the school year 2012-2013, a small increase in state school aid was agreed upon, including new aid for all districts (NYSED 2012-13). Totaling about $800 million, this partially reversed the prior 2 years' total of over $2 billion in reductions in state school operating aid. But on balance, in New York State disparities have widened since the CFE litigation ended in 2006. In response,

Ford has recently financed two reports designed to alert policymakers to the growing disparities (Baker, 2010; Baker & Corcoran, 2012). The 2012 report cited New York as one of the six most inequitable states for inter-district school funding equity.

Other Disequalizing Policies in New York State: The STAR Program and the Property Tax Cap

The push for more equitable state school funding was hindered by Pataki's announcement in his first term of a plan to use state revenue sources such as income and sales taxes to provide school property tax relief. Starting in 1999, New York residents have benefited from a multibillion dollar statewide school tax relief program (STAR) containing a regional cost adjustment that provides greater benefits for those owning homes in property-wealthy districts than it does for those living in property-poor districts. STAR, considered to be part of the state education budget, costs over $3 billion per annum, transferring state funds directly to compensate the state's school districts, which collect less local property tax revenue because local property taxpayers' bills are reduced by a STAR benefit. STAR applies to both homeowners and renters and provides greater benefits for senior citizens, but its regional cost adjustment by county ensures a disproportionate distribution of STAR benefits to wealthier school districts. During the *CFE* lawsuit, the litigators and their advisors determined that criticism of STAR would not be productive, given its popularity (Michael A. Rebell, personal communication, September 2012). STAR has been reformed to include a means test and annual percentage limits on upward adjustments, but it still counterweights the more progressive state school aid programs which direct more state resources to poorer districts (Baker & Corcoran, 2012).

Separately, Governor Andrew Cuomo (elected in 2010), in collaboration with business interests and tax reduction advocates, succeeded in imposing a 2% school property tax cap effective for 2011. Cuomo was not the first New York elected official to advocate for such a cap, but he was the first to overcome voices of opposition who preferred either no cap or a property tax circuit breaker tied to taxpayers' ratio of property tax burden to income.[5] Wealthier districts have more resources to override tax caps and raise taxes, provided they obtain a 60% supermajority of those voting on local school budgets. Poorer and middle-wealth districts may find this more difficult, and need even more help from state and federal equalization policies.

Impact of the ARRA on New York State

New York benefited from $31 billion of the American Recovery and Reinvestment Act of 2009 (Pub.L. 111-5) federal subsidies. In 2009-10 and 2010-11, it provided new education funding totaling $5.8 billion,[6] avoiding massive teacher and staff layoffs. When federal aid expired in 2011-12, local school districts lost both direct federal assistance and federal funds that had been passed through the State education budget, creating well over a $2 billion education budget gap. State decision makers and local school districts subsequently began to increase pressure on teachers to make financial concessions, including pension restructuring. Corporate voices, including that of the New York City Partnership, which supported the aims of the *CFE* lawsuit, aligned with the governor in efforts to lessen the influence of teachers' unions on school finance policy. A new tier of pension recipients was established, providing the newest teachers across the state with less generous retirement benefits. Ford has stayed clear of that heated political controversy, which continues to garner much more attention than school finance inequities.

Impact of Reduced Support for Public Engagement

Ford's current policy of deemphasizing funding for public engagement in the remedy phase of litigation has not helped the balance of power between low- and high-needs school districts. Despite strong support for litigation and public engagement up until 2006, Ford funding for school finance-related public engagement activities has diminished since 2007. The Campaign for Fiscal Equity (CFE), the entity that filed the 1993 adequacy lawsuit, encountered financial difficulties and did not receive Ford funding after 2010. CFE's remedy phase legal work was recently transferred to the Education Law Center. The reversal of hard fought gains in financial equity in New York State illustrates the impact of Ford's decision to reduce both the breadth of its strategic tools and the generosity of its grants.

APPLICATION OF WONG AND LEVIN MODELS TO NEW YORK STATE

Both the *Levittown* and *CFE* plaintiffs argued that New York State should change its policies to decrease social and territorial inequity. While Wong (1994) argues that federal (e.g., ARRA) and state aid to school districts do this, in New York State strong forces pull in the direction of increasing territorial inequities. Levin (1974b) predicted that powerful constituencies would maintain control even after years of litigation, but new constituencies have appeared in recent years, reducing union power somewhat. Students attending schools in New York State's high-needs districts including New York City as well as many poorer suburbs are, disproportionately, members of racial minority groups with low power in Levin's constituency model (Alliance for Quality Education, 2011). Starting in 2009-10, the $2 billion of reductions to the state school aid budget, while helping balance the state budget, disproportionately impacted districts most dependent on state aid, thereby increasing territorial distributional inequities.

NEW YORK STATE POLICY IMPACTS:
A CASE STUDY AT THE SCHOOL DISTRICT LEVEL

The following illustrates a typical pattern of interdistrict funding inequity tied to differences in the composition of student enrollment and community wealth in New York. While the Ford-supported *CFE* case raised spending levels, local control that maintains the policy of separate, small districts perpetuates financial inequities. Rye City and Village of Port Chester-Rye-Union Free (UF) School Districts (SD) are two adjacent school districts about 20 miles from New York City in wealthy Westchester County. Figure 6.3 compares the Census demographics of the districts; they show that both are "majority White." As of 2010, the Hispanic population was the great differentiator. In Port Chester public schools, 74% of students were Some Other Race Alone (in this case Hispanic), while in Rye, 6% of students were so classified (NYSED, 2010-11). A higher portion of Port Chester's education budget, 27% versus 16.1% for Rye, goes to support special education students. Port Chester English language learners also comprise a much higher percentage of the student population than Rye's (27% versus 4%), and the percentage of students eligible for the federal free lunch program is 48%, much higher than Rye's 2% (NYSED, School Report Cards). These factors, and lower property wealth and income, influence Port Chester's classification by NYSED (2010-11) as a "high-needs low-resource" district. Rye is a "low-needs high-resource" district.

Budget and Spending Comparisons

Given Port Chester's high-needs classification, there should be evidence of state augmentation of the district's local taxing resources. Looking back over nearly 20 years, pressure to narrow spending gaps between high- and low-needs districts has been effective, supporting the argument

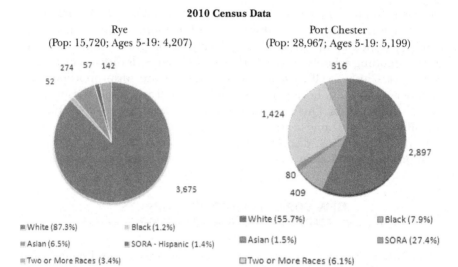

2010 Census Data

Rye
(Pop: 15,720; Ages 5-19: 4,207)

Port Chester
(Pop: 28,967; Ages 5-19: 5,199)

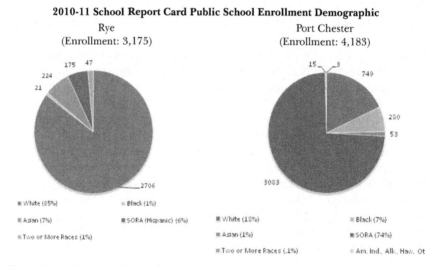

2010-11 School Report Card Public School Enrollment Demographic

Rye
(Enrollment: 3,175)

Port Chester
(Enrollment: 4,183)

Figure 6.3.   Comparative racial demographics.

that social movements backed by school finance reformers have helped to reduce interdistrict disparities in funding. Figure 6.4 shows that at the outset of the state *CFE* litigation, Port Chester's 1993-94 expenditures per pupil were only 70.5% of Rye's (NYSED, 1993-94). The spending ratio between Port Chester and Rye had progressively narrowed by 2011. Whereas Port Chester spent 82.5% of what Rye spent in 1999-2000, it spent 93% of what Rye spent in 2010-2011, a substantial improvement

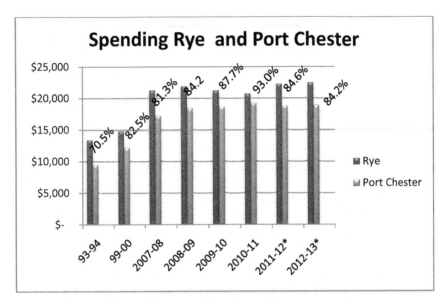

Source: New York State Education Department (93-94, 99-00, 2007-2011); Port Chester
and Rye School Budgets 2011-12 and 2012-13.
Note: *Figures used are from budgeted, not actual expenditures.

Figure 6.4.   Per pupil expenditures gap Port Chester as percentage of Rye 1993-
2013.

over 1993-1994's 70.5%. However, the average 2009-10 district total per
pupil spending differential, about $2,600, masked the effect of expendi-
tures for a greater proportion of special education students in Port Chester than in Rye (27% versus 16.1%). When only general education
expenditures per student are compared directly, the differential was
nearly $4,000 per pupil, with Rye spending $14,280 per general education pupil compared with Port Chester's $10,328 (NYSED, 2010-2011) in
2009-10, despite state and federal efforts to equalize educational opportunity for all students.

   While the two districts' funding gap narrowed between 1993-94 and
2010-11, Figure 6.4 suggests that it began to widen thereafter. The spending difference went from 87.7% in 2009-10, 93% in 2010-11, 84.6% in
2011-12 and 84.2% in 2012-13. Rye increased its 2011-2012 year's budget, $71.9 million ($22,228 per student), to $73.6 million ($22,453 per
student) for 2012-13 (with 3,277 projected pupils) while Port Chester's
proposed budget went from $79.6 million ($18,803 per pupil) to $81.3
million ($18,912) (2012-13 Property Tax Report Card), with 4,300 pro-

jected pupils. It is too soon to say whether the 2% property tax cap imposed last year (New York State Department of Taxation and Finance, 2012) will further widen the current interdistrict gap. However, a simple fact remains: in 2012-13, wealthier Rye will outspend poorer Port Chester by over $3,500 per pupil ($22,453 versus $18,912), supporting both Levin's notion that poorer parents have less power, and Wong's theory that localities increase inequity.

Impact of State Policies on District Programs

The 2011 property tax cap forced staff cuts and curtailed programs in school districts across the state; cuts disproportionately impacted disadvantaged students in poorer districts. Port Chester is no exception; the 2012-13 school budget cut 13.5 reading positions and one teacher's aide; it also considered eliminating full-day kindergarten, forcing tense negotiations with the teachers' union (Lavoie, 2012; Littman, 2012). Rye maintained its educational programming, but reduced secretarial, clerical, and computer support. Rye voters authorized new capital expenditures to rebuild its high school's aging science facilities (Rye, 2012). Parents throughout Westchester County donated tax-deductible gifts to school-related foundations (New York State Senate, 2012) to maintain programs that would otherwise have been curtailed or eliminated. It is too soon to know whether the Port Chester versus Rye spending gap (see Figure 6.4) will further widen in the future, but the tax-deductible contributions by parents to local public and private school foundations, likely more generous in Rye than in Port Chester, will mask the total effect of budget cutbacks on programs in these two school districts.

The Importance of Ford's Contribution to School Finance Equity

Based on Ford's self-assessment in 1980, its 1970 strategy of litigation, using social science research, public engagement, and advocacy worked. Their preferred metrics showed an increase in many states of the state's share of school funding and a commensurate decrease in local share. The strategy of empowering low-power constituents was an important part of this successful work. The rationale for grantmaking for such empowerment stemmed from Ford's long-standing commitment to civil rights activism. This chapter's detailed examination of New York State's efforts to reduce spending disparities in K-12 public education invites the question: have Ford's efforts from 1978-2012 to reduce funding inequities for New York's disadvantaged students been successful or quixotic?

At present, the evidence seems to point to a rather unsuccessful and incomplete strategy after 13 years of litigation. However, the current status of New York's school finance equalization efforts must be taken in the context of the nation as a whole. A weakened economy and decreases of federal and state funds have forced many districts to cut programs (Center on Budget and Policy Priorities, 2012), exacerbating social and territorial inequities, in Wong's (1994) terminology. As Levin predicted, long-term sustainability is challenged by powerful constituencies, be they local school districts or state policymakers. Both the STAR program and the newly instituted property tax cap were put in place by factions that were more concerned with tax payments than with the rights of students currently attending public schools. A setback in national and state economic conditions strengthened these constituents' hand.

While economic conditions may slow the trajectory of reform, there is no evidence that abandoning litigation and public engagement is the right solution. On the contrary, it is incumbent on those who wish to ensure the success of all students to continue to identify and address issues of equity. The case of Port Chester revealed that there continue to be school districts with concentrations of Hispanic students disproportionate to the state population, as was seen in San Antonio, Texas, 40 years ago in *Rodriguez*, and perhaps not coincidentally, clearly, interdistrict financial inequities persist. Therefore, advocating for measurable reforms continues to be an important mission for private foundations; they should use all available strategic tools.

NOTES

1.   Ford funded Joel S. Berke, Robert O. Berne, Susan H. Fuhrman, James W. Guthrie, Michael W. Kirst, Henry M. Levin, Allan R. Odden, Donna E. Shalala, and Leanna Stiefel to perform school finance research.

2.   *Quality Counts 2012 (Education Week*, 2012) reports enormous racial gaps in achievement, and half of the states fail to obtain a grade above a C in school finance equity. A Ford-funded report (Baker, Sciarra, & Farrie, 2012) shows that all but six states' fairness of school funding distribution is graded C or below based on 2009 data (p. 14). Baker and Corcoran (2012) underscore the role that state and local tax policies play in perpetuating inequities.

3.   The League of Women Voters of New York State submitted an *amicus curiae* brief in connection with the *Campaign for Fiscal Equity* lawsuit in 2003. This author was involved with the brief's preparation and participated from 1993 to 2006 in public engagement in connection with CFE.

4. According to CFE's lead counsel, Michael A. Rebell, the state did not meet the Court of Appeals' compliance deadline (July, 2004). The case was brought back to the trial court for noncompliance. The trial court appointed special masters; there were more extensive hearings, a special masters' report, a further trial court decision, an appeal to the New York State Appellate Division and a final appeal to the Court of Appeals in CFE III in 2006 (Rebell, personal communication, October 2012).

5. The Fiscal Policy Institute, New Yorkers for Fiscal Fairness, and the League of Women Voters of New York State have advocated this alternative to a property tax cap because the cap as designed places school districts with less assessed property value than others at a relative disadvantage in calculating allowable budget increases.

6. State Fiscal Stabilization Funds totaled $3 billion while $2.8 billion went to Pell Grants, Title I and special education funding provided directly to school districts. See 2010-11 New York State Executive Budget Briefing Book, pp. 133-134, retrieved from http://www.budget.state.ny.us/.

REFERENCES

ACCESS. (2012). National Education Access Network (homepage). Retrieved from http://schoolfunding.info/

Albada, M. (2010, December 5). Skeletons in the budgetary closet: Proposition 13 and the stifling of the California recovery. *Stanford Progressive*. Retrieved from http://www.stanford.edu/group/progressive/cgi-bin/?author=15

Alliance for Quality Education. (2011, March 2). Widening the funding gap: Race, poverty and Governor Cuomo's education cuts. Retrieved from http://www.aqeny.org/ny/wp-content/uploads/2011/03/Widening-the-Equity-Funding-Gap.pdf

Alliance for Quality Education, September 24, 2012. Testimony before Education Commission, Utica, New York. Retrieved October 5, 2012 from http://www.governor.ny.gov/puttingstudentsfirst#documents

Baker, B., & Corcoran, S. (2012, September). The stealth inequities of school funding: How state and local school finance systems perpetuate inequitable student spending. Center for American Progress. Retrieved September 20, 2012 from http://www.americanprogress.org/issues/education/report/2012/09/19/38189/the-stealth-inequities-of-school-funding/

Baker, B., Sciarra, D., & Farrie, D. (2010, September). *Is school funding fair? A national report card*. Newark, NJ: Education Law Center. Retrieved from http://www.schoolfundingfairness.org/

Baker, B., Sciarra, D., & Farrie, D. (2012, June). *Is school funding fair? A national report card*. Newark, NJ: Education Law Center. Retrieved March 13, 2012, from www.schoolfundingfairness.org

Berne, R. (2004, October). Statement before Supreme Court of the State of New York in *Campaign for Fiscal Equity, Inc., et al., v. The State of New York, et al.*, special referees Hon. William C. Thompson, Hon. E. Leo Milonas, John D. Feerick, Esq. Retrieved from http://finance.tc-library.org/ContentTypes.asp?cgi=5

Bott, M. (2012). *Private foundation activism in the early school finance equalization movement: A case study of the Ford Foundation's grantmaking between 1966 and 1980*. ProQuest Dissertations and Theses database. Retrieved from http://ezproxy.cul.columbia.edu/login?url=http://search.proquest.com/docview/1024429801?accountid=10226?accountid=10226 (1024429801)

The Broad Foundation. (n.d.). Retrieved from http://www.broadeducation.org/index.html

Brown v. Board of Education of Topeka, 347 U.S. 483 (1954).

Campaign for Fiscal Equity v. State of New York, 86 N.Y.2d 307 (1995) (CFE I); 100 N.Y.2d 893 (2003) (CFE II); and 29 AD3d 175 (2006) (CFE III). Retrieved from http://finance.tc-library.org/ContentTypes.asp?cgi=5

Center on Budget and Policy Priorities. (2011). *New school year brings more cuts in state funding for schools*. Washington, DC: Author. Retrieved from www.cbpp.org/cms/?fa=view&id=3569

Chambers, J. G., Parrish, T. B., Levin, J. D.; Smith, J. R., Guthrie, J. W., Seder, R. C., & Taylor, L. (2004). *The New York adequacy study: Determining the cost of providing all children in New York an adequate education. Volume 1: Final Report, and Volume 2: Technical Appendices*. Washington, DC: The American Institutes for Research. Retrieved from http://www.eric.ed.gov/ERICWebPortal/detail?accno=ED491623

The New York Community Trust. (2012). *Competitive grants*. New York, NY: Author. Retrieved from http://www.nycommunitytrust.org/GrantSeekers/RecentCompetitiveGrants/tabid/208/Default.aspx

Duncombe, W., & Yinger, J. (2004, April 18). State must reform formula for funding education (op-ed article). *Albany Times Union*. Retrieved from http://faculty.maxwell.syr.edu/jyinger/oped/reform.htm

Education.com. (2012). Demographics for Corpus Christi School, Port Chester, New York, 2010. Retrieved from http://www.education.com/schoolfinder/us/new-york/port-chester/corpus-christi-school/gear/#students-and-teachers

Education Law Center. (n.d.). Education Law Center (about). Retrieved from http://www.edlawcenter.org/about/mission-history.html

Feiden, D. (2001, March 11). There oughta be a law … Georgia attorneys rake in millions at expense of New York taxpayers and students. *New York Daily News*, p. 37.

Ford Foundation. (1968). *Annual Report 1968*. Available at Rockefeller Archive Center, Sleepy Hollow, New York.

Ford Foundation Archives. Microfilm reels for Program Actions (PA) 680-0248, Mexican American Legal Defense and Education Fund; 719-0064, Delegated Authority Projects; and 730-0555, League of Women Voters Education Fund. The first two digits indicate the beginning grant year. Available at Rockefeller Archive Center, Sleepy Hollow, New York.

Friends of Rye City School District. (2012). *The Rye school budget vote is on Tuesday, May 15*. Rye, NY: Author. Retrieved from http://friendsofryecityschooldistrict.blogspot.com/2012/04/rye-school-budget-vote-is-on-tuesday.html

Goldberg, M. F. (2002). Stirring the pot: An interview with Harold "Doc" Howe II. *Phi Delta Kappan, 82*(2), 160-162.

Guerra v. Smith, 474 F.2d 1399, 1973 U.S. App. LEXIS 10604 (5th Cir. Tex. 1973)

Guthrie, J., Kleindorfer, G., Levin, H., & Stout, R.(1971). *Schools and inequality.* Cambridge, MA: The MIT Press.

Horton v. Meskill, 376 A.2d 359 (Conn. 1977), aff'g 332 A.2d 813 (Super. Ct. Hartford Cty., Conn. 1974).

Janell Guerra, et al., v. Preston H. Smith, Governor of Texas, et al., Civil Action No. A-69-CA-9. [Memorandum to Christopher Edley from Pete Tijerina, July 8, 1969]. Program Action 680-0248, Ford Foundation Archives, Rockefeller Archive Center, Sleepy Hollow, NY.

Kelly, J. A. (1980). *Looking back, moving ahead: A decade of school-finance reform.* New York, NY: The Ford Foundation. Available at Rockefeller Archive Center, Sleepy Hollow, New York.

Kirst, M. (1980, Winter). A tale of two networks: The school finance reform versus the spending and tax limitation lobby. *Taxing and Spending,* 43-49.

Lankford, H., Loeb, S., & Wyckoff, J. (2002). Teacher sorting and the plight of urban schools: A descriptive analysis. *Educational Evaluation and Policy Analysis, 24*(1), 37-62.

Lavoie, L. (2012, April 20). Port Chester schools adopt budget, cut teachers. *Port Chester Daily Voice.* Retrieved from http://portchester.dailyvoice.com/schools/port-chester-schools-adopt-budget-cut-teachers

Levin, H. M. (1974a). Educational reform and social change. *Journal of Applied Behavioral Science, 10,* 304-320.

Levin, H. M. (1974b). Effects of expenditure increases on educational resource allocation and effectiveness. In J. Pincus (Ed.), *School finance in transition: The courts and educational reform* (pp. 171-198). Cambridge, MA: Ballinger.

Levittown Union Free School District et al. v. Ewald B. Nyquist, as Commissioner of Education, et al., 57 N.Y.2d 27 (1982).

Littman, A. (2012, May 14). Residents to decide fate of $81.3 M budget, three-way race for two school board seats. *Port Chester Patch.* Retrieved from http://portchester.patch.com/articles/district-set-for-budget-school-board-vote-on-Tuesday

McInnis v. Ogilvie, 394 U.S. 322 (1969). 1969 WL 120025 (Appellate Brief) Motion for Leave to File and Brief for School Improvement. The Urban Coalition, National Education Association of the United States, the Research Council of the Great Cities Program for School Improvement, the Lawyers' Committee for Civil Rights Under Law as Amici Curiae in Support of the Jurisdictional Statement (Mar. 07, 1969).

National Center on Time & Learning. (n.d.). Retrieved from http://www.timeandlearning.org/our-supporters

New York State Department of Taxation and Finance. (2012). Retrieved from http://www.tax.ny.gov/research/property/cap.htm

New York State Education Department. (2010-2011). Office of Educational Management. Property Tax Report Card Data. 2010-11PTRC%-19-10_post_access.xls. Retrieved from http://www.p12.nysed.gov/mgtserv/propertytax/docs/2010-11PTRC5-19-10_post_access.xls

New York State Education Department. (2012). Office of Educational Management. Property Tax Report Card Data. 2012-13PTRC5_10_12_Budget_

Data_Post.pdf. Retrieved from http://www.p12.nysed.gov/mgtserv/property-tax/#Data

New York State Education Department. (2012-13). Preliminary Estimate of 2011-12 and 2012-13 State Aids Payable under Section 3609 plus Other Aids. Run No SA121-3, March 27, 2012.

New York State Education Department. School Report Cards, 2000-2001 and 2010-2011, Port Chester-Rye Union Free School District and Rye City District. "Overview", "School District Profiles." Retrieved from https://reportcards.nysed.gov/files/2010-11/CIR-2011-661800010000.pdf, https://reportcards.nysed.gov/files/2010-11/FIS-2011-661800010000.pdf, https://reportcards.nysed.gov/files/2010-11/AOR-2011-661800010000.pdf, https://reportcards.nysed.gov/files/2010-11/AOR-2011-661904030000.pdf, https://reportcards.nysed.gov/files/2010-11/CIR-2011-661904030000.pdf, https://reportcards.nysed.gov/files/2010-11/FIS-2011-661904030000.pdf, http://www.p12.nysed.gov/repcrd2002/overview/661800010000.pdf, http://www.p12.nysed.gov/repcrd2002/cir/661800010000.pdf, http://www.p12.nysed.gov/repcrd2002/overview/661904030000.pdf, http://www.p12.nysed.gov/repcrd2002/cir/661904030000.pdf

New York State Education Department. (2012). Per pupil expenditures for Port Chester and Rye School Districts. Masterfile for 2010-2011. Retrieved from http://www.oms.nysed.gov/faru/Profiles/profiles_cover.html

New York State Regents. (2012). *2012-13 budget presentation, college and career readiness. Testimony before joint legislative committee on elementary and secondary education and the education committees of the senate and ways and means committees, New York State Legislature, Albany, NY.* Albany, NY: Author.

New York State Senate, Testimony before Joint Committees on Education and Finance, January 23, 2012. Retrieved from www.nysenate.gov/files/Marian%20Bott001.pdf

No Child Left Behind Act of 2001 (2002). P.L. 107-110, U.S. Department of Education. Retrieved from http://www2.ed.gov/policy/elsec/leg/esea02/index.html.

Petrovich, J. (2008). *A foundation returns to school: Strategies for improving public education.* New York, NY: The Ford Foundation. Retrieved from http://www.fordfound.org/pdfs/library/strategies_improving_public_education.pdf

Quality counts 2012. (2012). *Education Week, 31*(16), 62-63.

Rebell, M. (1999). Fiscal equity litigation and the democratic imperative. *Equity and Excellence in Education, 32* (3), 5-18. doi:10.1080/1066568990320302

Robinson v. Cahill, 287 A.2d 187 (Law Div. 1972), Supp. op, 289 A.2d 569 (Law Div. 1972), aff'd 303 A.2d 273 (1973).

Rodriguez v. San Antonio S.D., Gen. Civ. No. 68-175-SA (U.S.D.C. W.D. Tex, 1968); 337 F. Supp. 280, U.S. D.C. W.D. Tex, 1971.

Roza, M., Guin, K., Gross, B., & Deburgomaster, S. (2007). Do districts fund schools fairly? *Education Next, 7*(4), 68-73.

Rye City School District. (2012). Budget and election information. 2012-13 Budget Presentation/Discussion, April 3, 2012. Retrieved from http://ryecityschools.schoolfusion.us/modules/cms/pages.phtml?pageid=57542&sessionid=c6eeae11fd7ce359346712f2d2c24f93&t

Rye Country Day School. (n.d.). Retrieved from http://www.ryecountryday.org/page.cfm?p=198.RCDS Viewbook

San Antonio v. Rodriguez, 411 U.S. 1, 1973. Brief for Appellees Arthur Gochman, Warren Weir, Mark G. Yudof, Mario Obledo, and Manuel Montez, section 5, Minority Group Discrimination, 1971 WL 134333 (U.S. Appellate Brief).

Serrano v. Priest, 487 P2d 1241 (Cal. 1971) (Serrano I); Serrano v. Priest, 557 P.2d 929 (Cal. 1976) (Serrano II).

Shelley v. Kraemer, 344 U.S. 1, 1947.

Sracic, P. (2006). San Antonio v. Rodriguez *and the pursuit of equal education: The debate over discrimination and school funding.* Topeka, KS: The University Press of Kansas.

United States Census Bureau. (2010). Profile of general population and housing characteristics: 2010, census summary file 2, DP-1 for Port Chester village, New York and City of Rye, New York. American factfinder. Retrieved from http://factfinder2.census.gov/faces/tableservices/jsf/pages/productview.xhtml?fpt=table

United States Commission on Civil Rights. (1972). *Inequality in school financing: The role of law.* Washington, DC: U.S. Government Printing Office, Stock # 1780-1067. Retrieved from http://www.law.umaryland.edu/marshall/uscccr/titlelist.htm/#ICR1.2:SCH6/16

Walton Family Foundation. (2012). *Education reform.* Retrieved from http://www.waltonfamilyfoundation.org/educationreform/shape-public-policy

Wise, A. (1970). Rich schools, poor schools: The promise of equal educational opportunity (Second Impression 1972, xi; first published in 1967. Chicago, IL: The University of Chicago Press.

Wong, K. (1994). Governance structure, resource allocation, and equity policy. *Review of Research in Education, 20,* 257-289.

Yale Note. (1972). A statistical analysis of the school finance decisions: On winning battles and losing wars. *The Yale Law Journal, 81*(7), 1303-1341.

Zarb, F. G. (2004). *Final report of the New York State Commission on Education Reform.* Retrieved from http://www.lischooltax.com/Zarb%20Report.pdf

PART III

EDUCATIONAL ACCOUNTABILITY:
EFFECTS ON STUDENT OUTCOMES AND EQUITY

CHAPTER 7

THE ROOTS
OF SCORE INFLATION

An Examination of Opportunities
in Two States' Tests

Rebecca Holcombe, Jennifer L. Jennings, and Daniel Koretz

Since the 1970s, policymakers have relied on *test-based accountability* (TBA) as a primary tool for improving student achievement and reducing racial and socioeconomic achievement gaps. These policies have produced striking gains in scores on some accountability tests and, in some cases, seeming evidence of narrowing achievement gaps. As a result, support for test-based accountability has been widespread. Most policymakers are confident that score gains signify commensurate increases in achievement and will translate into improvements in children's long-term life chances, particularly for poor and minority children.

However, more than 2 decades of research indicate that TBA policies have not been the unqualified success that gains on high-stakes tests might suggest and have led to a variety of undesirable side effects. A recent National Research Council review concluded that the effects of TBA programs have ranged from zero to small (National Research Council, 2011). In addition, studies have identified distortions of educational

Charting Reform, Achieving Equity in a Diverse Nation
pp. 163–189
Copyright © 2013 by Information Age Publishing

practice, such as reducing instructional time allocated to material not emphasized on state tests (e.g., Koretz, Barron, Mitchell, & Stecher, 1996; Koretz, Mitchell, Barron, & Keith, 1996a; Stecher, 2002; Stecher, Chun, Barron, & Ross, 2000) in order to focus instruction on material that is predictably emphasized on the test. These practices can lead to *score inflation*—that is, gains in scores on the tests used for accountability that are markedly larger than the actual gains in student learning they are intended to signal (Koretz & Hamilton, 2006). Numerous studies have found that score gains on high-stakes tests often do not generalize to lower stakes assessments used as audit tests, such as the National Assessment of Educational Progress (NAEP) (e.g., Center on Education Policy, 2008; Fuller, Gesicki, Kang, & Wright, 2006; Jacob, 2007; Klein, Hamilton, McCaffrey, & Stecher, 2000; Koretz & Barron, 1998; Koretz, Linn, Dunbar, & Shepard, 1991; Lee, 2007). Although score inflation is highly variable across states (Ho, 2007), it is often severe. Some studies also have found that TBA programs can generate illusory improvements in equity (Klein, Hamilton, McCaffrey, & Stecher, 2000).

Score inflation has at least four important consequences. First, when scores are inflated, students have learned less than their scores suggest. Second, because schools serving poor and minority students face the most pressure to quickly increase test scores and greater barriers to doing so, inflation may affect them more severely, with negative implications for educational equity. Third, because inflation varies across schools, *relative* improvements become difficult to evaluate, and researchers and policymakers will misidentify effective and ineffective schools and teachers. Finally, accurate data on how students are performing is necessary for policymakers to identify and implement interventions that improve students' long-term outcomes. In the absence of such data, we may pursue interventions that are not effective or fail to implement policies that could improve student achievement.

To date, few studies have attempted to understand the sources of variation in score inflation across testing programs. In particular, research has not identified the specific characteristics of tests that facilitate or impede score inflation and inappropriate test preparation, that is, test preparation that inflates scores. Without this information, it is impossible to improve existing assessments to lessen these problems.

This chapter is the first attempt in the literature to systematically investigate the opportunities for score inflation within current tests. We evaluate released items from the mathematics tests of two states, Massachusetts and New York, in the years 2006-2008, to identify predictable recurrences that provide opportunities for narrowed instruction that might inflate scores. In this paper, we focus primarily on the eighth-grade tests in both states and the 10th-grade test in Massachusetts, but we also draw selectively from other grades for purposes of illustration. We selected Massachusetts and New York because they provide a strong contrast. The New York and Massachusetts content standards are very different; New York's are much narrower than those of Massachusetts, sometimes specifying a single fact or skill. At least through 2005, NAEP trends did not suggest inflation of Massachusetts Comprehensive Assessment System (MCAS) math scores in Grades 4 or 8 (Ho, 2007), although no audit studies have been conducted with the higher stakes 10th-grade MCAS test that is our focus. In contrast, New York State's eighth-grade math scores increased far more rapidly than its NAEP scores did after 2010. Both the Massachusetts MCAS tests and the state's reforms are generally well-regarded in the policy community. For example, Diane Ravitch asserted that "Massachusetts ... has earned its high marks the old-fashioned way, by improving its curriculum, testing incoming teachers, and sponsoring assessments far superior to those in most other states" (Ravitch, 2010). On the other hand, New York's testing program has been the focus of considerable controversy in the press and policy community. Unlike policymakers in many states, then-Commissioner David Steiner acknowledged in 2010 the likelihood of inflation in the state's test scores, and the New York State Department of Education has since that time pursued a policy of making its tests broader and less predictable in order to combat inflation.

PREVIOUS RESEARCH

The research literature on responses to high-stakes testing falls into three categories: (1) studies of the manipulation of the tested population, (2) studies of score inflation, and (3) investigations of changes in instructional strategies—including test preparation—and other aspects of practice.

The first category of studies, primarily in economics and sociology, examines strategies to remove students from the tested population in order to raise aggregate scores. For example, one study found that when schools are permitted to exclude special education students from testing, they assign more students to special education (Figlio & Getlzer, 2006). Other studies have found increased exclusion of low-scoring students (e.g., Jacob, 2005; Jennings & Beveridge, 2009). Although such strategies can create a modest bias in aggregate scores, they do not inflate the scores of individual students. Moreover, they are unrelated to the content of the specific tests. Therefore, they are not pertinent to the present study.

Studies in the second category (score inflation) follow a common logic. Achievement tests are small samples drawn from large domains such as "eighth grade mathematics" that are the target of users' inferences. The inference about mastery of the large domain based on scores is only valid to the extent that one can generalize from the small, tested sample to mastery of the largely untested domain. If score gains do signify increased mastery of the larger domain, reasonably similar gains should appear in other samples from that domain—that is, in scores on other tests intended to support similar inferences about achievement. Therefore, most studies of score inflation have investigated the extent to which gains in scores on a high-stakes test generalize to trends on a lower stakes audit test.

The first empirical investigation of inflation was conducted by Koretz et al. (1991) in a district with a testing policy that was high-stakes by the standards of the day, but much lower stakes than the norm today. The district administration pressured schools and teachers to improve scores, but there were no concrete sanctions or rewards for scores. When the district replaced one commercial, multiple-choice, basic skills achievement test battery with a quite similar competitor, math scores at the end of third grade dropped by half an academic year. Four years later, scores on the new test had reached the level that had been reached on the old test in its final year of use. This "sawtooth" pattern accompanying the adoption of new tests had been widely recognized in the psychometric community, but no prior studies examined whether the skills assessed by the earlier test remained stable or atrophied after the introduction of the new test. Koretz et al. administered the test that the district had abandoned 4 years earlier to a random sample of classrooms. Scores on that test had dropped by half an academic year while scores on the new test had risen by a like amount. Another random sample of classrooms was administered a parallel form of the new test (that is, a form designed to be equivalent) to evaluate whether performance on the researchers' tests were depressed by motivational factors. No motivational bias was found.

Since then, a substantial number of studies have followed the same approach, but using audit tests that were already in place rather than administering an alternative test experimentally. The most commonly used audit test has been NAEP. NAEP represents a degree of national consensus about what students should know, and scores are unlikely to be inflated because teachers have no incentive to prepare students specifically for it.

Because of a widespread belief in the policy community that the multiple choice format was responsible for inflation, Koretz and Barron (1998) evaluated score inflation in Kentucky's Kentucky Instructional Results Information System [KIRIS] high-stakes assessment program, which de-emphasized the multiple-choice format in some years and avoided it entirely in others. They found that gains on the KIRIS tests in mathematics in Grades 4 and 8 were three to four times as large as the state's gain on NAEP. Hambleton et al. (1995) examined performance gains in fourth grade reading in the same KIRIS assessment and found that scores on the state assessment increased by .76 of a standard deviation in the space of only 2 years—an extraordinarily rapid increase by historical standards (see Koretz, 1986)—while scores on the NAEP reading assessment did not increase at all.

Klein et al.'s (2000) study of Texas' state test and NAEP trends found a disparity in trends between the state's TAAS test and NAEP that was similar in magnitude to that found in Kentucky by Koretz and Barron (1998). In addition, they found that the widely cited "Texas miracle" of a rapidly shrinking gap between minority and non-Hispanic white students was not reflected in NAEP data. Similarly, Jacob (2005) analyzed data from the Chicago Public Schools' Iowa Test of Basic Skills (ITBS), which at that time was high-stakes and used for student promotion decisions as well as school accountability, and the low-stakes Illinois Goals Assessment Program. He found large gains on the high-stakes Iowa Test of Basic Skills following the introduction of accountability, but no similar effects of the accountability system on the Illinois Goals Assessment Program.

A number of other studies that compared trends across numerous states found that state test gains typically outpace national test gains, often by a large magnitude (Carnoy & Loeb, 2002; Center on Education Policy, 2008; Fuller et al., 2006; Grissmer & Flanagan, 1998; Hanushek & Raymond, 2004, 2005; Jacob, 2005, 2007; Rouse, Hannaway, Goldhaber, & Figlio, 2007). These disparities in trends are not uniform, however, and if NAEP is used as a comparison, some states appear to have escaped serious inflation (Ho, 2007).

The third category of studies examined a variety of behavioral responses to high-stakes testing that have the potential to inflate scores, including the use of explicit test preparation, other instructional strategies, changes in school management, and inappropriate testing practices. We are concerned here with test preparation and other instructional responses. Following the terminology introduced by Koretz and colleagues (Koretz & Hamilton, 2006; Koretz, McCaffrey, & Hamilton, 2001), we distinguish between three types of responses that can inflate scores: cheating, reallocation, and coaching. Cheating obviously inflates scores and is therefore not a focus of this study.

Reallocation refers to redistributing instructional resources, including instructional time, to better align with the content of the test. Reallocation is not necessarily undesirable. Indeed, one of the aims of TBA is to encourage teachers and students to align their activities with standards, that is, to focus more on material that has been deemed important and is therefore tested. However, reallocation (and alignment, which is a form of reallocation) can inflate scores, if it entails reducing the resources directed to portions of the domain that are important for the inferences based on scores but that are omitted from or given little emphasis in the test. Doing so makes performance on the tested sample unrepresentative of mastery of the domain as a whole (Koretz, 2005; Koretz et al., 2001).

The term *coaching* has been used in many ways, but we use it to mean focusing on incidental details of the test that are unimportant for the inference based on scores. These can be either aspects of format or unimportant details of content. We include under coaching test-preparation strategies such as process of elimination for multiple-choice items. Coaching inflates scores if it leads to higher performance than one would see if those unimportant details were changed. For example, a study by Shepard (1988) illustrated how severe a failure of generalizability across formats can be. Using data from a state test, Shepard found that when addition items were presented in a vertical format, 86% of students answered these addition questions correctly, but in horizontal format, only 46% of students did. In subtraction, the percentages were 78 and 30, respectively.

A number of studies have determined that teachers reallocate time within subjects in response to TBA, often at the expense of attention to important material (e.g., Koretz, Barron, et al., 1996; Koretz, Mitchell, et al, 1996a; Stecher, 2002). In a recent RAND survey of teachers in California, Pennsylvania, and Georgia, teachers reported that because there were so many standards, they identified "highly assessed standards" on which to focus their attention (Hamilton & Stecher, 2007). Earlier studies by Shepard and Dougherty (1991) and Romberg, Zarinia, and Williams (1989) found evidence of increased focus on basic skills to the exclusion of more complex skills in response to the emphasis placed on basic skills in state tests.

Studies have found a variety of forms of coaching in response to high-stakes testing. Studies by Darling-Hammond and Wise (1985), Shepard and Dougherty (1991), Smith and Rottenberg (1991), McNeil (2000), and Pedulla et al. (2003) all showed that teachers focused their instruction not only on the content of the test, but also on its format, by presenting material in formats as they will appear on the test and designing tasks to mirror the content of the tests.

While this research provides ample evidence of test preparation and other instructional responses that have the potential to inflate scores, the dividing line between inappropriate and appropriate test preparation remains unclear. Indeed, many state and local policies have blurred the distinction even more in recent years, such as, by encouraging the use of old test forms as instructional materials and announcing "power standards" well in advance of testing dates. In the end, the distinction is empirical: test preparation is desirable if it produces valid gains in scores and undesirable if it results in inflated gains. Research has not yet tied variations in score inflation to specific forms of test preparation.

OPPORTUNITIES FOR INFLATION
IN THE CONSTRUCTION OF A TEST

Tests used for accountability are necessarily only a small sample of a knowledge domain—for example, "eighth grade mathematics"—but must support inferences about students' command of the entire domain. Moreover, the tested sample is almost always systematically incomplete, because some types of knowledge and skills are harder to assess than others. Nonetheless, under low-stakes conditions, this incomplete sampling often works reasonably well. Because of the small sample, estimates of performance are subject to substantial measurement error, but this adds only imprecision, not bias. Because test authors create different samples from the domain, the results from different tests of the same domain often differ, but these differences are usually modest.

Using tests for accountability, however, poses a fundamental threat to the validity of inferences based on these tests. Even under low-stakes conditions, teachers may begin focusing on the specifics of the tested sample at the cost of material that is important but not emphasized on the test, thereby undermining the test's representation of the larger domain (e.g., Lindquist, 1951). However, under low-stakes conditions, the incentives to focus on the tested specifics are usually mild. In contrast, under high-stakes conditions like those created by test-based accountability, educators face strong incentives to focus instruction on the specific content and format of tested material rather than the full domain of knowledge and skills represented in the state standards. *If these aspects of the test are predictable* and teachers focus on them, scores will become inflated, and inferences about mastery of the domain will be undermined.

Koretz et al. (Koretz et al., 2001; Koretz & Hamilton, 2006) provided a formal framework for evaluating the effects of this sampling on validity under high-stakes conditions. They used the term *performance element* to denote each aspect of performance that affects performance on a test or is relevant to the inference the test scores are intended to support. An element's *test weight* is the emphasis given to it by the test—specifically, its influence on scores—while the *inference weight* is the importance of that element to the inference based on scores. Tests will often omit elements that are important for the inference or assign them weights that are not proportional to the importance of these elements to the inference. The validity of an inference about improved learning is the degree to which improvement on the tested elements, as weighted by the particular test, accurately signals improvement in command of the entire domain, as weighted by the inference. Following this framework, we label standards that are emphasized by the test as *high-weight standards* and items assessing them as *high-weight items*.

What specific opportunities do tests provide for inappropriate narrowing that can inflate scores? Test-preparation materials often suggest a variety of strategies, ranging from focusing on the standards most often emphasized by the test to taking advantage of item format, for example, by using process of elimination. To examine the opportunities systematically, it is useful to think of the construction of a test as comprising several successive stages of narrowing down from the broad "target" (Kane, 2006)—the largely unmeasured construct about which we want to draw conclusions based on scores—to the specific items presented to students. Although the process of building a test need not always follow this sequence, the steps provide a helpful way to categorize the opportunities for inappropriate narrowing presented to teachers and students.

The first opportunity for inflation can arise in the specification of a state's standards. This stage of sampling reduces a domain selected for testing, such as "eighth grade mathematics," to the subset of that domain included in a given state's content standards. This is represented as the step from Box 1 to Box 2 in Figure 7.1. (In each row of Figure 7.1, the included or emphasized material is in the left-hand box, while the material omitted or de-emphasized at that stage is in the shaded, right-hand box.) States vary in terms of both the breadth of their standards as a set and in the breadth of individual standards. For example, the Massachusetts standards for eighth-grade math include all five of the content strands represented in NAEP, while the New York standards omit one of the NAEP content strands—data analysis and statistics. Many of New York's standards are framed very narrowly, in some cases so narrowly that they come close to implying specific test questions. For example, geometry standard 8G4 requires that students, "Determine angle pair relationships when given two parallel lines cut by a transversal." In contrast, most of the individual standards specified by Massachusetts delineate somewhat broader categories of knowledge and skills. For example, the Massachusetts eighth measurement standard 8.M.3 states that students will:

> Demonstrate an understanding of the concepts and apply formulas and procedures for determining measures, including those of area and perimeter/circumference of parallelograms, trapezoids, and circles. Given the formulas, determine the surface area and volume of rectangular prisms, cylinders, and spheres. Use technology as appropriate.

(Note, however, that the second-to-last statement suggests a narrower operationalization of the standard.) Inflation that arises because educators no longer teach important content that is omitted from standards can only be identified by comparison to an external audit test that is judged to be a good measure of the relevant domain—in practice, most often the NAEP.

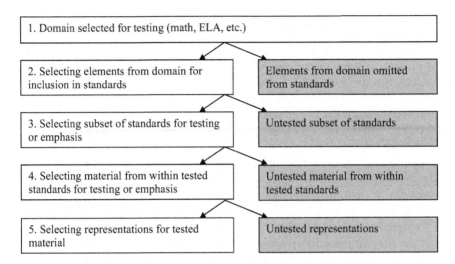

Note: "Tested" versus "untested" also represents emphasized versus de-emphasized.

Figure 7.1.   Taxonomy of opportunities for score inflation.

Because of limits on testing time, a second opportunity for narrowing arises: a given test is unlikely to sample exhaustively from the state's standards. Moreover, even among standards that are sampled, some standards may be sampled much more heavily than others, giving performance on these heavily emphasized standards disproportionate impact on students' overall scores. The selection of standards for inclusion or emphasis is represented by Box 3 in Figure 7.1. If this stage of sampling is unpredictable over time, it is unlikely to produce score inflation. For example, the students of teachers who focus unduly on standards emphasized in previous tests are likely to do poorly on previously unemphasized material included in the current-year test. Variations in test weights will also not inflate scores if they correspond to variations in inference weights—that is, if only material more important for the inference is given more emphasis by the test. However, if variations in emphasis are persistent, predictable, and unjustified by the inference, this stage of sampling provides an opportunity for reallocation that will inflate scores.

The third stage of sampling that provides opportunities for narrowed instruction is the uneven sampling of skills within standards (Box 4 in Figure 7.1). Some standards are written broadly, such that a single standard includes mastery of a cluster of skills and concepts. When a standard is written broadly, test designers sample from it in constructing a test, just as they sample among standards. If the within-standard sampling is predictable, that creates an incentive for teachers to focus on the emphasized aspects of the standard at the expense of those not emphasized or excluded. For example, if a given standard specifies that students learn rotation, transformation, and dilation of a polygon on a coordinate plane but only rotations are included in the test, teachers in high stakes contexts have an incentive to focus their instruction only on rotations. If they do, their students are likely to perform better on items representing that standard than they would on an alternative set of items representing the standard more fully.

The final stage of sampling, represented by Box 5 in Figure 7.1, is the choice of representations used to test each standard. We use the term *representation* to refer to both unimportant details of content and what we term *item style*. Item style is broader than item format, in the usual sense. For example, it includes the type of visual representation in the item, if any, the magnitude and complexity of the numbers used, and so on. Consider a hypothetical standard stating that students should understand the concept of slope in the context of simple linear equations. Problems involving slope could be presented verbally, graphically, or algebraically, or they could require translation among those representations. If the problems are presented graphically, they could be presented only with positive slopes in the first quadrant, or with a mix of positive, negative, and zero slopes in all four quadrants. In some cases, these choices are similar or identical from one year to the next. In extreme cases, the chosen representations may be so similar over time that new items are virtual clones of earlier ones.

The use of predictable representations facilitates coaching. If tests employ similar or identical representations in successive years, then using prior tests to practice renders these items familiar and may make them easier than other items with different item styles that were measuring the same underlying mathematical content. In addition, the use of predictable representations may make it easier to develop forms of test preparation that allow students to correctly answer items without gaining the knowledge or skills the item is intended to tap. As Shepard (1988) observed, policy makers should be interested in whether children can add and subtract, and not in whether they can add and subtract when items are presented in a vertical format.

DATA AND METHODS

We examined the 2006 through 2008 eighth-grade mathematics tests in Massachusetts and New York and the tenth-grade mathematics test in Massachusetts. Both Massachusetts and New York released item maps that link each test question to a state standard and a strand of mathematics (e.g., number sense and operations, measurement, statistics and probability, algebra, and geometry). Using these item maps, we constructed item-level datasets that organized all released items sequentially within individual standards. Released items in NY included all items used on the eighth-grade math test. Released items in MA at that time included all common items—that is, items taken by all students and used to generate students' scores. This database facilitates comparison of related items to identify recurrences of content or presentation that would afford opportunities for narrowed instruction and test preparation that might induce score inflation.

We examined recurrences largely following the schematic in Figure 7.1. We calculated the fraction of the strands and standards tested in each year and state, as well as the fraction of each area ever tested over 2006-2008. We examined the relative weighting of standards on the state exams both within and across years. To address differences in the narrowness of individual standards, we mapped the eighth-grade standards in New York onto those in Massachusetts and evaluated the breadth of the New York tests in terms of Massachusetts' broader standards. We isolated clusters of extremely similar items on each test in the years 2006-2008, and mapped backwards to the standards to identify cases where similar items were used to sample nominally different standards.

Because some standards, particularly in Massachusetts, represent broader bundles of skills and knowledge, we explored how well the tests evenly sample skills represented within a given standard. For example, a standard might require students to master tax, percent increase/decrease, simple interest, and sale prices, but consistently ask questions about interest rather than sale prices.

We examined the sequence of items within each standard in all of the tests to identify recurrences of representations. In theory, these recurrences can entail either aspects of item style or unimportant details of content—that is, details that are not warranted by the inference based on scores. However, in practice, the distinction between these two aspects of representation is often unclear, and we found that we could not reliably code it. Therefore, we do not make this distinction in the presentation of results.

RESULTS

We present results here in the order presented in Figure 7.1.

Elements From the Domain Included in the Standards (Box 2 in Figure 7.1)

Narrowing from the domain to the standards occurs in the selection of content for inclusion in the standards, the wording of the standards, and the operationalization of the standards in the test. To quantify the degree of narrowing between the larger domain in an area such as "eighth grade mathematics" and the domain described in a given state's standards, we would need a formal definition of what constitutes the larger domain, and in the United States, agreement about the domain is, at best, incomplete. Nonetheless, we can illustrate the process by comparing state standards to the framework of standards of the National Assessment of Educational Progress, which is intended to reflect a degree of national consensus about what students should know and be able to do. We can also compare the standards of the two states to compare the breadth, depth and complexity of skills and understandings they describe.[1] A comparison of eighth-grade standards from the two states provides striking examples of this stage of narrowing. In several respects, New York's standards and tests were markedly narrower than those of Massachusetts, and the details of that comparison offer concrete illustrations of the ways in which this narrowing can occur.

We have already an obvious instance of narrowing: the New York State eighth-grade mathematics standards entirely omitted the data analysis, statistics, and probability strand included in the NAEP, although the state's seventh-grade standards did include this strand. In contrast, the eighth-grade Massachusetts standards included five strands similar to those in the NAEP framework. Mapping from state standards to NAEP standards is inherently ambiguous because the two sets of standards divide content differently, and often there is a limited degree of overlap between two seemingly different standards. Nonetheless, it is clear that the New York standards were also somewhat narrower than the NAEP standards in the four strands they have in common. For example, the eighth-grade NAEP standards "Estimate square or cube roots of numbers less than 1,000 between two whole numbers" and "Visualize or describe the cross section of a solid" were not present in the New York eighth-grade standards.

A simple count of standards would suggest that New York's standards are broader than those of Massachusetts. The Massachusetts Mathematics Curriculum Framework (Massachusetts Department of Education, 2000) lists 39 eighth-grade content standards spanning five strands. New York State's Mathematics Core Curriculum (New York State Education Department, 2005) lists 48 eighth-grade content standards, even though this document excludes the data analysis, statistics, and probability strand.

More detailed examination, however, shows that the reverse is true: New York samples more narrowly from the domain. One reason is the wording of New York's standards, many of which were very narrowly worded, some so much so that they encompassed only one or a few pieces of information. For example, standard 8.G.1 was simply "Identify pairs of vertical angles as congruent." Moreover, this standard was just a subset of another, slightly less narrow standard, 8.G.6: "Calculate the missing angle measurements when given two intersecting lines and an angle" (New York State Education Department, 2005, p. 86).

In contrast, the Massachusetts standards were typically much broader. For example, Massachusetts standard 8.G.6 was "Predict the results of transformations on unmarked or coordinate planes and draw the transformed figure, e.g., predict how tessellations transform under translations, reflections, and rotations" (Massachusetts Department of Education, 2000, p. 64). This single Massachusetts standard encompasses fully six separate New York standards that are grouped under the heading "Students will apply coordinate geometry to analyze problem solving situations:"

- 8.G.7 "Describe and identify transformations in the plane, using proper function notation (rotations, reflections, translations, and dilations)"
- 8.G.8 "Draw the image of a figure under rotations of 90 and 180 degrees"
- 8.G.9 "Draw the image of a figure under a reflection over a given line"
- 8.G.10 "Draw the image of a figure under a translation"
- 8.G.11 "Draw the image of a figure under a dilation"
- 8.G.12 "Identify the properties preserved and not preserved under a reflection, rotation, translation, and dilation" (New York State Education Department, 2005, p. 86).

While not all cases were this extreme, we found that in general, the Massachusetts standards were broader, so the small number of standards in Massachusetts actually sampled more broadly from the domain than did the more numerous New York standards.

This difference in the breadth of standards was reflected in the allocation of items and raw score points on the tests in the two states. As detailed further below, we found that 40 to 50% of the raw score points on the New York eighth-grade tests in any given year mapped to only three Massachusetts eighth-grade standards.

The wording of standards may narrow content in subtle ways. For example, the Massachusetts standards include calculation of the volume of rectangular prisms but specify that the student will be given the formula:

> 10.M.2 *Given the formula*, find the lateral area, surface area, and volume of prisms, pyramids, spheres, cylinders, and cones, e.g., find the volume of a sphere with a specified surface area. (Massachusetts Department of Education, 2000, p. 75, emphasis added)

Including the italicized clause fundamentally narrows what is being measured. The student does not need to know the mathematical relationship between volume and dimensions to solve items addressing this standard; she needs only the elementary-school skills of "plugging" numbers into an equation and multiplying. Figure 7.2 shows a 10th-grade MCAS item assessing this standard, along with an item assessing similar content from Singapore's Primary School Leaving Examination, which students take at the end of sixth grade. Because the formula is given in the 10th-grade MCAS (it is not shown in Figure 7.2 because it is not contiguous in the test booklet), one could discard any mention of volume or the particular shape and simply ask students to solve the equation. By way of contrast, sixth graders in Singapore are not given the formula and are expected to know the mathematical relationship between dimensions and volume.

A simple listing of standards may understate the narrowing that can occur at this stage. The tests also create operational definitions of the standards, which may further narrow sampling from the domain. For example, items may predictably omit aspects of a standard that may be more difficult. The items in Figure 7.2 provide an example of this. The Massachusetts item (and the corresponding items in the New York tests, which are found in grade 6) require either calculating the total volume of a single prism or calculating one dimension given a full prism. In contrast, the Singapore item in Figure 7.2 requires comparison of two prisms and calculation of a fractional volume.

Although narrowing within standards in the writing of test items is discussed below, it is important to note here that the content of items may further narrow the span of the standards when items that purportedly measure two standards are so similar that they are effectively sampling the same content. For example, Figure 7.3 shows very similar items used to assess 10th-grade Massachusetts standards D.2 and P.2. These are not only different standards; they are also drawn from two different strands (data analysis and interpretation, and patterns and algebra, respectively). Similar items assessing nominally different standards are found in the New York tests as well.

---

a. 10th-grade MCAS (March retest), 2010: formula provided

33 A right rectangular prism has the
following dimensions:

  • The height is 5 feet.

  • The length is 6 feet.

The volume of the prism is 60 cubic feet.
What is the width of the prism?

A. 2 feet

B. 3 feet

C. 5 feet

D. 6 feet

---

b. 6th-grade Singapore Primary School Leaving Exam: no formula given

In Figure 1, Tank A is completely filled with water and Tank B is empty. Water is
poured from Tank A into Tank B without spilling. The heights of the water level in
the two tanks are now equal as shown in Figure 2.

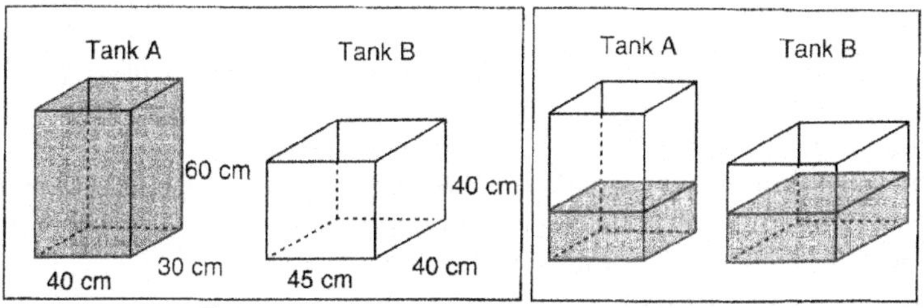

Figure 1   Figure 2

What is the height of the water level in Tank A in Figure 2?

Answer _____

Figure 7.2.   Comparison of volume items from 10th-grade MCAS and Singapore
6th-grade tests. Sample MCAS retrieved from MA Department of Education's
MCAS Question Search (2011). http://www.doe.mass.edu/mcas/search/. Sample
Singapore item is from Singapore Examinations and Assessment Board (2009).

Selection of a Subset of the Standards (Box 3 in Figure 7.1)

Tests may create incentives for teachers to narrow instruction by omitting certain standards, providing the opportunity for teachers to exclude
or de-emphasize content without negatively affecting students' test scores.

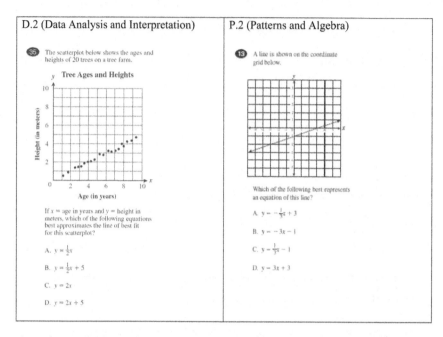

Figure 7.3.   Similar 10th-grade MCAS items used to sample nominally different standards. Item #35 on MCAS 10th-grade test in 2005 assesses standard D.2 by having students determine the equation from a linear scatterplot. Item #13 on MCAS 10th-grade test in 2006 assesses standard P.2 by having students determine the equation from a line. Retrieved from MA Department of Education's MCAS Question Search (2008). http://www.doe.mass.edu/mcas/search/

Table 7.1 shows that over the years 2006-2008, an average of 42% of New York eighth-grade standards, 67% of Massachusetts eighth-grade standards, and 60% of Massachusetts 10th-grade standards were tested.[2] That only a fraction of the state curriculum is tested in any given year would not enable score inflation so long as different standards are tested each year and teachers cannot predict which standards will be tested. For example, if the tests were based on a random sample of the standards each year, there would be no incentive for teachers to focus on a limited fraction of the curriculum.

Therefore, to assess whether sampling of standards was predictably incomplete, we examined the percentage of standards tested over the 3-year period of the study, 2006-2008. Over this 3-year period, 58% of relevant standards were sampled on the New York eighth-grade test, 83% were sampled on the Massachusetts 10th-grade test, and 90% were sampled by the Massachusetts eighth-grade test. All three tests created opportunities for reallocation by omitting content, although to varying degrees.

**Table 7.1.   Fraction of Total NY and MA Standards
Tested by Year and Over 2006-2008**

Set of Standards	Average per Year	Ever, 2006-2008
New York eighth-grade standards	42	58
Massachusetts eighth-grade standards	67	90
Massachusetts tenth-grade standards	60	83

Note: Number of standards tested in parentheses. MA excludes out of grade standards
that are sampled on the test, because these are extraneous to the validity of inferences
about student mastery of the standards in the tests' corresponding grade level framework.

However, these simple counts understate opportunities for inflation because they do not consider the relative emphasis the tests assign to the tested standards. If variations in emphasis—that is, test weights—are predictable, scores may become inflated if teachers emphasize highly sampled content, while decreasing emphasis on standards that are never (or only infrequently) sampled. Therefore, it is important to examine test weights in addition to omissions.

In both states, a small number of standards accounted for the majority of test points on the state tests. Figure 7.4 compares the distribution of standard weights on the three exams. The *x*-axis reports the number of standards ever actually assessed in the exams, sorted from the most to the least highly assessed. The *y*-axis indicates the percentage of points each standard is worth. The area below the step functions, therefore, corresponds to the percentage of test points covered by the number of standards at any point along the *x*-axis. The dotted drop lines indicate how many standards students must master to earn 50% of test points. On the New York eighth-grade test, about 50% of possible test points corresponded to only 10 of 48 standards. Similarly, on the Massachusetts eighth-grade math test, 8 of 29 standards account for a little more than 50% of test points, and on the 10th-grade test, 5 of 30 standards corresponded to about 50% of test points. The patterns are particularly stark for the Massachusetts 10th-grade mathematics tests, where the single standard with the highest test weight consistently contributed between 15 and 17% of test points per year, while the second highest weight standard consistently contributed between 7 and 17% of test points. To the extent that these weights represent consistent patterns of emphasis, teachers could profitably identify and teach to the cluster of standards that drives the highest number of test points, sacrificing instruction focusing on the others.

However, the extent of narrowing depends not just on the number of standards tested, but also on their breadth. As noted, the New York stan-

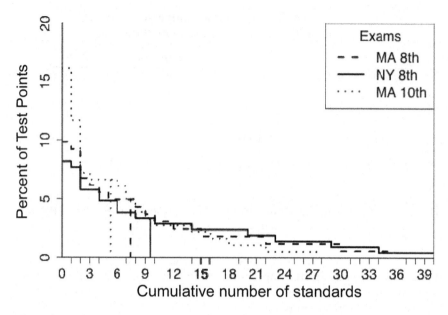

Figure 7.4.   Distribution of standards tested on NY and MA mathematics tests.

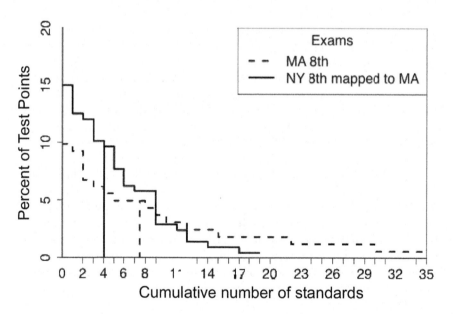

Figure 7.5.   Distribution of standards tested on NY and MA 8th-grade mathematics Tests (NY standards mapped to MA standards).

dards are generally narrower than those of Massachusetts, and a comparison between them should take this into account. To illustrate this point, Figure 7.5 represents the distribution of standards tested over 2006-2008 once the New York eighth-grade standards have been mapped onto those in Massachusetts. Here, we see that the uneven sampling of standards is much more dramatic on New York's eighth-grade test than on Massachusetts's; just 4 Massachusetts standards make up 50% of test points on the New York eighth-grade tests.

Coaching to high frequency items requires that teachers or students recognize the predicable patterns in the test. This is made easier when states release items that are similar to those that will be used in the future. In the period we studied, teachers in both states could download entire released forms that contain all the items used to calculate students' scores.[3] Moreover, in Massachusetts, teachers can use an online item search tool to download all items, if any, used in past years to assess mastery of a given standard. This type of sorting makes it easier for administrators and teachers to isolate aspects of their curriculum that are actually tested, as well as how and with what frequency performance on each standard is measured.

Selecting From Within Standards (Box 4 in Figure 7.1)

The previous section showed that standards are often unevenly sampled on state tests. When standards are framed broadly, tests may further narrow the sample by consistently excluding some skills from within a standard. This is more of a potential concern in Massachusetts than in New York because of the wording of standards. Many of New York's standards are written very narrowly, causing a narrowing of focus at the level of Box 3 and leaving less room for further narrowing at the level of Box 4. In contrast, most Massachusetts standards are written to include a cluster of skills, concepts, and representations, which creates a risk of score inflation if tests do not adequately sample from the skill set implied by the standards.

To evaluate how large a problem this was in Massachusetts, we examined items testing standards that contributed an average of 3% or more of test points per year in the years 2006-2008. We chose a 3% threshold because this represents sufficient weight to have a substantial effect on students' overall scores. We compared the test items to the specific standards they sampled, and noted which particular aspects of the standard the items sampled. (We did find a small number of examples of similar omissions on the New York tests even though the narrow framing of most standards made within-standard sampling less likely.)

We found evidence of incomplete sampling within standards on both the eighth-grade and tenth-grade Massachusetts tests. Four of the seven high-weight standards were incompletely sampled on the eighth-grade test. On the 10th-grade test, three of the six high-weight standards were incompletely sampled.

For example, eighth-grade standard 8.N.3 required students to "Use ratios and proportions in the solution of problems, in particular, problems solving unit rates, scale factors, and rate of change." Over this period, students were never asked to solve problems using the rate of change. In other cases, certain operations were excluded. Standard 8.N.12. requires students to "Select and use appropriate operations—addition, subtraction, multiplication, division, and positive integer exponents—to solve problems with rational numbers (including negatives)," but multiplication and positive integer exponents were never tested. In some cases, omission of a portion of a standard from items explicitly linked to that standard may not be problematic because of other items on the test. For example, the 10th-grade standard 10.D.1 required students to, "Select, create, and interpret as appropriate (e.g. scatterplot, table, stem-and-leaf plots, box-and-whisker plots, circle graph, line graph, and line plot) for a set of data...." The items linked to this standard omitted scatterplots, line graphs, and selection of appropriate representations, but these were sampled in the context of other items addressing other standards.

Selecting Representations (Box 5 in Figure 7.1)

All of the previous steps entail narrowing of what is tested on state tests, relative to the domain about which inferences based on test scores are made. The final stage, the selection of representations, entails *how* that content is tested. As noted, we use the term representation broadly to refer not just to item format and the appearance of material in the test item, but also to the recurrent use of minor details of content that are incidental to the construct the item is intended to assess.

In extreme cases, representations are so similar that items are essentially clones of those used in earlier years. A particularly extreme example of clone items was found in the seventh-grade mathematics tests in New York. Two of the four items that appeared over a 4-year period are shown in Figure 7.6. Note that the stems are essentially identical except for the substitution of "watermelon" for "cheese," and the distracters are similar except for the doubling of rulers in the second year. One of the remaining two items was also a clone of these two. The fourth was similar but more complex, requiring students to recognize that the appropriate measure is grams rather than kilograms.

A more subtle form of recurrent presentation can be seen in the items testing New York standard 8.N.4, "Apply percents to: tax, percent

a) Item 27 in 2008

Which tool is most appropriate for measuring the mass of a serving of cheese?

A   ruler

B   thermometer

C   measuring cup

D   weighing scale

Item 9 in 2009

Which tool would be most appropriate for Natasha to use when finding the mass
of a watermelon?

A   scale

B   inch ruler

C   meter stick

D   measuring cup

Source: New York State Department of Education (2008, p. 21 and 2009, p. 11).

Figure 7.6.   Clone items assessing NY's standard 7.M.9: "Determine the tool and
technique to measure with an appropriate level of precision: mass."

increase/decrease, simple interest, sale price, commission, interest rates,
gratuities." This was one of the two most frequently tested standards in
the eighth-grade tests, tested with 12 items during the 4 years from 2006
through 2010. Of those 12 items, only one required students to calculate a
rate or percentage. The other 11 provided a base quantity and a percentage and required that the student calculate either a change (e.g., a discount or a tip) or a final quantity (e.g., a total bill including the tip). The
use of a consistent form narrows what students need to know and facilitates teaching mechanical solutions that do not require a solid understanding of rates or percentages.

DISCUSSION

This study documents that the tests in New York and Massachusetts– and
in particular, the New York eighth-grade and Massachusetts tenth-grade
tests—do provide opportunities for narrow test preparation that could

lead to inflated scores. We found multiple similarities in the types of opportunities afforded by both tests. Predictable sampling of standards and predictable representations of skills, were present on all tests, though their severity varied. We also identified test-specific opportunities that derived from the way the standards are framed in each state.

Substantial resources have been devoted to identifying these patterns—by state agencies, districts, and commercial firms—and anecdotal evidence suggests that some teachers are aware of them. For example, the Quincy, Massachusetts district website lists the test weights of each section of secondary mathematics textbooks used in the district and shows all of the relevant test items from a 4-year period (Quincy Public Schools, 2004). In an interview with the first author, a data coach in the Boston Public Schools provided pie charts illustrating the proportion of the total possible points on the test that could be attributed to each standard, which was used to decide what to emphasize in the classroom. As another data coach in the Boston Public Schools told us, "(The attitude is) just focus on the questions and content with the most potential to drive up scores. Why teach anything else?" In other cases, commercial test preparation resources alert teachers to recurrent patterns.

These predictable patterns in tests used for accountability create incentives to narrow instruction in ways that can deprive students of good instruction, disadvantage good teachers and inflate scores. When teachers, administrators and schools are evaluated based the gains their students demonstrate on these tests, they face strong disincentives to provide students with opportunities to master the full breadth and depth of math learning described in each state's framework of standards. Thus, tests that provide substantial opportunities for score inflation increase the likelihood that performance evaluation systems based on test score gains will misidentify successful teachers and schools and perversely reward teachers who teach to the test, while penalizing teachers who attempt to instruct students in the entire domain outlined in state standards. As Shepard (1990) notes, schools or teachers that teach to the full framework of a curriculum and thus provide a broad, rich curriculum beyond the specifics of the tested sample might be at a disadvantage on a test used for accountability purposes. Because these teachers seek to provide students with a broader educational experience, they spend proportionally less time on the specific content that offers the greatest return in terms of test score gains.

This study provides only a first glimpse of the opportunities for inappropriate test preparation provided by current high-stakes tests. Ample research, however, shows that the results—inappropriate instruction and score inflation—are widespread and often severe. Improving test-based accountability will require more widespread evaluation of these opportunities, monitoring educators' responses, and redesigning of tests and the accountability systems in which these tests are embedded to reduce incentives to narrow instruction,

We close by pointing toward important areas for future research on equity, which is the focus of this book. What remains incompletely researched is whether historically disadvantaged groups are more likely to receive test-specific instruction, and to what extent score inflation affects the measurement of between-group inequality in outcomes. To the extent that poor and minority students are concentrated in the lowest scoring schools that face the greatest pressure to raise scores, they may be the most severely affected (e.g., Rouse et al., 2007). Nonetheless, many policymakers and educators continue to view test score data as accurate measurements that track student performance as well as racial and socioeconomic inequities. While test scores are intended to provide more transparency about student performance, this chapter demonstrates the ways that predictability in test design supports test-specific instruction. Any score inflation caused by test-specific instruction interferes with our ability to accurately measure educational inequality.

ACKNOWLEDGMENTS

The research reported here was supported by the Institute of Education Sciences, U.S. Department of Education, through Grant R305AII0420, and by the Spencer Foundation, through Grants 201100075 and 201200071, to the President and Fellows of Harvard College. The opinions expressed are those of the authors and do not represent views of the Institute, the U.S. Department of Education, or the Spencer Foundation.

NOTES

1. A majority of states have committed to adopting the Common Core Standards, and this could provide a more widely accepted operational definition of the target of inference. However, Porter, McMaken, Hwang, & Yang (2011) reported that alignment between the Common Core and NAEP is only modest, albeit a bit higher than the average alignment between the Common Core and the average state's standards. The disparity between NAEP and the Common Core is not yet widely understood, and it remains unclear whether educators, policymakers, and others will decide that NAEP content omitted from the Common Core is relevant to the domain.

2. Because the New York state math test was administered in March during this time period, New York identified a subset of standards that were eligible for inclusion in the state test. These standards included seventh-grade

standards scheduled to be taught after March of the previous year, as well as eighth-grade standards taught before March. All told, 68.8% of the eighth-grade standards are eligible for testing. In addition, the eighth-grade test includes standards taught in the seventh-grade curriculum after the March test. To provide comparability across states, we focus on the percent of the total *8th* standards that were tested each year. Were we to use a denominator that includes seventh-grade post-March standards and eighth-grade pre-March standards, 83% of standards were covered between 2006-2008.

3. Beginning in 2011, New York stopped releasing test forms. In most grades and subjects, Massachusetts began releasing only half of the common items in 2009.

REFERENCES

Carnoy, M., & Loeb, S. (2002). Does external accountability affect student outcomes? A cross-state analysis. *Educational Evaluation and Policy Analysis, 24*, 305-331.

Center on Education Policy. (2008). *Has student achievement increased since 2002? State test score trends through 2006-07*. Washington, DC: Author.

Darling-Hammond, L., & Wise, A. E. (1985). Beyond standardization: State standards and school improvement. *The Elementary School Journal, 85*, 315-336.

Figlio, D., & Getzler, L. (2002). Accountability, ability and disability: Gaming the system. *National Bureau of Economic Research Working paper 9307*. Retrieved from http://www.nber.org/papers/w9307

Fuller, B., Gesicki, K., Kang, E., & Wright, J. (2006). *Is the No Child Left Behind Act working? The reliability of how states track achievement*. Retrieved October 11, 2009, from: http://www.eric.ed.gov/PDFS/ED492024.pdf

Grissmer, D., & Flanagan, A. (1998). *Exploring rapid achievement gains in North Carolina and Texas: Lessons from the states*. Washington, DC: National Education Goals Panel.

Hambleton, R. K., Jaeger, R. M., Koretz, D., Linn, R. L., Millman, J., & Phillips, S. E. (1995). *Review of the measurement quality of the Kentucky Instructional Results Information System, 1991-1994*. Frankfort, KY: Office of Education Accountability, Kentucky General Assembly.

Hamilton, L. S. & Stecher, B. M. (2007). *Measuring instructional responses to standards-based accountability*. Santa Monica, CA: RAND.

Hanushek, E. A., & Raymond, M. E. (2004). The effect of school accountability systems on the level and distribution of student achievement. *Journal of the European Economic Association, 2*, 406-415.

Hanushek, E. A.,& Raymond, M. E. (2005). Does school accountability lead to improved student performance? *Journal of Policy Analysis and Management, 24*(2), 297-327.

Ho, A. D. (2007). Discrepancies between score trends from NAEP and state tests: A scale-invariant perspective. *Educational Measurement: Issues and Practice, 26*(4), 11-20.

Jacob, B. A. (2005). Accountability, incentives, and behavior: Evidence from school reform in Chicago. *Journal of Public Economics, 89,* 761-796.

Jacob, B. A. (2007). *Test-based accountability and student achievement: An investigation of differential performance on NAEP and state assessments* (NBER Working Paper w12817). Retrieved from http://www.nber.org/papers/w12817

Jennings, J. L., & Beveridge, A. A. (2009). How does test exemption affect schools' and students' academic performance? *Educational Evaluation and Policy Analysis, 31,* 153-175.

Kane, M. (2006). Validation. In R. L. Brennan (Ed.), *Educational measurement* (4th ed., 17-64). Westport, CT: American Council on Education/Praeger.

Klein, S. P., Hamilton, L. S., McCaffrey, D. F., & Stecher, B. M. (2000). *What do test scores in Texas tell us?* (Issue Paper IP-202). Santa Monica, CA: RAND. Retrieved November 15, 2011, from http://www.rand.org/publications/IP/IP202/

Koretz, D. (1986). *Trends in educational achievement.* Washington, DC: Congressional Budget Office.

Koretz, D. (2005). Alignment, high stakes, and the inflation of test scores. In J. Herman & E. Haertel (Eds.), *Uses and misuses of data in accountability testing*: *Yearbook of the National Society for the Study of Education* (Vol. 104, Part 2, pp. 99-118). Malden, MA: Blackwell.

Koretz, D., & Barron, S. I. (1998). *The validity of gains on the Kentucky Instructional Results Information System (KIRIS)* (MR-1014-EDU). Santa Monica, CA: RAND.

Koretz, D., Barron, S., Mitchell, K., & Stecher, B. (1996). *The perceived effects of the Kentucky Instructional Results Information System (KIRIS)* (MR-792-PCT/FF). Santa Monica, CA: RAND.

Koretz, D., & Hamilton, L. S. (2006). Testing for accountability in K-12. In R. L. Brennan (Ed.), *Educational measurement* (4th ed., 531-578.) Westport, CT: American Council on Education/Praeger.

Koretz, D., Linn, R. L., Dunbar, S. B., & Shepard, L. A. (1991, April). The effects of high-stakes testing: Preliminary evidence about generalization across tests. In R. L. Linn (Chair), *The effects of high-stakes testing.* Symposium presented at the annual meetings of the American Educational Research Association and the National Council on Measurement in Education, Chicago.

Koretz, D., McCaffrey, D., & Hamilton, L. (2001). *Toward a framework for validating gains under high-stakes conditions* (CSE Technical Report 551). Los Angeles, CA: Center for the Study of Evaluation, University of California.

Koretz, D., Mitchell, K., Barron, S., & Keith, S. (1996a). *The perceived effects of the Maryland School Performance Assessment Program* (CSE Tech. Rep. No. 409). Los Angeles, CA: University of California, National Center for Research on Evaluation, Standards, and Student Testing.

Koretz, D., Mitchell, K., Barron, S., & Keith, S. (1996b). *The perceived effects of the Maryland School Performance Assessment Program* (CSE Technical Report No. 409). Los Angeles, CA: Center for the Study of Evaluation, University of California.

Lee, J. (2007). *The testing gap: Scientific trials of test-driven school accountability systems for excellence and equity.* Charlotte, NC: Information Age.

Lindquist, E. F. (Ed.). (1951). Preliminary considerations in objective test construction. In *Educational measurement* (2nd ed., pp. 119-158). Washington, DC: American Council on Education.

Massachusetts Department of Education. (2000). *Massachusetts Mathematics Curriculum Framework*. Malden, MA: Author.

Massachusetts Department of Education. (2006). *MCAS question search*. Retrieved January 18, 2008 and November 10, 2011 from http://www.doe.mass.edu/mcas/search/

McNeil, L. M. (2000). *Contradictions of school reform: The educational costs of standardized testing*. London, England: Routledge.

National Research Council. (2011). *Incentives and test-based accountability in public education*. Committee on Incentives and Test-Based Accountability in Public Education, Michael Hout and Stuart W. Elliot, Editors. Board on Testing and Assessment, Division of Behavioral and Social Sciences and Education. Washington, DC: The National Academies Press.

National Research Council. (2011). *Incentives and test-based accountability in education*. In M. Hout & S. W. Elliott (Eds.), *Committee on Incentives and Test-Based Accountability in Public Education, Board on Testing and Assessment*. Washington, DC: The National Academies Press.

New York State Education Department. (2005). *Mathematics core curriculum*. Albany, NY: The State University of New York.

New York State Department of Education. *(2008)*. *New York State Testing Program: Grade 7 mathematics test*. Retrieved from http://nysedregents.org/Grade7/Mathematics/20080306book1.pdf

New York State Department of Education. (2009). *New York State Testing Program: Grade 7 mathematics test*. Retrieved from http://nysedregents.org/Grade7/Mathematics/20090309book1.pdf

Pedulla, J. J., Abrams, L. M., Madaus, G. F., Russell, M. K., Ramos, M. A., & Miao, J. (2003). *Perceived effects of state-mandated testing programs on teaching and learning: Findings from a national survey of teachers*. Chestnut Hill, MA: National Board on Educational Testing and Public Policy. Retrieved July 15, 2010. http://www.bc.edu/research/nbetpp/statements/nbr2.pdf

Porter, A., McMaken, J., Hwang, J., & Yang, R. (2011). Common Core Standards: The new U.S. intended curriculum. *Educational Researcher, 40*(3), 103-116.

Quincy Public Schools. (2004). *MCAS Math Concordance*. Quincy, MA: Author. Retrieved January 23, 2012, from http://66.241.201.139/powerpoint/MCAS/Math%20Concordance%20-%20Show.ppshttp://66.241.201.139/powerpoint/MCAS/Math%20Concordance%20-%20Show.pps

Ravitch, D. (2010). Is education on the wrong track? *A TNR Symposium*. Retrieved March 16, 2010, from http://www.tnr.com/article/politics/education-the-wrong-track-0

Romberg, T. A., Zarinnia, E. A., & Williams, S. R. (1989). *The influence of mandated testing on mathematics instruction: Grade 8 teachers' perceptions*. Madison, WI: University of Wisconsin, Center for Educational Research, School of Education, and Office of Educational Research and Improvement of the United States Department of Education.

Rouse, C. E., Hannaway, J., Goldhaber, D., & Figlio, D. (2007). *Feeling the Florida heat? How low-performing schools respond to voucher and accountability pressure* (NBER working paper no. 13681). Retrieved from http://www.nber.org/papers/w13681

Shepard, L. A. (1988). *The harm of measurement-driven instruction.* Paper presented at the annual meeting of the American Educational Research Association, Washington, DC.

Shepard, L.A. (1990). Inflated test score gains: Is the problem old norms or teaching the test? *Education Measurement: Issues and Practice, 9,* 15-22.

Shepard, L. A., & Cutts-Dougherty, K. (1991). *Effects of high-stakes testing on instruction.* Paper presented at the annual meeting of the American Educational Research Association, Chicago. Retrieved from http://www.colorado.edu/education/faculty/lorrieshepard/testing.html

Singapore Examinations and Assessment Board.(2009). *PSLE Examination Questions 2005-2009.* Singapore: Author.

Smith, M. L., & Rottenberg, C. (1991). Unintended consequences of external testing in elementary schools. *Educational Measurement: Issues and Practice, 10,* 7-11.

Stecher, B. (2002). Consequences of large-scale, high-stakes testing on school and classroom practice. In L. Hamilton, B. M. Stecher, S. P. Klein (Eds.), *Test-based accountability: A guide for practitioners and policymakers* (pp. 79-99). Santa Monica, CA: RAND. Retrieved from http://www.rand.org/publications/MR/MR1554/MR1554.ch4.pdf

Stecher, B. M., Chun, T. J., Barron, S. I, & Ross, K. E. (2000). *The effects of the Washington State Education Reform on schools and classrooms: Initial findings.* Santa Monica, CA: RAND.

CHAPTER 8

RACIAL AND SOCIOECONOMIC GAPS IN SOCIAL SKILLS DEVELOPMENT

A Longitudinal Study of K-5 Children's Growth Trajectories and the Effects of Parents and Schools

Xiaoyan Liu and Jaekyung Lee

The No Child Left Behind Act (NCLB) was enacted based on the belief that setting high standards and establishing measurable goals could help improve all students' academic achievement and close achievement gaps. While performance-driven accountability policy such as NCLB relied heavily on high-stakes testing, the policy did not evidence any significant impact on narrowing racial achievement gaps (Lee & Wong, 2004). Under NCLB, students' academic skills have been increasingly emphasized even in lower grades, particularly in states where specific literacy and other academic skills standards for young children are in place (Jacobson, 2004; Kessenich, 2006). In contrast, few states developed standards for social-emotional dimensions of development and little attention has been given to the impact of children's social skills on their academic success (Chiu,

Charting Reform, Achieving Equity in a Diverse Nation
pp. 191–218
Copyright © 2013 by Information Age Publishing
All rights of reproduction in any form reserved.

2001; Kessenich, 2006). While many studies have attempted to identify key school and family factors that influence racial and socioeconomic achievement gaps, fewer studies have examined the role and effects of social skills that may account for racial and socioeconomic differences in academic performance. The present study addresses this gap in knowledge by examining the trajectory of students' social skills development and the factors that influence social skills development among students with diverse racial, cultural, and socioeconomic backgrounds.

The primary purpose of this study was to advance our understanding of issues that are relevant to social skills development of young children in the United States. The goals of this study were twofold. The first goal was to examine developmental trajectories of work-related skills and interpersonal skills among diverse groups of young children from kindergarten through fifth grade. The second goal was to provide educators with insight into how an extensive array of environmental factors influenced children's specific social skills developmental trajectories and explained changes in gaps over time.

THE IMPORTANCE OF STUDENTS' SOCIAL SKILLS

When children enter the school system, they are expected to have certain skills and experiences that enable them to negotiate the academic and social task demands of the school environment (Lane, Givner, & Pierson, 2004). However, transitioning from the family environment to the school system is not easy for most children, particularly those who come from disadvantaged backgrounds. According to a study by Rimm-Kaufman, Pianta, and Cox (2000), up to 46% of kindergarten teachers reported that at least half of the students in their class entered with problems related to an unsuccessful transition into school. Teachers identified poor social skills, trouble following directions, and difficulty with independent and group work as factors contributing to this poor transition. Existing research has demonstrated that children who lacked social skills were often rejected by peers, had trouble interacting with teachers and families, suffered emotional difficulties, and had greater tendency to externalize and internalize social and emotional problems (Warnes, Sheridan, Geske, &Warnes, 2005).

In addition to home-school transition and school adjustment, an extensive body of literature links students' social skills with school academic achievement (Claessens, Duncan, & Engel, 2006; Duncan et al., 2007; Foulks & Morrow, 1989; Horn, Atkins-Burnett, Karlin, Ramey, & Snyder, 2007; McClelland, Acock, & Morrison, 2006; McClelland, Morrison, & Holmes, 2000; McWayne, Fantuzzo, & McDermott, 2004;

Michelson, Sugai, Wood, & Kazdin, 1983). For example, research conducted in the early 1970s demonstrated a significant relationship between social skills, teacher and student interaction, and academic achievement (Michelson et al., 1983). Children who demonstrated lower social skills in elementary school were more likely to demonstrate academic underachievement in middle school and to experience deviant peer relationships with peers in adolescence, and were also less likely to be employed after leaving school (Horn et al., 2007). Students' deficits in social skills likely result not only in lower academic competence, poor adjustment to the school environment, and social/educational problems in the short term, but social skill deficits are also related to future adjustment problems in academic competence, social competence, and future employment in the long term.

Teaching essential social skills for diverse groups of students would also contribute to enhancing social equity. Beyond contributing to academic success in schools, investment in social skills development for all students may pay off for the future civic engagement and social justice. Amy Gutman (1987) proposed the "democratic threshold principle" that inequalities in the distribution of educational goods can be justified only if they do not limit the ability of every individual to participate effectively in the democratic process. Martha Nassbaum (2006) also developed an argument for basic human capabilities that include social skills such as affiliation and control over one's environment. While there are many different pathways to the development of social skills and traits for civic engagement, schooling experiences can play a crucial role in the process (Verba, Schlozman, & Brady, 1995).

Furthermore, parents and teachers often overlook deficits in young children's social skill development until the child requires major interventions to counteract current problems (Horn et al., 2007). In other words, early signs of students' social skills deficits are being missed entirely. Since research demonstrates that children's social problems become resistant to change over time (Horn et al., 2007), the more researchers know about factors influencing the development of social skills in younger children, the more information we will have on early detection and intervention addressing children's social skills deficits.

RESEARCH FRAMEWORK AND QUESTIONS

Although most researchers recognize the importance of students' early social behavior in relation to school adaptation and achievement, little research has been done to construct a theory of a child's social skills development over time. Previous studies have examined a variety of aspects of social behavior, including self-control, prosocial behavior, aggression, antisocial behavior, attention, behavioral persistence, externalizing problems, and internalizing problems (Bloom, 1964; Chan, Ramey, Ramey, & Schmitt, 2000; Hoglund & Leadbeater, 2004; Howes, 1990; Ladd & Price, 1987; La Paro & Pianta, 2000; McWayne et al., 2004; Miles & Stipek, 2006; Murphy, Eisenberg, & Fabes, 1999; Zhou, Hofer, & Eisenberg, 2007). Findings from these studies have led researchers to recommend further examination of the relationship between particular aspects of students' social skills and academic success (Bain & Agostin,1997; Lane et al., 2004; Lane, Wehby, & Colley, 2006). Previous research has demonstrated that the racial and SES achievement gap emerges prior to school entry and persists or even widens during school years (McClelland et al., 2000). However, little research has examined how racial and socioeconomic gaps in social skills change over time or how schools and parents influence students' social skills development, and the data used in existing studies investigating these gaps rarely covers more than a 3-year time frame (Hoglund & Leadbeater, 2004; La Paro & Pianta, 2002; McClelland et al., 2000).

In light of these concerns, the present study examined kindergarten children's developmental trajectory of social skills and the factors that influence social skills development. The present study differentiated two specific types of social skills: work-related social skills (WRS) and interpersonal skills (INS) and identified the associations between environmental factors and the development of these two specified social skills over an extended period of time and across diverse groups of students. The study used longitudinal data from the nationally representative Early Childhood Longitudinal Study (ECLS-K), and spanned over 6 years. This allowed for the examination of both overall trends and individual differences in the developmental trajectories of two specific sets of social skills. The aim of this study is to provide a complete picture of how social skills develop intraindividually and interindividually across different racial and SES groups in an ecological framework.

WRS refers to a set of skills that are important for children to achieve academically. WRS not only stem from children's executive function skills, such as attention, memory, and inhibitory control, but also reflect the behavioral and social manifestation of these skills, such as listening and following directions, participating appropriately in groups, staying on task, self-control, cooperation with others, and organizing work materials (Bronson, 1994, 1996; Cooper & Farran, 1988, 1991; McClelland et al., 2006). In addition, WRS include the ability of children to self-regulate their behavior as well as their ability to work responsibly, independently, and cooperatively (McClelland et al., 2006). INS include students' ability to interact positively with peers, to share, and to respect other children

(McClelland et al., 2006). Research has consistently demonstrated that students who have higher WRS at an early age appear to demonstrate longer attention spans, greater persistence and self-control, and greater engagement with learning tasks than students who have lower WRS (Claessens et al., 2006; Duncan et al., 2007; McClelland et al., 2000; McClelland et al., 2006; McWayne et al., 2004). Compared to studies on WRS, there are fewer studies examining the impact of INS on academic success. Findings on the relationship between INS and academic success have been mixed (Ladd & Price, 1987; Foulks & Morrow, 1989; Pettit, Bates, & Dodge, 1997; McWayne et al., 2004). Since INS does not consistently predict young children's academic success in either early or the late elementary grades, it is necessary to distinguish WRS and INS from general aspects of social behaviors so that researchers can provide more specific implications for educators and parents regarding the utility of two specific sets of social skills.

Students develop social skills in multilayered and multifaceted educational settings. Bronfenbrenner's bioecological theory emphasized the complexity of interaction between the individual and the environment and provides a framework for understanding how environmental factors impact a child's social skills development. The bioecological framework can be used to understand how family, classroom, teacher-child interaction, and current level of social skills influenced the development of children's social skills. Since young children spend most of their time at home and in school, home and school locations may be regarded as the structures of the microsystem(s) that encompass the relationships and interactions a child has had with her/his immediate surroundings (Berk, 2000; Bronfenbrenner, 1993). To account for the importance of the interactions between the individual and environment, this study concentrated on the microsystems' support and connections between family and school that directly or indirectly affected children's social skills development. The present examination of social skills developmental trajectory took into account the influence of students' prior social skills scores, socioeconomic status, ethnicity, parental involvement, parent-child interaction, class size, and class behavior and was based on input from multiple sources of information and data including teacher and parent interviews, school records, school administrator interviews, and student self-reports. The key research questions were as follows:

1. How do students' social skills trajectories differ across racial and SES groups over the course of early elementary education?
2. Which factors, parenting or school factors, account for variations in students' social skills development and how do parenting and

school factors contribute to narrowing the gaps among different racial and SES groups?

METHODS

Data Source and Sample

This study utilized data from the Early Childhood Longitudinal Study-Kindergarten class of 1998-1999 (ECLS-K). The ECLS-K study focused on children's early public or private school experiences beginning in kindergarten and following the children through eighth grade. This nationally representative sample dataset was developed by the National Center for Education Statistics (NCES, 2002). One of the primary goals of the ECLS-K was to provide a better understanding of how children's early experiences influence their transition into kindergarten and their progression through the early elementary school years. A total of 21,260 kindergartners throughout the nation participated.

The target sample for this study was derived from ECLS-K K-fifth grade public-use dataset. This dataset is a longitudinal study that follows the same nationally representative cohort of children from base year (kindergarten, fall 1998 and spring 1999), through first grade (spring 2000), third grade (spring 2002), and fifth grade (spring 2004). This enables researchers to study how a wide range of family, school, community, and individual factors are associated with children's performance and provides longitudinal information on the growth and development of children's social skills and cognitive competency across different grades.

To track typical students' growth trajectories, this study included only those students who (a) did not repeat kindergarten in fall 1998; (b) were assessed in the fall of kindergarten on social skills thus providing the baseline social skills scores; and (c) stayed in the same school over the course of data collection. As shown in Table 8.1, the total sample consists of 5,181 students from 725 schools. Male students accounted for half of the sample. 68% were White, 11% were African American, 17% were Hispanic, and the reminders were Asian/Pacific Islanders (3%) and American Indian or Alaska Native (2%).

Measures

Dependent Variables: WRS and INS From Teacher Report Rating

The ECLS-K used the Social Rating Scale (SRS) to assess children's social skills. The SRS asked teachers how often a student exhibited certain social skills and behavior in the classroom. Three SRS subscales captured positive aspects of children's social skills development: approach to learning, self-control, and interpersonal skills. The items were rated on a scale of 1 to 4 (1 = *never*, 2 = *sometimes*, 3 = *often*, and 4 = *very often*). A higher rating on the SRS indicated a higher level of social adjustment. Due to the copyright of the SRS, specific individual item scores were not available for public users. Scores on the WRS were computed by averaging two subscales: approach to learning and self-control. The approach to learning scale measures behaviors that affect the ease with which children can benefit from the learning environment. The self-control scale is indicative of the child's ability to control behavior by respecting the property rights of others, controlling temper, accepting peer ideas for group activities, and responding appropriately to pressure from peers. The INS scale captured behaviors such as interacting positively with peers, sharing, and respecting other children (McClelland et al., 2006). This study used teacher reports from the SRS interpersonal subscale, which included five items related to (1) forming and maintaining friendships, (2) getting along with people who are different, (3) comforting or helping other children, (4) expressing feelings, ideas, and opinions in positive ways, and (5) showing sensitivity to the feelings of others. The internal consistency reliability of WRS and INS were acceptable with alpha coefficients ranged from .79 to .89 from fall K through fifth grade (NCES, 2002).

Independent Variables

It is important to note that ECLS-K is a multisource and multimethod study. The data was collected from children, their parents, teachers, and schools using a variety of formats, including computer-assisted telephone interviews for parents, one-on-one assessment for the children, self-administered paper/pencil questionnaires for teachers, school administrators or their designees, and the collection of student records from schools. Therefore, definitions for the independent variables used in this study were derived these various sources, and are described below. All categorical variables were defined dichotomously.

Demographic Variables

1. *Race/Ethnicity.* Race/ethnicity information was derived from the composite race variable collected during parent interviews, including White, Black or African American, Hispanic, Asian/Pacific Islander, and American Indian/Alaska Native. Race/ethnicity was dummy-coded in the analysis with White students serving as the reference group.

2. *Socioeconomic Status (SES).* ECLS-K calculated the composite variable of socioeconomic status (SES) by using the data for the set of parents who completed the parent interview. The SES variable reflected the SES of the household at the time of data collection. The components used to create the SES variable were as follows: father/male guardian's education, mother/female guardian's education, father/male guardian's occupation, mother/female guardian's occupation, and household income (NCES, 2002). Continuous average SES measures collected from fall K through fifth grade were used.

3. *Other Demographic Variables.* This study takes into account other demographic variables, including gender, disability status, day care and preschool participation, siblings, and primary language at home, that may be important when evaluating children's social skills development.

Time

Elapsed time was calculated as the number of days between the assessment date of the different data collection rounds and the children's date of birth and then converted into months by dividing the total number of days by 30. The time information was available from kindergarten through fifth grade.

Parenting Variables (5 Variables)

To examine the effects of parenting on social skills development, this study included five composite variables, with a moderate internal reliability ranging from .64 to .78, as follows:

1. *Parental involvement (PI) at home.* Example items of PI at home included how often the parents read books, told stories, and played games or did puzzles with the child.

2. *Parental involvement (PI) in school.* Six items were used to measure PI in school, such as the frequency of parent(s) attendance at an open house or back-to-school night, attendance at a meeting of a parent-teacher organization, and attendance at a parent advisory group meeting.

3. *Parent-Child interaction.* ECLS-K used a 13-item scale that measured the expression of warmth a parent exhibited during the parent interview. Example items included parents' responses to the following statements: "My child and I often have warm, close times together," "Most of the time I feel that my child likes me and wants

to be near me," and "I am usually too busy to joke and play around with my child." Negative statements were coded reversely.

4. *Parent discipline.* Parent inductive discipline was measured according to parents' responses to the question: "If your child got so angry that she/he hit you, what would you do?" Possible choices included whether or not the parent would "spank child," "take child's time out," "hit child back," "discuss what child did wrong," "ignore it," "make child do chores," "make fun of child," "make child apologize," "take away a privilege," "give a warning," or "yell at child." The discipline variable was dichotomously coded with strict discipline as the reference group.

5. *Parent belief of school readiness.* Two composite variables were created to examine the level of parents' belief about children's academic and social readiness respectively. Parents responded to questions about the importance of their children counting to 20, knowing letters, knowing how to use a pencil and paint brush, how to share, how to sit still and pay attention, and how to communicate his/her needs and thoughts well.

School Variables (6 Variables)

In order to evaluate the impact of school factors on students' social skill development, this study examined six school variables, with an acceptable internal reliability ranging from .51 to .84, as follows:

1. *Class size.* Class size was dichotomously coded with the large class size ($N > 21$) as the reference group.

2. *Classroom equipment.* The composite variable of classroom equipment score was computed by averaging eighteen items to indicate whether classrooms had adequate textbooks, trade books, workbooks/practice sheets, and video tapes/films.

3. *Class group behavior.* On a scale of 1-5, with 1 equals "*class group misbehaves very frequently*" and 5 equals "*group behaves exceptionally well,*" a composite measure of class group behavior was computed from kindergarten through fifth grade with a high score indicating better class group behavior.

4. *Teacher-child interaction.* Since teacher beliefs about child development are significantly predictive of teacher's practices and teachers who hold stronger beliefs about children's developmental readiness are more likely to engage in developmentally appropriate practices in their classrooms (Winsler & Carlton, 2003), teacher-child interaction were measured by averaging relevant items.

5. *School type*. School type was recoded into three dummy variables: catholic (=1), public (=2), and other type (=3) with public school as the reference group.

6. *School location*. School location was recoded into three dummy variables: urban (= 1), suburban (= 2) and rural (= 3) with urban school as the reference group.

Analytical Models

Several basic analyses were conducted initially including descriptive statistical analysis and mean score comparisons across racial groups in terms of the parenting variables, school variables, and social skills scores. Since the ECLS-K is not a simple random sample, researchers must take extra steps to address oversampling and use cluster sampling when making inferences about the population to ensure that estimates reflect accurate standard errors (Hahs-Vaughn & Onwuegbuzie, 2006). This study applied AM, a statistical software package for analyzing data from complex samples with ECLS-K panel weight, strata, and cluster information.

The ECLS-K sample has a hierarchical data structure where the children were nested in classrooms and schools. Children nested in hierarchies tend to be more similar to each other because of the common availability of resources, SES, family background, and race or ethnicity than people randomly sampled from the entire population (Raudenbush & Bryk, 2002). From this perspective, observations based on these nested children are not fully independent, which violates the basic assumption of ordinary least squares regression. To address this problem, hierarchical linear models (HLM) were used, where each level of the hierarchical structure is formally represented by its own submodel. These submodels express relationships among variables within a given level, and specify how variables at one level influence relations occurring at another (Raudenbush & Bryk, 2002).

Preliminary analyses based on AM indicated that there were two different growth slopes within students' social skills developmental trajectory from kindergarten through the fifth grade: students' social skills increased from fall to spring in kindergarten, but seemed to decrease from first grade through fifth grade. To compare growth rates during these two different periods (kindergarten and first through fifth grade), this study used HLM three-level piecewise linear growth models (Raudenbush & Bryk, 2002).

To answer the research questions, a sequence of growth models were estimated for "work-related skills" (WRS, Model a) and for "interpersonal social skills" (INS, Model b) as separate outcomes. First, Model 1 (base model) included two elapsed time variables as the only predictors at Level 1 to examine social skills development patterns across the whole sample. The time span of the developmental trajectories examined in this study was 6 years. The time of the initial assessment was set as zero and the elapsed time was separated into two time periods: kindergarten and Grades 1-5. The variations in growth parameters during and after kindergarten were captured in the Level 2 and Level 3 model and the average growth slopes in the two time periods were specified as randomly varying across schools.

Second, Model 2 (race/SES effects model) added students' race/ethnicity and SES variables as predictors at Level 2 to see how the social skills trajectories differed among different racial and SES groups. In this model, both ethnicity and SES coefficients were "fixed" at Level 3 with the assumption that race and SES effects were constant among schools. In order to examine the demographic composition effect, school-level aggregate variables of race/ethnicity and SES were added at Level 3.

Third, Model 3 (child/parenting effects model) added child and parenting variables as Level 2 predictors to estimate the extent to which racial and SES gaps in WRS and INS development could be explained by child characteristics and parenting variables. In Model 3, student race, family SES, and gender were regarded as time-invariant predictors while other demographic and parenting variables were regarded as time-varying predictors (Singer & Willett, 2003). All of the variables were grand mean centered and all the Level 2 slopes were fixed at Level 3.

Fourth, Model 4 (school effects model) added a series of school variables at Level 3 in order to estimate the extent to which the racial and SES gap in WRS and INS development could be explained by school characteristics. It is possible for children to change classroom and teachers over time, therefore, all of the school characteristics were time-varying predictors.

Last, Model 5 (final model) contained factors that were significantly predictive of social skills and allowed comparison of the relative contributions of family and school contexts on narrowing the racial and SES gap of WRS and INS development over time.

RESULTS

Descriptive Analysis

As shown in Table 8.1, a large number of children (76%) had preschool experience, attending either Head Start or a day care center. A majority

Table 8.1. Child, Parenting, and School Characteristics of Sample by Racial Groups and by Total

	White N = 3,450 Weighed N = 632,591 (68.3%)	Black N = 499 Weighed N = 96,966 (10.5%)	Hispanic N = 807 Weighed N = 153,497 (16.6%)	Asian/Pacific N = 335 Weighed N = 26,920 (2.9%)	Indian/Alaska N = 90 Weighed N = 15,637 (1.7%)	Total N = 5,181 Weighted N = 925,611
Child Level						
Male	50.2%	54.3%	49.2%	46.2%	50.1%	50.3%
Disability (yes)	38.6%	36.7%	33.2%	24.8%	46.7%	37.3%
Preschool (yes)	78.4%	83.2%	61.5%	62.6%	77.1%	75.6%
SES	.22	−.35***	−.30***	.18***	−.21***	.06
	(.70)	(.61)	(.66)	(.73)	(.61)	(.72)
Siblings (yes)	89.8%	84.2%	91.2%	88.4%	91.1%	89.4%
Parent involvement at home	3.58	3.61***	3.36***	3.57	3.50***	3.54
	(.99)	(1.10)	(1.05)	(1.01)	(1.05)	(1.01)
Parent involvement at school	.73	.58***	.63***	.65***	.61***	.69
	(.18)	(.22)	(.20)	(.20)	(.17)	(.20)
Parent-child interaction	3.54	3.49***	3.49***	3.44***	3.53**	3.53
	(.29)	(.36)	(.36)	(.41)	(.34)	(.31)
School Level						
Small class size	47.7%	47.1%	56%	39%	65%	49.1%
Class group behavior	3.59	3.29***	3.55***	3.66***	3.32***	3.55
	(.49)	(.49)	(.49)	(.46)	(.48)	(.50)
Catholic	18.8%	6%	13.1%	14.6%	7.8%	16.2%
Other private	10.8%	4.2%	4.8%	5.1%	0	8.7%

Note: This table only lists the variables used in the final models. Other variables, such as parent belief of student readiness, inductive discipline, classroom equipment, teacher-child interaction, and location were not significantly related to social skills. Percentage by each racial group presented the percent of student within each racial group; percentage by total presented the percent of student in the whole sample. Mean and SD (in the parenthesis) were calculated for numerical variables. All the means were compared to White by using post hoc LSD, $*p < .05$, $**p < .01$, $***p < .001$.

202

of children (89%) had one or more siblings at home. Less than half of the students (49%) attended kindergarten where class size was less than 21. Around 16% of them attended Catholic schools and 9% attended other private schools.

In order to characterize all independent variables that would be used for later HLM models, mean score comparisons were conducted first by using the White students as the reference group. Minority groups had significantly lower SES than White students. White parents had significantly higher PI at school, more frequent parent-child interactions, and were more likely to believe their child was ready for school than the racial-minority parents. In terms of the school level variables, White and Asian/Pacific Islander children were more likely to have adequate classroom equipment and have more class materials to use compared to other racial-minority students. Asian/Pacific Islander children were most likely and Black students were least likely to attend class with good group classroom behavior.

Initial analyses indicated that the relationship between overall WRS, INS, and time did not follow a consistent linear growth pattern. As mentioned earlier, the social skills items were rated on a scale of 1 to 4 (1 = *never*, 2 = *sometimes*, 3 = *often*, and 4 = *very often*). A higher rating on the social skills scale indicated a higher level of WRS and INS. Table 8.2 lists means and standard deviations of WRS and INS for the whole sample and by race/ethnicity. Compared to the growth pattern for WRS and INS, which decreased from first through fifth grade, the growth pattern for WRS and INS increased from the fall of kindergarten through spring of kindergarten, with effect sizes ranging from .16 to .22.

Figure 8.1 and 8.2 show comparisons of WRS and INS scores among five racial groups. Overall, White and Asian/Pacific Islanders students exhibited the highest number of WRS and INS. The Hispanic and American Indian/Alaska Native subgroups exhibited INS in class less often than White or Asian students, and Black students exhibited the fewest number of WRS or INS in class than all other groups. Racial gaps in the growth rate of WRS and INS are discussed in greater detail in the next section.

HLM Analyses of Social Skills Development

Average Initial Scores and Growth Rate

As shown in Table 8.3, Model 1 (base model) provided preliminary information on the growth of social skills. This model also provided baseline statistics for evaluating subsequent Level 2 and Level 3 models, information on the mean initial scores, and statistics on the mean trajectory growth rate during kindergarten and during Grades 1 to 5.

**Table 8.2.   Mean and *SD* of WRS and INS
for Total Sample and Racial Subgroups**

Outcome	White	Black	Hispanic	Asian/ Pacific	Indian/ Alaska	Total	Gains (Effect size)
WRS Fall K	3.18	2.94	3.04	3.15	3.03	3.13	
	(.55)	(.60)	(.55)	(.54)	(.59)	(.56)	
WRS Spring K	3.29	3.02	3.15	3.29	3.28	3.24	.16
	(.55)	(.64)	(.57)	(.55)	(.63)	(.57)	
WRS Grade 1	3.21	2.91	3.12	3.26	3.06	3.17	.10
	(.56)	(.63)	(.59)	(.58)	(.58)	(.58)	
WRS Grade 3	3.20	2.91	3.14	3.34	3.19	3.17	.00
	(.55)	(.63)	(.58)	(.55)	(.64)	(.57)	
WRS Grade 5	3.20	2.931	3.16	3.38	3.05	3.17	.01
	(.56)	(.61)	(.58)	(.54)	(.54)	(.58)	
INS Fall K	3.10	2.93	2.95	3.02	2.95	3.06	
	(.61)	(.62)	(.58)	(.61)	(.58)	(.61)	
INS Spring K	3.25	3.08	3.16	3.21	3.11	3.22	.22
	(.60)	(.63)	(.61)	(.65)	(.59)	(.61)	
INS Grade 1	3.19	2.95	3.12	3.19	2.94	3.16	.09
	(.62)	(.65)	(.65)	(.62)	(.69)	(.63)	
INS Grade 3	3.15	2.87	3.15	3.22	3.08	3.13	.04
	(.62)	(.69)	(.64)	(.59)	(.75)	(.64)	
INS Grade 5	3.14	2.87	3.14	3.26	3.01	3.12	.01
	(.62)	(.65)	(.62)	(.61)	(.56)	(.63)	

Note: Analyses were based on AM software. Mean values were calculated on a 1-4 scale. 1 = *never*, 2 = *sometimes*, 3 = *often*, 4 = *very often*. *SD* is in the parentheses. Effect size is calculated using Cohen's *d*: mean gain score divided by the pooled standard deviation.

Students often exhibit WRS and INS in the classroom while enrolled in the fall kindergarten, as indicated by two average initial scores of 3.13 for WRS and 3.08 for INS (see Table 8.3). In terms of average growth rates, children gained an average of .011 (for WNS) and .02 (for INS) points per month during kindergarten but then lost .0007 (for WNS) and .002 (for INS) points per month during Grades 1 to 5. This suggests that children's social skills, as rated by teachers, changed little between Grades 1 and 5.

Students had significantly different average initial status and average growth rates within and between schools. Thirty-seven percent of the total variance in initial INS occurred between schools, whereas 29% of the variances in initial WRS occurred between schools. Both family and school accounted for small and similar variance in social skills growth during the two time periods; however, school variables accounted for more of the

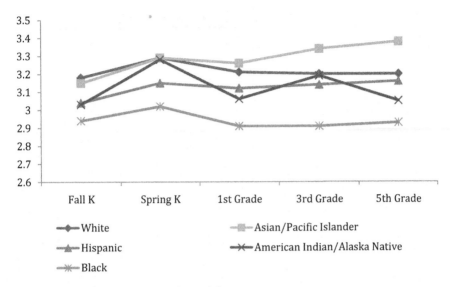

Figure 8.1.   WRS comparison by racial groups.

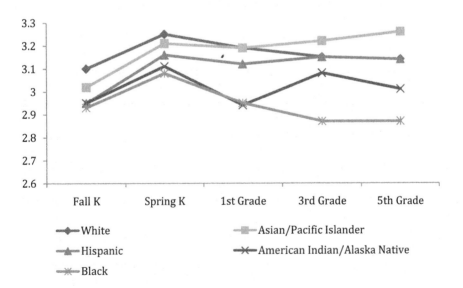

Figure 8.2.   INS comparison by racial groups.

Table 8.3.   Three-Level HLM Fixed and Random Effects of Base Model

	WRS (Model 1a)	INS (Model 1b)
Fixed Effects		
Initial Status	3.127*** (.014)	3.079***(.016)
Growth during K	.011*** (.002)	.020*** (.002)
Growth during Grades 1-5	-.0007** (.0002)	-.0017***(.0003)
Random Effects		
Within School Variance		
Initial Status	.169 ***	.152***
Growth during K	.0001	.00008
Growth during Grades 1-5	.00002***	.00002***
Between School Variance		
Initial Status	.07***	.09***
Growth during K	.0006***	.0008***
Growth during Grades 1-5	.00002***	.00003***
ICC	.29	.37

Note: The table lists coefficients and standard errors (in parenthesis) for fixed effect. ICC is intraclass correlation coefficient, which equals Level 3 variance divided by total variance. *$p < .05$. **$p < .01$. ***$p < .001$.

variance in social skills growth during kindergarten than demographic and parenting variables.

Racial and SES Gap

Black students had both significantly lower initial WRS and INS and Hispanic students had a significantly lower initial INS score than White students at the beginning of kindergarten after accounting for the effect of SES (Table 8.4, Model 2). However, the actual differences in initial scores between racial gaps were small, with the effect sizes ranging from .227 to .292 in the Black-White gap for both WRS and INS and .177 in the Hispanic-White gap for INS, respectively. The findings indicated that Black and Hispanic students, on average, exhibited WRS and INS almost as often in class although they performed less well than White students. Significant racial and SES gaps between schools were not found except for the small negative effect of enrollment of Asian/Pacific Islander students on initial WRS and INS.

Figure 8.1 and 8.2 indicated that, except for Asian/Pacific Islander students, other minority groups stay in almost the same order from kindergarten through fifth grade. As shown in Table 8.4, Model 2a and 2b,

Asian/Pacific Islander students demonstrated significantly faster growth from first grade through fifth grade than other racial groups although the effect sizes were very small (effect size =.004 and .005). By the fifth grade, Asian/Pacific Islander students had the highest and White students had the second highest WRS and INS scores.

Model 2a (race/SES effects model in WRS) also indicated that there were small positive relationships between SES and initial WRS during kindergarten, suggesting that one standard deviation increase in SES was associated with a .133 standard deviation increase in initial WRS score. Similarly, one standard deviation increase in SES was associated with a .006 standard deviation increase in the WRS growth rate after controlling for race/ethnicity. Model 2b (race/SES effects model in INS) indicated that one standard deviation increase in SES was associated with a .130 standard deviation increase in initial INS after controlling for race/ethnicity. The variance of initial WRS in Model 2a decreased from .169 to .165, indicating that 2.4% variance in initial WRS was attributable to students' ethnicity and SES. Similarly, students' ethnicity and SES explained 2.6% of the variance in initial INS.

The Impacts of Parenting and School

Models 3 and 4 estimated the extent to which child, parenting, and school characteristics explained racial and SES gaps in students' development in WRS and IRS over time. The relative contribution of the child, parenting, and school context to the development/growth of WRS and INS are summarized in Table 8.4.

Children who were male and had a disability performed less well on initial WRS and INS compared to female students and children without an identified disability. Children who had sibling(s) had higher initial scores on both outcomes. In terms of the parenting variables, students who had higher PI at school and greater parent-child interaction performed better on both WRS and INS than students with lower PI at school and lower parent-child interaction. While child and parenting variables had small yet significant effects on students' initial WRS and INS, these variables almost had no effects on WRS and INS growth rate during kindergarten. Except for the enrollment of Asian/Pacific Islander students, other school level variables had no significant influences on either WRS or INS growth over time, suggesting that the social skills growth rate was similar between different schools.

A summary of regression coefficients of ethnicity and SES on WRS and INS among four models is presented in Table 8.5. This table compares how the effects of race and SES change after adding child, parenting, and school variables in four models so that we can determine which specific variables accounted for the racial and SES gaps in social skills. As shown

Table 8.4.   Effect Sizes of Significant Findings in Model 2 (Race/SES Effects Model) and Model 5 (Final Model)

	WRS (Model 2a)	WRS (Model 5a)	INS (Model 2b)	INS (Model 5b)
Initial Status				
Intercept $\beta 00$				
Black	-.227*		-.292*	-.230*
Hispanic			-.177*	-.160*
SES	.133***	.079**	.130***	.067**
Male		-.330***		-.309***
Disability		-.361***		-.268***
Preschool experience		-.070**		-.082**
Sibling		.131***		.129**
Parental involvement at home		-.030*		-.027*
Parental involvement at school		.148***		.151***
Parent-child interaction		.062***		.078***
School-other type		-.292**		-.370***
School-%Asian/Pacific	-.078**	-.088*	-.067*	-.088*
School-class size		-.123*		
School-class group behavior		.070*		
Growth during K				
SES	.006*	.008*		
School-Asian/Pacific		.008*	.010*	.010*
Growth during Grades 1-5				
Asian/Pacific	.004**	.004*	.005**	.004*
Male		-.003***		-.003***
Disability		.002**		
Primary language		-.004***		-.004***
School-other type				-.001*

Note: The table lists effect sizes which were calculated by using standardized regression coefficients. *$p < .05$. **$p < .01$. ***$p < .001$. Only significant findings were shown in the table. Black and Hispanic gaps in WRS and SES gap in INS disappeared in the model 5 (final model) after adding parenting and school level variables. Public school was the reference group for school type comparison.

in the comparison between Model 2 (race/SES effects model) and Model 3 (child/parenting effects model), three racial gaps narrowed: Black-White gap in initial WRS, Black-White gap in initial INS, and Hispanic-White gap in initial INS. The reduction of racial gaps is indicative that these newly added child and parenting variables, particularly parental involvement at school and parent-child interaction, accounted for the racial gap in initial scores. The comparison of racial and SES gaps between Model 4

Table 8.5.   Comparisons Between Racial and SES Gaps Within Schools

	WRS				INS			
	Model 2a	Model 3a	Model 4a	Model 5a	Model 2b	Model 3b	Model 4b	Model 5b
Initial Status								
Black	-.227*	-.129	-.228*	-.149	-.292*	-.202	-.29*	-.23*
Hispanic					-.177*	-.138	-.175*	-.16*
SES	.133***	.076**	.133***	.079**	.130***	.072**	.130***	.067**
Growth during K								
SES	.006*	.007**	.007*	.008*				
Growth during Grades 1-5								
Asian/ Pacific	.004**	.004*	.005**	.004**	.005*		.004*	.004*

Note: The table lists effect sizes which were calculated by using standardized regression coefficient and directions of coefficients. "-" means HLM coefficient is negative. *$p < .05$, **$p < .01$, ***$p < .001$. Blank means there is no significant gap.

(school effects model) and Model 2 (race/SES effects model) indicated that school factors, such as class equipment, location, and teacher-child interaction, did not contribute to narrowing the racial and SES gaps in initial social skills scores between White students and other students. None of the child, parenting, and school variables were attributable to the variance in WRS and INS growth rate.

DISCUSSION AND IMPLICATIONS

Racial and Socioeconomic Gaps in Social Skills

Consistent with other research on the development of children's social competence (Hoglund & Leadbeater, 2004; McClelland & Morrison, 2003; Zhou, 2007), this study revealed that WRS and INS emerged before children entered kindergarten, and that their developmental trajectories were relatively stable over 6 years. However, it also found racial and SES gaps in students' social skills developmental trajectories. White, Asian/ Pacific Islander students, and students from higher socioeconomic backgrounds entered kindergarten with higher average social skills scores than Black, Hispanic, and low-income students. Black students, on average, scored significantly lower on WRS and INS compared to White students, and Hispanic students had significantly lower INS scores than White students at the beginning of kindergarten. These Black-White and Hispanic-White gaps in social skills persisted throughout the K-5 period. Consistent with previous studies (Chan et al., 2000; Connell & Prinz, 2002; McClelland et al., 2000; Mistry, Biesanz, & Chien, 2008), students' SES was significantly positively related to WRS, with higher income students showing more growth in WRS than lower income students.

The patterns of racial group differences in intraindividual change indicated that the ranking of social skills for each racial group stayed in almost the same order from kindergarten to the fifth grade compared to other groups. Black students exhibited the least development in social skills over time, whereas the White group and Asian/Pacific Islanders were consistently top ranked. These differences in social skills development may be related to how different cultural and racial groups are socialized, and to mismatches between students' home and school cultures. Cartledge (2001) estimated that more than 40% of our public school student population will be from racially, culturally, and linguistically diverse backgrounds by the year 2050. On the other hand, a majority of teachers are and will continue to be White, upper-middle class females (Woolfolk, 2011). Students who come from different cultural and racial groups may not have been explicitly taught the rules of the dominant (i.e., teacher) culture or socialized to recognize cultural differences in expected behavior. Teachers might mislabel a student who failed to connect to the mainstream culture as having a behavior problem or poor social skills. Since language plays an important role in influencing teachers' social skills rating (Cartledge, 2001; Chan et. al, 2000), language barriers might prevent minorities from understanding teacher's directions and communicating effectively with teachers. Teachers' race and personal biases may also negatively impact social skills ratings. Cartledge (2001) found that Black teachers' social skills ratings were not influenced by race, whereas White female teachers rated Black students considerably lower than White students, and gave Black boys particularly low ratings. Cultural misunderstandings, language barriers, and other personal biases and expectations, which potentially disrupt an informant's perception of children's social skills (Michelson et al., 1983), are plausible explanations for why Black students received significantly lower initial WRS and INS scores and why different racial groups behave differently in terms of social skills. A deeper explanation of this can be found in the theory of epistemological racism, which explains how educational research and practice can be racially biased (Scheurich & Young, 1997). Epistemological racism suggests that the social history and culture of the dominant race has profoundly negative consequences for those of other racial cultures with different epistemologies. As one of possible negative consequences, teachers may implicitly favor White students and thus some children of color appear not to perform or relate as well in school.

Despite these differences among racial groups, it is worth noting that Black and Hispanic students, on average, exhibited WRS and INS in class almost as often as White students although they performed less well. Given the absence of common national standards or developmental benchmarks for social skills, it is unclear whether Black and Hispanic students have the level of social skills needed to successfully participate in school.

Implications for Policy and Practice

This study has several implications for how educational policy can improve academic performance and social equity. First of all, since child, parenting, and school characteristics all accounted for some of the variance in early social skills development across racial and SES groups, nurturing children's social readiness at an early age and enhancing their early social skills at home and in school is very important (Hogland & Leadbeater, 2004).

Second, this study provides evidence for the types of interactions and PI at school that are most suitable for improving the social skills of different racial groups. Parent(s) interaction with children, such as reading and taking children to multicultural events helps children integrate in classrooms and society. Roopnarine, Krishnakumar, Metindogan, and Evans (2006) showed that parent-child interaction have been identified as critical in determining children's cognitive and social development in diverse ethnic and cultural groups. However, there are disagreements about how different parent-child interaction influence cognitive and social development in different racial groups (Roopnarine et al., 2006). This study confirmed Connell's findings (2002) that parent-child interactions characterized as warm, structured, and emotionally responsive were positively related to children's social skills. These types of interactions even narrowed the African American-White gap on initial WRS scores. These findings suggest that promoting parent-child interactions that are warm and emotionally responsive, such as having warm and close time with a child together and establishing close relationship with a child are important for narrowing racial gaps in social skills. This suggests that national, state, and school policies that promote parental involvement should be continued and expanded.

The role of discipline on the development of WRS and INS is less clear (Connell, 2002). More research is necessary to understand how discipline influences WRS and INS development and how parents should balance warmth and discipline at home. Since not all types of parental involvement have positive influences on students' social skills development, it is important for parents to find an optimal level of involvement that warrants the investment of adequate time and resources for social interactions with their children but at the same time avoids authoritarian control over their child's behaviors.

Similar to the Black and Hispanic subgroups, cultural misunderstanding and language barriers also might contribute to Asian/Pacific Islander students' having lower initial fall kindergarten scores than their Whites peers. The example of Asian/Pacific Islander students, who were able to catch up with their White peers and demonstrated relatively faster social skills growth during Grades 1 to 5, points to the importance of environmental influences on social skills growth. Asian/Pacific Islanders were more likely to come from the families with higher SES and attend higher quality schools with better classroom equipment, better group classroom behavior, and better teacher-child interaction than other racial-minority students. Asian/Pacific Islander parents also reported higher parental involvement at home, more engagement in school activities, and rated their child higher on school readiness skills. Additionally, Asian/Pacific Islander students were less likely to display discipline problems, were somewhat less disruptive, and more likely to attend classes with better group behavior. The current study found that teachers tended to rate Asian/Pacific Islanders with the highest WRS and INS scores during Grades 1 to 5. From this perspective, school resource allocation, parental involvement, parent-child interaction, and teachers' perceptions played important roles in enhancing social skills' growth and narrowing the White-Asian/Pacific Islander gap. However, our study did not found statistically significant evidences of environmental effects on social skills' growth during or after kindergarten. There are several reasons for this mismatch. First, WRS and INS were evident in the years before children entered kindergarten, and the developmental trajectories were relatively stable over 6 years. Children who experienced higher initial WRS and INS scores had a slightly lower growth rate during kindergarten. As a result, there is little variance that explains social skills growth after kindergarten. Second, previous research also found that demographic variables, including gender, ethnicity, SES, child age, and child personal characteristics (e.g., self-esteem or assertiveness) accounted for more of the variance in social skills than environmental influences (Boyle, Jenkins, & Georgiades, 2004; Connell & Prinz, 2002; Ketsetzis, Ryan, & Adams, 1998). Third, it is possible that other important factors that could impact student social skills may be missing from this study. Previous studies found that other variables such as family relationship, parental marital status, parent depression, parenting stress, teacher instruction time in class, and teacher certification influenced children's social progress (Crosnoe & Cooper, 2010; Hoglund & Leadbeater, 2004). The model might be improved by adding variables that tap into diverse aspects of parenting and school attributes in the future.

The significant amount of variance between schools implies that some schools may provide environments that are conducive to social skills improvement. Indeed, recent federal mandates such as the No Child Left Behind Act of 2001 (PL 107-110) called for increased effort by educators to improve the social and behavioral climate in school (Luiselli et al., 2005). There have been different strategies to help children learn and improve social skills in the classroom and community, such as teaching social skills as part of daily instruction, integrating social skills into everyday classroom events, and applying purchased social skills curricula (Luiselli, McCarty, Coniglio, Ramirez, & Putnam, 2005; Williams & Reisberg, 2003). However, the effect of these types of interventions and direct social skills training in school on achieving racial and socioeconomic equity in social skills development remains to be examined in the future.

Limitations and Outstanding Issues

This study has some limitations that need to be noted, and can help direct future studies on students' social skills development. First, similar to other secondary analyses, this study used data that had been collected using a strong sampling method yet at the same time suffered from weak measurements. For example, since this study examined the effect of parenting on social skills among racial groups, some ECLS-K measures might not assess the same construct over time or address the same content across different racial groups. The ECLS-K parent interview questions might not adequately capture unique parenting styles and parent involvement activities among racial-minority families, resulting in a cultural bias against certain racial minority groups. The measurement of ECLS-K itself might not measure what it is meant to measure for different racial groups. Second, because of the paucity of prior empirical work, there was little guidance in the literature on the degree to which social skills reflect individual differences in the child or reflect characteristics of the family or sociocultural environment (McClelland et al., 2006). Thus, this study was exploratory in searching for multiple variables in different models and testing for effects. Third, there was a potential threat to the external validity in this study. The analytical sample chosen for longitudinal analysis was comprised of students who remained at the same schools over the K-5 period. The students who changed schools over time might have different developmental patterns from those who remained at the same schools. This limits the generalization of this study's results about social skills developmental trajectories and environmental influences.

Last but not least, the reliance of this study on a teacher-rated social skills scale for measuring outcomes has several limitations: teacher's rating scales measure current levels of functioning but do not assess etiology; rating scales cannot explain why social skills deficits occur; and rating scales do not dictate intervention strategies. Future study calls for gathering information on social skill functioning from multiple sources, settings, and through the use of diverse methods (Demaray, Ruffalo, & Carlson, 1995; Merrell, 2001).

Given these limitations, our study findings have to be interpreted carefully. Researchers and educators should avoid confirming stereotypes about racial groups or beliefs that "it's the parents fault." Although "school effects" were not significant for social skills development based on teacher rating measures, it may also reflect the current schooling practices that narrowly emphasize academic skills over other skills. Further study and discussion of how schools and teachers can and should work with parents and contribute to social skills development may contribute to broadening the education agenda. While the linkage between social skills and academic achievement remains tenuous and controversial, more investment in character education and social skills development can be an antidote against students' affective and behavioral problems that are often exacerbated by poverty and impoverished learning environments at school. Another point to consider is the implications of these findings for homogeneous schools that are becoming more diverse, both in terms of race and SES. In this case, it may be that attention to social skills development—in the schools—is important to improve social equity since teachers in these schools may be inadequately prepared to address the social skills of a diverse student population. Although our school location variable per se did not show significant differences across urban, suburban, or rural schools, subsequent research that examines social skills development across school settings may contribute to understanding how school settings interact with social skills development of diverse populations.

The finding that there is little development/growth in social skills between Grade 1 and Grade 5 does not necessarily suggest that social skills development/growth only takes place in kindergarten, and not in other grades. In this study, the nonlinear growth pattern based on the Social Rating Scale might indicate that teachers have different expectations at different grade levels. During kindergarten, teachers might perceive social skills growth because they could compare and rate children's growth over time to initial status measures, as suggested by the finding that WRS and INS positively increased between the fall and spring of kindergarten. However, while the same teacher rated students at two different points in time in kindergarten, different teachers rated students only once in Grades 1, 3, and 5. Moreover, the higher grade teachers might adjust their expectations for child behavior based on appropriate grade level behavior (Chan et al., 2000). As a result, these higher expectations of teachers in higher grades might create lower ratings than prior teachers for the same student. Additionally, the nonlinear growth pattern might reflect that schools over emphasize test scores after kindergarten and ignore the importance of social skills training under pressure from the NCLB act.

REFERENCE

Bain, S. K., & Agostin, T. M. (1997). Predicting early school success with developmental and social skills screeners. *Psychology in the Schools, 34*(3), 219-228.

Berk, L. E. (2000). *Child development* (5th ed., pp. 23-38). Boston, MA: Allyn & Bacon.

Bloom, B. (1964). *Stability and change in human characteristics*. New York, NY: Wiley.

Boyle, M. H., Jenkins, J. M., & Georgiades, K. (2004). Differential-maternal parenting behavior: Estimating within- and between-family effects on children. *Child Development, 75*(5), 1457-1476.

Bronfenbrenner, U. (1993). The ecology of cognitive development: Research models and fugitive findings. In R. Wonziak & K. Fischer (Eds.), *Development in context: Acting and thinking in specific environments* (pp. 3-44). Hillsdale, NJ: Erlbaum

Bronson, M. B. (1994). The usefulness of an observational measure of young children's social and mastery behaviors in early childhood classrooms. *Early Childhood Research Quarterly, 9*, 19-43.

Bronson, M. B. (1996). *Manual for the Bronson Social and Task Skill Profile (teacher version)*. Chestnut Hill, MA: Boston College.

Cartledge, G., & Loe, S. A. (2001). Cultural diversity and social skills instruction. *Exceptionality, 9*(1&2), 33-46.

Chan, D., Ramey, S., Ramey, C., & Schmitt, S. (2000). Modeling intra individual changes in children's social skills at home and at school: A multivariate latent growth approach to understanding between-settings differences in children's social skill development. *Multivariate Behavioral Research, 35*(3), 365-396.

Chiu, S. (2001). *Exploring kindergartner's social and cognitive competence: An application of ECLS-K* (Unpublished PhD dissertation). University of Maryland.

Claessens, A., Duncan, G. J., & Engel, M. (2006). Kindergarten skills and fifth grade achievement: Evidence from the ECLS-K. Retrieved November 11, 2008, from http://www.northwestern.edu/ipr/publications/papers/2004/duncan/kindergartenskills.pdf

Connell, C. M., & Prinz, R.J. (2002). The impact of childcare and parent-child interaction on school readiness and social skills development for low-income African American children. *Journal of School Psychology, 40*(2), 177-193.

Cooper, D. H., & Farran, D. C. (1988). Behavioral risk factors in Kindergarten. *Early Childhood Research Quarterly, 3,* 1-19.

Cooper, D. H., & Farran, D. C. (1991). *The Cooper–Farran behavioral rating scales.* Brandon, VT: Clinical Psychology.

Crosnoe, R., & Cooper, C. E. (2010). Economically disadvantaged children's transitions into elementary school: Linking family processes, school contexts, and educational policy. *American Educational Research Journal, 47*(2), 258-291.

Demaray, M. K., Ruffalo, S. L., & Carlson, J. (1995). Social skills assessment: A comparative evaluation of six published rating. *School Psychology Review, 24*(4), 648-671.

Duncan, G. J., Dowsett, C. J., Claessens, A., Magunuson, K., Huston, A. C., Klebanov, P., ... Japel, C. (2007). School readiness and later achievement. *Developmental Psychology, 43*(6), 1428-1446.

Foulks, B., & Morrow, R. D. (1989). Academic survival skills for the young child at risk for school failure. *Journal of Educational Research, 82,* 158-165.

Gutman, A. (1987). *Democratic education.* Princeton, NJ: Princeton University Press.

Hahs-Vaughn, D. L., & Onwuegbuzie, A. J. (2006). Estimating and using propensity score analysis with complex samples. *The Journal of Experimental Education, 75*(1), 31-65.

Hoglund, W. L., & Leadbeater, B. J. (2004). The effects of family, school, and classroom ecologies on changes in children's social competence and emotional and behavior problems in first grade. *Developmental Psychology, 40*(4), 533-544.

Horn, M. L. V., Atkins-Burnett, S., Karlin, E., Ramey, S. L., & Snyder, S. (2007). Parent ratings of children's social skills: Longitudinal psychometric analyses of the social skills rating system. *School Psychology Quarterly, 22*(2), 162-199.

Howes, C. (1990). Can the age of entry into child care and the quality of child care predict adjustment in kindergarten? *Developmental Psychology, 26*(2), 292-303.

Jacobson, L. (2004). Pre-K standards said to slight social, emotional skills. *Education Week, 23*(42), 13.

Kessenich, A. T. (2006). The impact of parenting practices and early childhood curricula on children's academic achievement and social competence (Unpublished PhD dissertation). University of Maryland

Ketsetzis, M., Ryan, B. A., & Adams, G. R. (1998). Family processes, parent-child interactions, and child characteristics influencing school-based social adjustment. *Journal of Marriage and the Family, 60* (2), 374-387.

Ladd, G. W., & Price, J. M. (1987). Predicting children's social and school adjustment following the transition from preschool to kindergarten. *Child Development, 58*(5), 1168-1189.

Lane, K. L., Givner, C. C., & Pierson, M. R. (2004). Teacher expectations of student behavior: Social skills necessary for success in elementary school classrooms. *The Journal of Special Education, 38*(2), 104-110.

Lane, K. L., Wehby, J. H., & Cooley, C. (2006). Teacher expectations of students' classroom behavior across the grade span: Which social skills are necessary for success? *Council for Exceptional Children, 72*(2), 153-167.

La Paro, K., & Pianta, R. (2000). Predicting children: Competence in the early school years—A meta-analytic review. *Review of Educational Research, 70*(4), 443-484.

Lee, J., & Wong, K. K. (2004). The impact of accountability on racial and socioeconomic equity: Considering both school resources and achievement outcomes. *American Educational Research Journal, 41*(4), 797-832.

Luiselli, J. K., McCarty, J. C., Coniglio, J., Ramirez, C. Z., & Putnam, R. F. (2005). Social skill assessment and intervention: Review and recommendation for school practitioners. *Journal of Applied School Psychology, 21*(1), 21-38.

McCellland, M. M., Acock, A. C., & Morrison, F. J. (2006). The impact of kindergarten learning-related skills on academic trajectories at the end of elementary school. *Early Childhood Research Quarterly, 21,* 471-490.

McClelland, M. M., & Morrison, F. (2003). The emergence of learning-related social skills in preschool children. *Early Childhood Research Quarterly, 19,* 206-224.

McCelland, M. M., Morrison, F., & Holmes, D. L. (2000). Children at risk for early academic problems: The role of learning-related social skills. *Early Childhood Research Quarterly, 15*(3), 307-329.

McWayne, C. M., Fantuzzo, J. W., & McDermott, P. A. (2004). Preschool competency in context: An investigation of the unique contribution of child competencies to early academic success. *Developmental Psychology, 40*(4), 633-645.

Merrell, K. W. (2001). Assessment of children's social skills: Recent developments, best practices, and new directions. *Exceptionality, 9*(1&2), 3-18.

Michelson, L., Sugai, D. P., Wood, R. P., & Kazdin, A. E. (1983). *Social skills assessment and training with children.* New York, NY: Plenum Press.

Miles, S. B., & Stipek, D. (2006). Contemporaneous and longitudinal associations between social Behavior and literacy achievement in a sample of low-income elementary school children. *Child Development, 77*(1), 103-117.

Mistry, R. S., Biesanz, J. C., & Chien, N. (2008). Socioeconomic status, parental investments, and the cognitive and behavioral outcomes of low-income children from immigrant and native households. *Early Childhood Research Quarterly, 23*(2), 193-212.

Murphy, B. C., Eisenberg, N., & Fabes, R. A. (1999). Consistency and change in children's emotionality and regulation: A longitudinal study. *Merrill-Palmer Quarterly, 45*(3), 413-444.

Nassbaum, M. C. (2006). *Frontiers of justice: Disability, nationality, species membership.* London, England: Belknap Press.

National Center for Education Statistics. (2002). Retrieved January 18, 2010, from http://nces.ed.gov/ecls/Kindergarten.asp

Pettit, G. S., Bates, J. E., & Dodge, K. A. (1997). Supportive parenting, ecological context, and children's adjustment: A seven-year longitudinal study. *Child Development, 68*(5), 908-923.

Raudenbush, S., & Bryk, A. (2002). *Hierarchical linear models: Applications and data analysis methods* (2nd ed). Thousand Oaks, CA: SAGE.

Rimm-Kaufman, S. E., Pianta, R. C., & Cox, M. J. (2000). Teachers' judgments of problems in the transition to Kindergarten. *Early Childhood Research Quarterly, 15.*

Roopnarine, J. L., Krishnakumar, A., Metindogan, A., & Evans, M. (2006). Links between parenting styles, parent-child interaction, parent-school interaction, and early academic skills and social behaviors in young children of English-speaking Caribbean immigrants. *Early Childhood Research Quarterly, 21*(2), 238-252.

Scheurich, J. J, & Young, M. D. (1997). Coloring epistemologies: Are our research epistemologies racially biased? *Educational Researcher, 26*(4), 4-16.

Singer, J. D., & Willett, J. B. (2003). *Applied longitudinal data analysis: Modeling change and event occurrence.* Oxford, England: Oxford University Press.

Verba, S., Schlozman, K. L., & Brady, H. E. (1995). *Voice and equality: Civic voluntarism in American politics.* Cambridge, MA: Harvard University Press.

Warnes, E. D., Sheridan, S. M., & Geske, J. (2005). A contextual approach to the assessment of social skills: Identifying meaningful behaviors for social competence. *Psychology in the Schools, 42*(2), 173-187.

Williams, G. J., & Reisberg, L. (2003). Successful inclusion: Teaching social skills through curriculum integration. *Intervention in School and Clinic, 38*(4), 205-210.

Winsler, A., & Carlton, M. P. (2003). Observations of children's task activities and social interactions in relation to teacher perceptions in a child-centered preschool: Are we leaving too much to chance? *Early Education & Development, 14,* 155-178.

Woolfolk, A. (2010). *Educational psychology* (11th ed.). Columbus, OH: Pearson/ Allyn & Bacon.

Zhou, Q., Hofer, C., & Eisenberg, N. (2007). The developmental trajectories of attention focusing, behavioral persistence, and externalizing problems during school-age years. *Developmental Psychology, 43*(2), 369-385.

CHAPTER 9

DEVIL IS IN THE DETAILS

Examining Equity Mechanisms in Supplemental Educational Services

Rudy Acosta, Patricia Burch, Annalee Good, and Mary S. Stewart

INTRODUCTION

Market-based school improvement reforms that rely on principles of competition, choice and limited regulation as central levers for improving student outcomes have emerged as a potential mechanism for addressing the needs of diverse learners. The Supplemental Educational Services (SES) provision of No Child Left Behind (NCLB) is an example of a market-based school improvement reform. The policy offers parents "mini-vouchers," or a choice of tutoring programs from a host of third-party organizations that use public money to provide additional academic help to eligible students in the form of after-school tutoring. In this chapter, we explore how the design of the SES policy impacts access to quality instruction for eligible low-income students and their families. Drawing on data from a mixed-method, multi-site study on the implementation and impact of SES, we consider how well the design

Charting Reform, Achieving Equity in a Diverse Nation
pp. 219–249
Copyright © 2013 by Information Age Publishing
219

elements that advance commercial interests mesh if at all, with the equity orientation and goals of NCLB. The chapter provides new perspectives for understanding the tensions within market-based accountability strategies in education reforms that target children in underperforming and underresourced schools.

POLICY BACKGROUND

Under No Child Left Behind, schools identified as in need of improvement for two or more years are required to offer parents of children in low-income families the opportunity to receive extra academic assistance, or SES. Both preexisting and new organizations offering after-school study and tutoring programs compete for SES funds and the opportunity to deliver tutoring services to eligible students, including both for-profit and nonprofit providers. The structure and characteristics of these organizations varied widely along multiple elements such as hourly rates, tutor qualifications, tutoring session length, instructional strategies, and curricula. The law required that these organizations align the content and educational practices of SES to the state's academic content standards, as well as applicable federal, state, and local health, safety, and civil rights laws, [§1116(e)(12)(B)(i)] and should be based on high-quality research with evidence of their effectiveness in increasing student academic achievement [§1116(e)(12)(C)]. In addition, the law required states to withdraw approval from SES providers that failed to increase student academic achievement for 2 or more years. Consistent with a market-based orientation, the law also restricted schools, district and states from regulating provider programming—based on the idea that doing so would dampen competition, which is viewed as essential to improving the supply and quality of tutoring.

The SES provision of NCLB is rooted in the original conceptualization of the Elementary and Secondary Education Act of 1965 (ESEA). The initial push for equity in ESEA was defined as leveling the playing field so that students in communities struggling economically could have access to supplemental, high quality instruction intended to make up for what were perceived at that time as cultural and economic disadvantages, relative to their middle class counterparts (Goodlad & Keating, 1990). Under NCLB, SES was included as part of a compromise between Republican members of Congress, who supported vouchers and Democrats who resisted this effort. Unlike vouchers, which replaced public schooling provisions with private approaches to schooling, SES represented an expansion of more responsibility for local and state educational agencies (Henig, 2006). Supplemental instruction was intended as a means of improving the quality of instruction for low-income students, by allocating a portion of Title I funds out of district control and distributing it among competing third-party educational organizations. Public funds were earmarked for these organizations to design and deliver instructional programs before, during, and after the school day. As noted above, districts and states were afforded limited authority to regulate these providers under the principle that market forces would provide accountability. Furthermore, districts and states were also responsible for creating the conditions where there was an adequate and responsive supply of services for parents, who are in other words, the "consumers" of SES.

Federally-funded compensatory policies that incorporate market-based accountability strategies present a particular paradox. From one perspective, market-based accountability strategies are intended to redistribute resources and ensure that government programs prioritize towards low-income students in order to level the playing field. From a different perspective, these compensatory policy designs are anchored in theories of market-based accountability where the market is the primary mechanism ensuring access to high quality tutoring. The greater the competition among different kinds of providers (government and nongovernment), the greater is the supply and the more likely that weak providers (with low attendance) will exit the field. Third party entities bear central responsibility for the design and delivery of services to students in public schools. Under this second perspective, incentives for SES service providers, particularly for-profit organizations, to serve high-needs students differ somewhat from those intended in the original ESEA law. For these companies, the bottom-line is staying alive in a competitive market, reducing costs, and increasing profit margins. The case of SES represents a problematic paradox in market-oriented reforms aimed at improving equity and access. Principles of free market competition prefer limited government regulation and prioritize competition. The ideals of equity and access epitomized, although somewhat unrealized in ESEA, identify government and government regulation as critical to improving the quality of education for low-income students. Leveling the playing field means reducing barriers to unequal access via government intervention and funding. In commercialist principles, leveling the playing field connotes limiting government intervention and lowing barriers to entry for vendors. These ideas can be reconceptualized and further understood as the principles of equity and commercialism.

Equity Principle

Equity-oriented policies are based on the principle of fairness, that children, regardless of income, should have equal access to high quality schools. Under ESEA, the first categorical and compensatory programs operated from a deficit orientation. The programs were designed to equalize opportunities by using educational interventions to make up for what were considered to be student's social and personal "deficits." In ESEA's latest iteration, NCLB launched a Federal drive to draw attention to cultural and socioeconomic barriers (e.g., language proficiency, living in poverty, and learning disabilities) that have frustrated student access to quality education and perpetuated persistent achievement gaps. In particular, NCLB requires that all children, including historically under-served populations such as English language learners (ELL) and students with disabilities, be considered fully in any measure of school "success," as determined by their proficiency on state standardized tests scores. Toward this end, SES aims to level the playing field by giving low-income parents the option of after-school tutoring—which middle and upper class parents long have employed through private funds—to increase student advantage.

Commercial Principle

The SES provision illustrates the commercial principle in NCLB. Under this principle, the goal of achieving equal access to quality services in principle is achieved through mechanisms anchored in the commercial workings of the free market. Market-based policies address the problem of bureaucratic oversight because stakeholders operate outside the parameters of the perceived inefficiencies of public schools that, many have argued, failed to improve the academic achievement of students. SES functions under the market-based assumption that parents will select the best services for their child based on quality information about the nature of these services. Ineffective providers will be weeded out by supply and demand, leaving the most effective supplemental service providers. Student achievement will improve because of the tutoring they received. The intended outcome in the commercial realm is that these choices will provide parents, specifically those from low-income families, with more opportunities to remedy the structural inequities that historically have existed in their children's schooling. Table 9.1 provides a summary comparing these two principles within the context of SES.

This chapter further examines the policy conditions under which reforms (such as SES) use market-based accountability as a central mechanism for improving the quality of instruction. We utilize the idiom, "the devil is in the details" to identify and explain the levers in the policy design that are in tension with equity principles. We argue that there is a tension between the overarching equity goals in federal compensatory policy and the nuts and bolts (or details) of using market-based reforms and/or strategies to achieve equity.

Table 9.1.   Juxtaposition Between Equity and Commercialist Goals

Study Variables	Equity Goals	Commercial Goals
SES Policy	Provide supplemental tutoring services to all eligible students in low-income and *underperforming* schools	Establish market oriented interventions where third party organizations provide instruction to eligible families that opt for services
SES in practice: Access to adequate amounts of learning opportunities	All eligible students receive an allotment of instructional time necessary to make adequate academic gains	Third party organizations determine the amount of instructional time based on Title I per-pupil allocations and their own hourly rates
SES in practice: Access to quality learning opportunities	All eligible students have access to tutoring opportunities regardless of learning needs (e.g., ELL and students with disabilities)	Third party organizations determine the curriculum based on supply and demand. Third party organizations not required to provide services to all students
SES in practice: Quality of Information	Information disseminated to eligible families through different formats, avenues and languages	Third party organizations *advertise* information about services

Note: Comparison between the equity and commercialist principles as they specifically pertain to SES policy and data from this specific integrated mixed-methods study.

REVIEW OF QUALITATIVE WORK ON EDUCATION PRIVATIZATION

Privatization of education is multifaceted and understanding privatization reforms requires multidimensional approaches (Hentschke & Wohlstetter, 2007). Quantitative inquiry provides valuable data regarding inputs and outputs of a policy at play; however, it can be overly linear and rational in relation to the nuanced and nonrational implementation process of educational policy. The in-depth nature of qualitative research not only compliments statistical data, but may help attend to the experiences of those who are supposed to benefit from market-based reforms, as compared to the intentions and actions of those who implement and deliver them. This is especially the case when examining issues of equity in policy design and how it plays out in the instructional setting, not only in terms of teaching practices and philosophies, but in the nomenclature of the curriculum utilized for learning and the physical surroundings of instruction.

Qualitative research further provides a deeper understanding of power differentials and dynamics as policies are implemented. Relevant to the overarching issue of equity—understanding how power is mediated among the stakeholders, the policy, and the places of implementation—research is able to understand the effectiveness of policy objectives beyond that of academic improvement (Honig, 2006; Koyama, 2011). One iteration of power is the parent's or consumer's ability to "buy" services that will improve upon the academic achievement of those students that need it most. Private companies, however, such as those delivering SES, are not subject to the same regulatory oversight as public schools. Qualitative research aimed at investigating the processes and practices of private companies may offer a better understanding of how parents access, consume, and act on information about private tutoring services, and how public and private entities interact to implement public policy. It is in the nuances of this process that research can begin to unveil not only the power dynamics among schools, private companies, and parent-consumers, but why and how market-oriented implementation strategies obscure, and at times work against intended equity goals.

Specifically, qualitative research on market practices can describe and assess patterns in what and how students are taught, the capacity of tutors in these settings, and the nature of their interactions with students in diverse settings. These patterns are critical to understanding the links (or lack thereof) between the intent of SES policy (improved student achievement) and the early results from statistical analyses. Qualitative studies also lead to the development of best practices and provide researchers and policymakers with important insights into school, community, and classroom level characteristics associated with student achievement.

Unfortunately, qualitative research on SES has been very limited to date. Early research on SES was largely descriptive, exploratory, and focused on the challenges of SES implementation in a context of limited capacity and/or will on the part of district and state providers in informing parents about their options and in monitoring and reporting on the quality of tutoring provided (see Burch, 2007; Burch, Steinberg, & Donovan, 2007; Center on Education Policy, 2007; Fusarelli, 2007; Government Accountability Office, 2006; Gill et al., 2008; Potter et al., 2007; Sunderman, 2006; Sunderman & Kim, 2004; Zimmer et al., 2007). Common challenges identified in this research included low student enrollment, unclear curriculum and alignment problems, lack of knowledge and communication among parents, providers and schools, inadequate monitoring and oversight of providers, as well as other problems related to market incentives and competition.

Existing qualitative studies have a number of limitations, including the absence of in-depth, context-rich data on the nature and quality of tutoring in that the majority of studies were conducted far from the instructional setting. Previous qualitative studies (Burch et al., 2007; Center on Education Policy, 2007; Fusarelli, 2007; Government Accountability Office, 2006; Gill et al., 2008; Potter et al, 2007; Sunderman, 2006; Sunderman & Kim, 2004;

Zimmer et al., 2007) relied on the reports (through interviews) of providers, school administrators, and district and state officials. We view the reliance on interviews with policymakers, school administrators, and district and state officials on what was happening in tutoring sessions as a shortcoming that limited understanding of the meaning and value of SES for its intended beneficiaries—students in chronically underperforming schools—and the ways in which the identities and conditions at play in these settings contribute to its relevance and quality. In addition to interviews with policymakers, administrators, and other officials, and to address previous design limitations, we incorporated parent focus groups, observations of SES tutoring sessions, and archival data to add further depth to understanding the details within SES policy.

RESEARCH DESIGN

This chapter draws on a subset of data from a multisite, mixed-method case study design that integrates quantitative and qualitative methods to examine the implementation and efficacy of SES. This research was conducted in five urban school districts (in four states), representing different student demographics—Milwaukee, Wisconsin; Minneapolis, Minnesota; Chicago, Illinois; and Austin and Dallas, Texas—and involved three linked and overlapping phases of research. Phase 1 began in year 1 and continued into year 2, consisting of an in-depth qualitative study designed to define key elements of SES program models and the policy and practice variables that mediate implementation of these models. The data collected in Phase 1 informed the measures of SES treatment constructed for the quantitative analysis. Phase 2 likewise began in year 1 and continued in year 2; it was a major quantitative investigation of selection into SES (i.e., who registers and participates), SES program impacts on student achievement (i.e., effects of standardized test scores in English and math), and the characteristics of SES that correlate with SES impacts.

The research phases were tightly integrated to augment the knowledge generated in this study. For example, issues or patterns in tutoring practice that were identified in the fieldwork (e.g., through observations of tutoring sessions, interviews with district staff, etc.) were discussed with the quantitative research team members, who in turn designed analyses (with the available data, which included but were not limited to hours of service per provider, test results by site, and attendance rates) to explore whether these issues or patterns influenced the variables accounting for measurable effects across different districts and SES providers. Similarly, findings produced in the quantitative analysis were discussed with the qualitative research team, who in turn, fine-tuned qualitative instruments to further explore in data and observations factors that might explain the emerging results.

In what follows, we discuss a number of findings illuminated through this collaborative approach to mixed-method research. We begin by discussing the qualitative design of the study upon which findings for this chapter are largely based.

Questions Guiding Our Study

A distinguishing feature of our multisite, multimethod case study of the implementation and effectiveness of SES is an in-depth qualitative component designed to define key elements of SES program models and to identify how policy and implementation potentially mediate or influence SES impacts. We examined the following implementation questions:

1. What does SES tutoring look like in practice? The in-depth qualitative component of this case study allowed us to investigate much of what is missing in existing evaluations of SES: how much actual instructional time students received and the nature of the instruction itself. We wanted to see what was happening in an invoiced hour of SES and how instruction varied across different SES providers (by setting, format, and approach). As we analyzed the quality of instruction, we also focused on the nature of programming for particular student populations, mainly ELLs and students with disabilities, and how variations in these elements relate to program effectiveness. This led us to ask the following subquestion: how, if at all, are ELL and students with disabilities being served? From an equity standpoint, we examined the level to which SES provides students *access* to sufficient amounts of quality learning opportunities.

2. If quality of information is a key tenant of parent choice, what can we learn about the levels of information that eligible SES parents are obtaining? By assuming that parents are consumers, as framed by the SES policy, what do parents want and need to know in order to make informed decisions? And is available information responsive to the needs of all parents, including parents of students with special needs?

3. Finally, what are the implications of this analysis for the future of market-based education reforms? What short and long-term levers can policy reformers incorporate that will make the private sector centrally responsive and directly accountable to the needs of historically underserved diverse learners?

Sample

We used an embedded sampling approach consistent with our interest in understanding SES tutoring practices in context. Within each district, we sampled three to six providers. To capture a diverse sample, we selected providers that had a high share of the provider market in each district, high attendance levels relative to other providers in the same district, and 2 or more years providing SES in the district. In addition, we sought to include an equal number of digital, in-home, in-school, and community-based tutoring, as well as for-profit, nonprofit, district-provided, and, when applicable, faith-based organizations (see Table 9.2 for site specifics). We also attempted to include providers that advertised services for ELL populations and students with disabilities in order to examine how SES plays out for these critical student populations. Yet, obtaining a sample perfectly representative of these provider characteristics proved challenging. Limitations obtaining this sample included reluctance on the part of providers; low numbers of providers with more than one year of service in smaller urban districts (i.e., districts that only recently had to start offering SES); and limited numbers of providers that target ELL students and students with disabilities.

METHODOLOGY

We applied a constant comparative method (both within and across method) to develop and refine our understanding of patterns and dissimilarities in tutoring practices across providers. Further, the same data were analyzed and discussed simultaneously by different researchers in an effort to consider and develop multiple interpretations of events observed. As with any qualitative study, data analysis occurred both concurrently to and after the data collection process. The following section provides a more nuanced description of the observations, interviews, and documents analyzed for the study.

Observations

Building on decades of instructional research, we sought a research design that captured: (1) the complex social and structural contexts in which after-school tutoring occurs, (2) the importance of analysis based on consistent findings across multiple sources of information, and (3) the importance of qualitative analytic strategies in the analysis of observation data rather than reliance solely on statistical generalizations and statistics

Table 9.2. Sample of SES Providers Across District Sites (2009-10 and 2010-11)

District Sites	Total Providers in Sample	For-Profit Vendors	Nonprofit Providers	District Operated Providers	Onsite Format*	Digital Format**	Serving Special Needs***
Austin	6	5		1	5	2	5
Chicago	6	4	1	1	4	2	6
Dallas	5	5			4	2	3
Milwaukee	7	4	3		7	1	4
Minneapolis	6	3	3		4	2	6

Note: Numbers do not necessarily match the totals because there are some providers that fit more than one criterion.
*Onsite format instruction took place at school, at home, or in another community setting.
**Refers to programs that include at least some element of digital instruction (i.e. online or software-based).
***Refers to providers serving either or both ELLs and/or Students with disabilities.

(see also Noam, 2004). To this end, we created an instrument that allowed us to assess the quality of the program as a whole (Burch & Good, 2009; Good, Burch, Heinrich, Stewart, & Acosta, 2011). This instrument was based on collecting multiple observations, across sites, and using these observations to develop descriptive vignettes of tutoring practices. The observation instrument included indicator ratings at two 10-15 minute observation points, as well as, materials collection, a rich description in the form of a vignette, and follow-up information provided by the tutor(s).[1] Our observation instrument draws on these best practices to systematically collect information on teaching methods and instructional materials in use and to identify the correlation of different formats, resources (curriculum materials, staffing, etc.), and instructional methods on students' observed levels of engagement. Field researchers conducted observations of 94 tutoring sessions in the 5 urban school districts across a range of provider characteristics described previously.

Interviews and Focus Groups

We conducted 73 semistructured, in-depth interviews with tutoring staff from each of the providers sampled in each district. The interviews focused on: (a) the nature of the tutoring program (instructional formats, curriculum, etc.); (b) staff professional background and training; (c) the level of interaction with schools, teachers, students, and families; and (d) particular adaptations for the needs of special education students or ELLs. These interviews provided distinct perspectives on the actual, ground-level work of the SES program and offered data and insight on the benefits and limitations of the program models employed by the various providers. Wherever possible, we conducted interviews with tutoring staff for individuals whose tutoring sessions we had observed.

We conducted 52 semistructured, in-depth interviews with the program administrator(s) for each SES provider in the sample for each district. Administrator interviews focused on the instructional format and setting, as well as providers' formal curriculum. Administrators were also asked about recruitment and retention strategies; staff training; communication strategies with the district, school, and families; the guiding principles of their program; and diagnostic strategies.

To understand the context within which SES policy was implemented, we conducted semistructured interviews with 20 district officials and 4 state-level personnel, representing each district and state in the sample. Interviews focused on inter-organizational coordination, organizational capacity, interaction with policy requirements, and policy intentions.

Finally, to examine the factors influencing parents' decision to participate in the SES program, the criteria they used to select providers, and
their assessment of program quality, we conducted focus groups with parents of students who were eligible to receive SES and/or who received SES
services during the 2009-2010 school years. We scheduled two parent
focus group sessions per district, with one focus group in each of two geographic regions of each district. One hundred and sixty eight parents
across five districts participated in the focus groups.

Documents

For each provider, we collected data on staffing levels, curricular focus,
length of tutoring sessions, student grouping practices, and physical
descriptions of where the tutoring took place (i.e., in-person, online, etc.).
We also collected information on recruitment and retention strategies,
communication formats (e.g., flyers about services or individual progress
reports) with various stakeholders (e.g., parents), and assessment strategies (both diagnostic and summative). Other documents included materials developed by providers to market their programs, train tutors, and
record student attendance.

FINDINGS

Equity is providing equality of opportunity; access goes a step further—
insisting on not just equal services but also equal opportunities to leverage opportunities or access them—with policy providing some of the
infrastructure in order to help make this happen. Although test-based
accountability and evidence on "what works" are at the core of the NCLB
reauthorization, the intent of SES focuses more on the means, rather
than, the end result of increased test performance: that is, to facilitate as
extensive a choice as possible for students and parents in selecting providers and program types. As noted above, it is the presence of this parental
choice, and therefore a market of services, that SES promises will insure
quality after-school opportunities to historically underserved populations,
such as students with disabilities and ELLs. Yet our findings, primarily
from the qualitative portion of our study, suggest that access to adequate
amounts *and* quality of after-school learning opportunities is limited, in
many ways, as a result of these very policy design elements.

What Does SES Tutoring Look Like in Practice

Access to Adequate Amounts of Learning Opportunities

In assessing what SES tutoring looks like in practice, we examined three variables: the number of hours of tutoring each student received (or invoiced hours), the actual amount of instructional time students received in each of those invoiced hours (determined by our observations of SES sessions), and the difference between the advertised length of tutoring sessions and actual instructional time.

Research suggests that a minimum of 40 hours per academic school year is critical to producing a measurable effect on student achievement as measured by test scores (Heinrich & Burch, 2009). In this study, through observations and invoice documents, we found that out of the five districts in our study only in Chicago were substantial numbers of students receiving at least 40 hours of SES (56% of elementary students), compared to 11% in Milwaukee and 14% in Minneapolis, 8% in Austin, and 5% in Dallas.

Beyond measuring the amount of invoiced hours students receive, we also compared the advertised time to the actual instructional time according to two distinct measures: the discrepancy between advertised and actual instruction and the ability of students to maximize their instructional time (what we call "attendance flux"). Regarding the first measure, advertised sessions ranged from 60 to 150 minutes of instruction per session. The format of observed sessions varied by design (i.e., online or traditional "offline" instruction) and instructional setting (i.e., schools, homes, or community centers). We found that irrespective of the format, students received less instructional time than what was advertised by providers. The magnitude of these differences varied by format and by district (specific figures by format are presented in Table 9.3). With regards to attendance flux, almost half of all observations with two or more students (primarily traditional offline, school-based settings), students that started a session were observed arriving late, leaving for part of the session, or leaving the tutoring session altogether. Of the 63 observations with 2 or more students, 26 students (41.3%) engaged in attendance flux. Through interviews with tutors and provider administrators, we confirmed that school-based SES programs often compete with other after-school programs (e.g., athletics, clubs) for students' time, and classrooms with multiple students required coordination and set-up that cut into instructional time.

We consistently observed a difference between the advertised time of a tutoring session and the actual instructional time. Providers are required to advertise the average length of their sessions (U.S. Department of Education [USDE], 2009).[2] Districts are invoiced at an hourly rate, based on the time students spend in tutoring. Yet, advertised time does not always equal instructional time, and sometimes even invoiced time differed from advertised time based on our preliminary analysis (Good et al., 2011). These differences tend to vary by format (which we sampled by design or setting. See Table 9.3). In online organizations, instruction started the minute the student came online and ended promptly at the end of the (typically) hour-long advertised time. The tight focus on instructional time also was observed in home-based settings. Instruction started immediately after the tutor arrived and ended on average 5 or 6 minutes early, leaving time for the collection of materials, record-keeping, and departures. In school and community settings, instructional time was bookended by classroom management activities or logistics such as transportation, accounting for, on average, 19 minutes in the case of school-based tutoring and approximately 46 minutes in the case of community based tutoring. One example from our observations of tutoring sessions in community-based settings revealed that less time was devoted to organization and classroom management issues. However, the variety of grouping patterns, instructional approaches, and other details of community-based vendors was too broad to make conclusions regarding the cause of these discrepancies between instructional versus advertised time in this setting. Overall, based on instructional format (with some formats having greater discrepancies of time than others, either by design or setting), students participating in SES may not be fully receiving the instructional time as advertised by SES vendors.

Access to Quality Learning Opportunities

Although there is little research on best practices specific to SES, prior research on out-of-school programs generally tells us that high-quality

Table 9.3.   Difference Between Advertised and Instructional Time

Format of Instruction	Advertised Time by SES Providers (Minutes)	Actual Instructional Time (Minutes)	Difference (Minutes)
Online	67.5	57.83	9.67
Offline	90.6	70.8	19.8
Home	64.29	60.64	3.65
School	95.56	76.33	19.23
Community	116.67	70	46.67

Note: Advertised sessions ranged from 60 to 150 minutes. "Online" refers to computerized instruction. "Offline" refers to the more traditional teacher-student instruction. The last three formats specifically refer to the setting of where instruction takes place. "Community" refers to settings outside homes or schools, such as a library or a community center. Data is from 2009-10 academic school years.

programs are characterized by: (1) consistent and sustained instructional time; (2) small grouping patterns (no larger than 10:1, but smaller is better); (3) curriculum that is content-rich, differentiated to student needs and connected to students' regular school-day learning; (4) instruction (or content delivery) that is varied (e.g., structured and unstructured, independent and collective, etc.), active (guided teacher led instruction as opposed to worksheets), focused on skills development, sequenced to achieve skill development objectives, and explicit in its targeting of specific skills; (5) positive relationships between tutors, students and peers; and (6) teachers/tutors with both content and pedagogical knowledge and continuous support, as well as constructive evaluation, from their administrators (Beckett et al., 2009; Good et al., 2011; Lauer et al., 2006; Noam, 2004).

Across all districts, we observed tutoring practices that were conventional, focused on tutoring in the tested subjects (mathematics and reading), and delivered via whole group instruction. We did not find consistent evidence of innovative practices, active learning, or a curriculum that complemented the regular school day. Instead, SES tutors used traditional, teacher-directed instruction and content that was isolated from the students' school day instruction. In sum, our findings suggest that students did not receive adequate amounts of quality instructional time. Due to observed inconsistencies of instructional times, students were not receiving enough SES hours to make significant gains.

Lack of Services for English Learners and Students With Disabilities

In relation to the quality of instruction, we sought to explore how SES catered to the needs of ELLs and students with disabilities. As stated above, our observation instrument draws on previously established work on best instructional practices (Good et al., 2011), to capture teaching methods that cater to diverse learners. Figure 9.1 draws and represents observation data providing a snap-shot analysis of best instructional practices that cater to the needs of ELLs and students with disabilities. The first four specifically pertain to practices catering to students with disabilities. The latter four pertain to instructional strategies for ELLs. Observers noted whether each of the eight indicators were either present or not during SES instruction. Observers also noted if the instructional indicators could not be observed since a major obstacle for providers, tutors, and researchers was identifying students with documented ELL or special education needs. The majority of tutors we observed and interviewed did not have access to Individualized Educational Plans or district data on ELL identification.

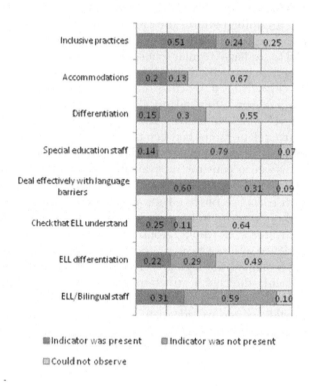

Figure 9.1.   Observed best-practice indicators for students with special needs in SES sessions based on 94 observations between 2008-10.

Regarding students with disabilities, out of those indicators that were observed, SES instructors were able to provide examples of inclusive practices. Some examples of these practices were smaller teacher ratios or the SES tutor was a regular school day teacher who knew about the student's special educational needs. With regards to ELL practices, SES instructors navigated language barriers with the help of other students or with a second bilingual tutor in the setting of instruction. In the majority of our observations, however, tutors were not prepared for the academic or behavioral challenges of diverse learners. From our interview data, we found that few providers offered adequate professional development to meet the needs of students in these populations. Based on observation data, out of 94 observations, only 13 tutors participating in our observations were trained in special education practices, which is roughly 14% as stated by the special education indicator in Figure 9.1. ELL practices were double that at 31%, with 29 tutors asserting that they were trained to provide services for language learners.[3] Further observation data indicated that for students with disabilities, approximately 19 (From Figure 9.1 this is 0.2 of 94) of the observations included accommodations, and about 14 (0.15 of 94) contained differentiation practices. For ELL students, 24 (0.22 of 94) of the observations included differentiation practices during lessons.

Some providers compensated for the fact that tutors were underprepared by reducing the group size for students with disabilities to one-on-one and/or encouraging tutors to "slow" instruction down, using a lower grade level curriculum, or in other ways modifying the curriculum. Yet, modifying the curriculum, which, depending on the situation, may hinder student progress because students may be no longer working on the objectives in which they will be assessed. As previously mentioned, providers struggled to obtain adequate information needed to appropriately service students with disabilities and ELLs. Changing the curriculum level for these students without the specific knowledge of a student's needs may fail to adequately provide instruction that addresses a student's ability level,[4] thus contradicting research based on sound instructional practices.

Even though providers advertise to ELL and students with disabilities, we found that most of the tutors in our observations offered general, not individualized, instruction that did not differentiate for struggling students. According to providers' advertised services, 14 out of 20 providers in our sample advertised that they could serve ELL students, at least in a limited way or for limited languages. Thirteen out of 20 (though not necessarily overlapping the 14 mentioned above) providers advertised that they could serve students with disabilities, at least in a limited way or for limited special needs. Yet, we encountered very few tutors with training or experience in instruction differentiated to ELL or students with disabilities, and with very few exceptions, neither curriculum nor instruction were tailored to the unique needs of these students.

Failing to properly identify and amend instruction for this sub-population of students is particularly disturbing given that through our quantitative data, across all five districts, ELL and students with disabilities were more likely to register and attend sessions than non-ELL students (Stewart et al. 2012). As seen in Tables 9.4a and 9.4b, during the 08-09 and 09-10 academic school years, a substantial number of ELLs and students with disabilities registered for SES. In the case of Austin, during the 08-09 school year, 45% of the students registered were identified as ELL. In Chicago, during the 09-10 school year, 29% of the students registered were identified as having a disability. The same tables also show that beyond registering, ELLs and students with disabilities were attending SES in substantial numbers. For the 08-09 school year 14.8% of students attending

Table 9.4a. Participation and Attendance Rates Across Districts (Academic Year 2008-09)

| | Registered for SES | | | | | | Attended SES | | | | | |
	Total Students	% ELL	# ELL	% SWD	# SWD	Total Students	% ELL	# ELL	% SWD	# SWD		
Austin	2,842	45.3	1,287	14.1	401	2,009	46.1	926	13	261
Chicago	25,492	10.9	2,779	15.2	3,875	22,515	11.3	2,544	15.1	3,400
Dallas	2,809	18.3	514	13.9	390	1,755	18.8	330	13.2	232
Milwaukee	4,123	5.1	210	20.7	853	2,620	6.2	162	19	498
Minneapolis	2,352	31.5	741	16.7	393	1,591	34.9	555	16.4	261
Total	37,618	14.7	5,531	15.7	5,912	30,490	14.8	4,517	15.3	4,652

Table 9.4b. Participation and Attendance Rates Across Districts (Academic Years 2009-10)

	Registered for SES					Attended SES				
	Total Students	% ELL	# ELL	% SWD	# SWD	Total Students	% ELL	# ELL	% SWD	# SWD
Austin	1,463	34.5	505	11.2	1,164	1,318	35.5	468	10.6	140
Chicago	11,324	17.1	1,936	29.4	3,329	10,357	17.7	1,833	29.9	3,097
Dallas	11,143	20.5	2,284	11.8	1,315	10,781	20.8	2,242	11.7	1,261
Milwaukee	6,933	11.8	818	19.8	1,373	4,998	13.2	660	19	950
Minneapolis	4,698	38.5	1,809	19.4	911	3,320	42.1	1,398	18.6	618
Total:	35,561	20.7	7,352	19.9	7,092	30,774	21.5	6,601	19.7	6,066

SES were identified as ELLs and 15.3 percent as students with disabilities. These numbers increased in the 09-10 school year with 21.5% of students attending SES identified as ELLs and 19.7% as students with disabilities.

As part of our mixed-method study, and to compliment our qualitative analysis, we used odds-ratios to further emphasize the importance of differentiated instruction in an SES setting (as seen in Table 9.4c). First, for the 2008-09 school year we found that ELLs were 1.438 times more likely to register and 1.437 times more likely to attend SES than students not categorized as ELLs. During the same academic year, however, ELLs were .87 times less likely to receive 40 or more hours of SES than non-ELL students. During the same academic year, students with disabilities were 1.121 times more likely to register than students not identified as disabled. Students with disabilities were also 1.066 times more likely to attend SES than students not identified as disabled which translates to having 7 percent greater odds of attending SES. Students with disabilities were also .86 times *less* likely to reach higher thresholds (40+ hours) of SES than other students not identified as disabled.

In the 2009-10 school year, this latter relationship appears to change, with both ELL and students with disabilities increasing their odds of participating. Referring back to Table 9.4c, ELL students were 2.510 times more likely to register and 2.530 times more likely to attend SES than students not categorized as ELLs. In contrast from the previous year, ELLs were now 1.310 times more likely to receive 40 or more hours of SES than non-ELL students. For students with disabilities the odds of registering, attending, and receiving 40 or more hours of instruction doubled. Students with disabilities were 2.219 times more likely to register, 2.358 times more likely to attend, and 2.004 times more likely to receive 40 or more hours of SES than students not identified as disabled. It is important to note, however, that this result is driven by Chicago public schools, which prioritized students with disabilities in the 2009-10 school year. Even if Chicago public schools prioritized specific subgroups, the demand of SES for ELLs and students with disabilities has increased based on registration and attendance numbers.

The data above again points to the unresolved tensions between equity and commercialism in the design of SES. Equity is not simply about creating options; it is about ensuring access to high quality instruction. In the case of SES, some parents were taking advantage of the option to participate. Yet, our findings regarding the lack of differentiated instruction testify to the continued problem of the opportunity to access high quality instruction. To summarize, tutors lacked access to a student's IEP, which provides information on a student's specific disability and appropriate accommodations for meeting their academic needs. They also did not have any information on whether a student was identified as ELL. Most

Table 9.4c. Student Selection Into SES (Odds of Registering for and Attending SES)

Student Characteristic	Registered for SES		Attended SES		Attended 40 or More Hours	
	2009-10 (N = 85,906)	2008-09 (N = 100,988)	2009-10 (N = 85,906)	2008-09 (N = 100,988)	2009-10 (N = 33,273)	2008-09 (N = 43,671)
	Coefficients Reported as Odds Ratios					
Female	1.016	1.109	1.102	1.092	1.008	1.072
Asian	0.582	0.315	0.673	0.335	0.991	1.071
White	0.451	0.455	0.509	0.520	0.889	1.164
Black	reference	reference	reference	reference	reference	reference
Hispanic	0.598	0.607	0.641	0.689	1.585	1.921
Other race	1.066	0.837	0.963	0.804	0.407	0.853
English language learner	2.510	1.438	2.530	1.437	1.310	0.870
Free lunch	0.727	1.247	0.661	1.310	2.562	2.912
Students w/disability	2.219	1.121	2.358	1.066	2.004	0.860
Retained	1.049	1.014	1.154	0.959	1.163	0.691
Attended SES prior year	1.469	2.397	1.569	2.464	2.389	1.928
Percent absent prior year	0.284	0.928	0.121	0.909	0.000	0.881
Grade K-5	1.497	1.284	1.541	1.378	1.254	1.694
Grade 6-8	reference	reference	reference	reference	reference	reference
High school	1.104	0.653	0.752	0.478	0.193	0.126

Note: The reference category for grade level is middle school students (Grades 6-8); odds ratios for K-5 and high school students are interpreted relative to middle school students. Similarly, the odds ratios for the race variables are interpreted relative to black students. Data from five district study sites are combined.

*Coefficients (odds ratios) reported in bold are statistically significant predictors of student selection.

tutors were either unsure how to access such information or were unaware such information existed. If they did have access, it typically was because they happened to be a teacher at the school site where tutoring took place. From the providers' perspective in our sample of districts, district administrators did not have a systematic process for providing this information. This could be the result of legal issues with sharing confidential IEP information. This data also points to the tensions between the equity and commercialist realms. The equity policy levers are aimed at insuring that diverse learners are thoroughly accommodated through Individualized Educational Plans and ELL identification measures. The commercialist levers are aimed at providing choices, however, not all of these options are receptive to the needs of diverse learners.

Under the policy guidelines of SES, providing services that accommodate instruction to ELLs and students with special needs is not the responsibility of the providers (USDE, 2009).[5] This is another example of how the devil is in the details. The details within the commercialist levers of the policy limit options for the families of students that require differentiated instruction. Even if SES vendors offered services for ELLs or students with disabilities, there is no guarantee that the student will receive instruction from a highly qualified teacher since the NCLB highly qualified teacher requirements do not apply to SES providers (USDE, 2009). Consistent with our case study approach, we sought to use qualitative data to provide further depth and understanding to SES teaching practices. Based on our analysis from data gathered from observations and interviews, SES tutoring sessions often lacked a highly qualified instructor. We now turn to the second part of our inquiry, which details the experiences of low-income parents of children eligible for SES programming.

Levels of SES Information for Parents

SES is based on the assumption that improving public schooling hinges in part on giving low-income parents the opportunity and choice of instructional services. Utilizing data from parental focus groups in each of our sites, we sought to further understand the levels of information parents received about SES. Based on analysis of the data obtained from these focus groups we found the following: (1) Parents received incomplete information, including limited information on provider options and on the services different providers offered. Related to this finding, we found that asymmetries in information affected the access of students identified as ELL or those with disabilities to SES. (2) Parents observed and acknowledged gaps in the communication among stakeholders. In other words, parents observed the lack of communication between school and provider administrators and personnel affecting SES instruction.

(3) And there was a lack of access allowing parents a voice in influencing and improving the quality of the structure of services (how the program is designed and eventually how it functions).

Confusion about SES manifested itself in a variety of ways. In some cases, parents reported that they lacked a clear understanding of their options under SES. In other instances, parents did not know that they had options when it came to a choice of providers. They were eager to obtain tutoring for their child and went with the first vendor that contacted them, unaware that there were other vendors that might be a better fit for their child in terms of scheduling, focus, and format. Examples of these informational gaps were especially evident in Austin, where parents voiced that they knew little about SES. In Milwaukee, one parent mentioned that she had liked the services offered to her child but discovered half way into the program that math services were also available. She reported that if she had known about math services, she would have ensured that her child had participated in them as well. Similar issues arose in districts where information about SES services was disseminated to parents in large quantities, which made it difficult for parents to process. Parents suggested that districts streamline information so they would know which vendor the information was referring to or provide a greater level of detail about SES vendors. For instance, a parent in Chicago stated, "They could have actually broke it down and gave more detail about why they chose this one, that one, and that one for your child. You know, instead of just having to decide on your own."

Conflated with the issue of incomplete or asymmetric information, the lack of attention to access issues (how information about services is disseminated) in the design of the policy was especially poignant with parents of students identified as ELL or with special needs. For example, in focus groups, many parents of ELL students stated that they simply wanted their children to receive additional help in school in their native tongue. Parents received information from a variety of sources, which made it difficult to siphon out which providers could cater to their children's language needs. For parents of students with disabilities, parents were not thoroughly comfortable with the information they were receiving. Parents of this specific subgroup just wanted to know if SES tutors were going to differentiate instruction in order to meet their child's specific needs. During the focus groups, some parents of students with disabilities mentioned that they had taken the trouble to visit their child's SES instructor on the first day to make sure that their child received the necessary services catered to her or his specific needs. However, this did not always insure students were well served. For example, one parent who felt that her child was not receiving adequate services based on her specific need decided to remove her from the program.

Beyond incomplete and asymmetric dissemination of information, parents observed and acknowledged gaps in the communication among stakeholders. While parents appreciated the availability of SES, many felt that there were a number of problems that needed to be worked out before the program could benefit their child. For example, one suggestion noted across focus groups was for districts to improve communication between vendors and school personnel in the hopes of helping the district to prioritize and select students who would benefit from SES the most. Parents' experiences corroborate the trend noted by district, school, provider, and tutoring staff that lack of communication among stakeholders was a major barrier to successful implementation.

Finally, across districts, parents did not feel that they could influence the structure of the program (how the program is designed and how it functions) or the quality of the services their child received beyond removing their children from the program or confronting individual SES instructors. For example, in Minneapolis, some parents opted to remove their children from the tutoring program either because scheduling was inflexible or because providers were unprofessional. As a whole, parents felt that their voiced concerns could only be made on the part of their individual children and would not have an appreciable effect on the program overall. The law provides various guidelines and suggestions for states and districts to help ensure that parents have a genuine opportunity at maximizing their SES choice. Yet, the attempt falls short. For example, the law allows for providers to self-report whether they can offer differentiated instruction for ELLs and students with disabilities (USDE, 2009). Districts thus inform parents that there are providers offering differentiated instruction for their children's needs. Yet, from our observations (see Figure 9.1 in the observation indicators labeled "Special Education Staff" and "ELL/Bilingual Staff"), we constantly found that ELLs and students with disabilities receiving SES lacked having a qualified instructor directing instruction. The information is thus not reflective of the teaching practices advertised and therefore not responsive to the actual needs of the students. Parents wanted assurance that if they selected a provider that advertised offering services for diverse learners, that their child received those services.

BETWEEN EQUITY AND COMMERCIALSIM

The case of SES, as we argue in this chapter, illuminates the risks of reforms that attempt to incorporate the principles of both equity and commercialism. Specifically, our research suggests that absent explicit policy mechanisms that ensure access to quality programming for historically underserved populations and address information power asymmetries between low-income parents and SES vendors, equity goals are trumped by commercial aims. As we have shown, our findings suggest that the SES policy design places a premium on limiting regulation of third party entities. Thus the limits of regulation and the demand for learning opportunities provide a further incentive for third party entities that receive federal public dollars to provide supplemental after-school instruction to low-income students. Based on our study, however, based on our study, not all eligible students received adequate amounts of quality instruction under SES.

Although NCLB explicitly attempts to equalize the playing field for low-income students by providing the option to obtain supplemental academic help, in reality the policy does not address unequal power dynamics between the market levers of the policy and parent access to information. The rhetoric of NCLB is that all eligible students, particularly those who have been underserved in the past, should have equal access to programming. Knitted to the idea of equal opportunity, however, is the ideology that access is enabled in large part through parent choice and creating more competition in the education "marketplace" of tutoring services. Extending educational opportunity in the area of out-of-school time means giving poor urban families in eligible schools the opportunity to participate in *out of school* programming free of charge and the right to choose a vendor for their child, as opposed to having the district choose for them.

Regardless of the reasons, findings of our multisite study suggest that students are not receiving enough hours of SES instruction to produce significant gains in their learning, and given that invoiced hours may not equal instructional time, this is not a problem that will be resolved *only* by setting minimum standards for the number of instructional hours SES should provide. Under an equity-based framework, eligible students would receive an adequate number of hours necessary to make significant academic gains. The number of hours students attend SES (after registering) is influenced by a number of factors, including the dollars allocated per-student by the district for SES. As mandated by Federal policy, each district has a maximum allocation per student for SES and providers who charge higher hourly rates can provide fewer hours before hitting the maximum allocation. In this specific case, the commercialist reality of the policy trumps equity-based levers by allowing the price of services to establish the number of hours of instruction that students receive, from district to district, based on Title I per-pupil allocations.

As noted above, it is encouraging that ELL students are more likely than non-ELL students to sign up and register for SES. Based on our qualitative analysis, however, the quality of tutoring that they receive during sessions is clearly inadequate. Districts cannot, except by waiver, set programming criteria based on principles of equity and opportunity. In other words, SES providers do not have to cater services to those students that may need them the most, further asserting the tensions between the equity and commercial principles of the policy. Providers are not required to offer services to students with disabilities or ELLs, but if providers do offer these services, the law requires them to be advertised, and districts are responsible for providing these services if no provider is able or willing to do so. The policy required districts to use public funds but does not require the recipients of those public funds to be equitable in offering services to all student populations.

Connected to district struggles between the equity and commercialist principles, our research illustrates how district staff persons responsible for SES contend that their hands are tied in monitoring providers. District staff point out that most SES tutors do not have to meet "highly qualified" standards or have specific or sufficient training to be academic tutors. In our study, district staff (corroborated by provider staff) felt some state educational agencies have been lax in evaluating providers and setting minimum standards for tutoring quality and have failed to request essential information on applications for assessing and monitoring quality or to follow through on district complaints about provider incompetence or misconduct. With very few resources for program administration, let alone monitoring and evaluation, district staff has been stretched to find time to observe SES providers and better understand what is taking place in an hour of SES for which districts are invoiced. Even among well-meaning and compassionate staff, and among providers stating under contract that they could and would serve students with special needs, huge barriers to learning for these subgroups existed.

As an issue of accountability, families also have inadequate access to information and a lack of effective levers for holding providers, districts *and* states accountable for their responsibilities. As in the case of other education policies, and we would argue particularly in the context of SES, "some parties have more power than others in determining the course of implementation" (Dumas & Anyon, 2006, p. 165). In the case of SES, parties such as providers have greater resources (time and organizational capacity, as well as legal and financial knowledge), and therefore power, than low-income parents. Ironically, the *choice* that is supposed to give parents more power actually leaves them feeling less powerful. Parents enroll but then are not assured that their children have equal opportunities to learn; advertised time does not equal instructional time. Advertised services such as serving ELL or students with disabilities intended to draw families, are not adequately resourced. Parents seeking to remedy problems in the policy and make it more equitable have little recourse for doing so, leaving them feeling powerless and disadvantaged in a program aimed at affording them more opportunity and more say in the character and quality of supplemental instruction.

CONCLUSION

The complexities and contradictions within the design of SES exemplify the traits of a new kind of education policy, one in which political power can no longer be assumed to be national, state or local governments but includes various private actors as well (Burch, 2009b). Yet, the role and authority of government does not disappear. More so with SES, local governments are expected (as in a marketplace) to negotiate and compete with private firms. School districts continue to ensure that the necessary resources are allocated to those schools that need them the most in order to abide by state accountability standards. Concurrently, districts need to abide by federal guidelines and establish the SES market, which allows third party organizations to compete in the allocation of resources to the schools and students that need them the most.

Leveraging the empirical findings and theoretical insights noted above, what most deserves our attention? Choice programs such as SES that leave much of the content of instruction unregulated may create fertile ground for perpetuating inequities and the achievement gap. The challenge facing policy makers in strengthening reforms is to ensure that wherever private firms are involved in the design of remedial services, they are held to high and consistent standards for the very students whom ESEA is supposed to help the most—the historically underserved in education.

We should also reconsider the rationale behind and the serious implications of allowing providers to fully determine their hourly rates and instructional strategies. The evaluation of effects in this study and others clearly point to a minimum threshold of tutoring hours after which tutoring appears to produce small, but measurable effects on student achievement. Federal lawmakers should reconsider allowing states and districts to cap the hourly rates providers can charge.

In addition, the interactions and relationships among instructional variables are fundamental to intervention quality, including student grouping patterns, location, time spent on instruction, attendance flux during sessions, and student engagement and patterns of *out of school time* best practices. The level of instructional differentiation for students with special needs (i.e., ELL and students with disabilities) warrants particular attention to the opportunities of differentiation within the curriculum and whether this specific student population is attaining measurable gains. This is a critical, and in our examination, neglected piece of tutoring program quality.

Finally, researchers need to focus significant energy on the processes of, and state capacity for, accountability, from the initial approval process to the monitoring and evaluation of providers. Many of the variables in our study—curriculum, instructional strategies, tutor qualifications, attendance—are included in specific sections of state applications; however, we have little evidence that these variables are part of the monitoring process. If we are to accurately evaluate the design and implementation of SES, we must have a better idea of where the weak (and strong) links lie in the accountability system (as currently designed). This includes rethinking assumptions that market-based forms of accountability automatically work for parents as consumers. Absent incentives to do so, third party providers appear to have little incentive to provide continuous high quality information to parents.

In summary, the juxtaposing frameworks of accountability (one based on equity, the other based on commercialist perspectives) are not obvious at first. Seeing the contradictions requires attending to the details—and it is again in the details—where the promise and problem of policy lie. The intent behind the policy was to allow the quasi-voucher essence of SES tutoring to provide innovative methods of instruction, which, the policy assumed, schools lacked the capacity to implement, in order to abridge historic achievement gaps. Nearly a decade after its inception, the tensions have become more apparent in the ongoing implementation of the policy and further understood through fieldwork, such as the type presented through the scope of this study.

Education privatization policies are promoted as a means to increase access to varied and high quality education for disadvantaged children, increase the accountability of the organizations that work with children, and increase the liberty of parents to choose educational experiences matched to their children's needs (Burch, 2009a). Within this emergent category of policy design, for profit and not for profit firms are offered commercial benefits in exchange for serving historically disadvantaged students. If the goal of these reforms is to make public education better so that all children succeed, we need better evidence that education privatization policies do more than simply provide space for educational vendors to make a profit.

Major federal policies, such as SES, that stretch between equity and commercialism are problematic staging areas for addressing historical disadvantages. There may be room for some commercialism in education reforms. However, any education policy that incorporates market-based mechanisms also needs to include accountability mechanisms to ensure that commercial interests do not subsume equity objectives. This means identifying and incorporating the necessary incentives, mandates and capacity building that will encourage and hold third party providers receiving Federal funds jointly accountable for providing equal opportunities for historically disadvantaged students.

ACKNOWLEDGMENTS

The authors thank the Institute of Education Sciences, PR/Award number: R305A090301, Education Policy, Finance, and Systems Research Program, Goal 3 for support for research funded in this project. Study web page: www.sesiq2.wceruw.org

NOTES

1. To date, we have conducted three reliability training sessions with the qualitative research team to ensure consistency in ratings. In each session the research team rated the same video segment of an instructional session and went through each indicator to compare ratings. Validity of the instrument is ensured by the development process, whereas its structure and content is based on well-tested, existing observation instruments for out of school time (OST), existing literature on the best practices for OST, and the theory of action in the SES policy. We continue to test and refine the data collection process as the study progresses.

2. The wording of the law states that "the parent should be made aware of the anticipated duration of services and this information should be detailed in the child's individual student agreement." However, as mentioned throughout the scope of this chapter, it is unclear whether districts (through equity principles) or providers (through commercialist principles) are directly accountable for this provision.

3. This difference in percentage may also reflect the definition of the indicator, which includes both bilingual tutors as well as tutors trained in ELL instruction.

4. Although most tutors we observed did not have specific training or certification in working with students with disabilities, it should be noted that we observed many sessions with certified teachers as tutors. Most of these tutors would have had training related to special education as part of their certification process and in many cases considerable experience working with students with disabilities in their regular classrooms.

5. The state and each district are responsible for ensuring that eligible Limited English Proficiency (LEP) students receive supplemental educational services and language assistance in the provision of those services through either a provider or providers that can serve LEP students with or without the assistance of the district or state; or, if no provider is able to provide such services, including necessary language assistance, to an eligible LEP student, the district would need to provide these services, either directly or through a contract.

REFERENCES

Beckett, M., Borman, G., Capizzano, J., Parsley, D., Ross, S., Schirm, A., & Taylor, J. (2009). *Structuring out-of-school time to improve academic achievement: A practice guide.* Washington, DC: National Center for Education Evaluation and Regional Assistance, Institute of Education Sciences.

Burch, P. (2007). *Supplemental educational services under NCLB: Emerging evidence and policy issues.* Education Policy Research Unit. Retrieved from http://epsl.asu.edu/epru/documents/EPSL-0705-232-EPRU.pdf

Burch, P. (2009a, April). *Getting to the core: The role of instructional setting in federally mandated tutoring* (Working paper). Presented at the 2009 American Educational Research Association Conference, San Diego, CA.

Burch, P. (2009b). *Hidden markets: The new education privatization.* New York, NY: Routledge.

Burch, P., & Good, A. (2009). *Supplemental education services observation instrument.* Retrieved from http://www.sesiq2.wceruw.org/documents/SES_Multisite_Study_OI.pdf

Burch, P., Heinrich, C.J., Good, A., & M. Stewart. (2011, February). *Equal access to quality in federally mandated tutoring: Preliminary findings of a multisite study of supplemental educational services* (Working paper). Presented at the 2011 Sociology of Education Conference, Monterey, CA.

Burch, P., Steinberg, M., & Donovan, J. (2007). Supplemental educational services and NCLB: Policy assumptions, market practices, emerging issues. *Educational Evaluation and Policy Analysis, 29*(2), 115-133.

Center on Education Policy. (2007). *Behind the numbers: Interviews in 22 states about achievement data and No Child Left Behind Act policies.* Washington, DC: Author.

Dumas, M., & Anyon, J. (2006). Toward a critical approach to education policy implementation: Implications for the battlefield. In M. Honig (Ed.), *New Directions in education policy implementation* (pp. 149-169). Albany, NY: SUNY.

Fusarelli, L. (2007). Restricted choices, limited options: Implementing choice and supplemental educational services in No Child Left Behind. *Educational Policy, 21*(1), 132-154.

Gill, B., McCombs, J. S., Naftel, S., Ross, K. E., Song, M., Harmon, J., ... O'Day, J. (2008). *Title I school choice and supplemental educational services under No Child Left Behind: Progress toward implementation* (RB-9334-EDU). Santa Monica, CA: RAND Corporation.

Good, A., Burch, P., Heinrich, C., Stewart, M., & Acosta, R. (2011, April). *Instruction matters: Lessons from a mixed-method evaluation of supplemental educational services under No Child Left Behind.* Paper presented at the 2011 American Educational Research Association Conference, New Orleans, LA.

Goodlad, J. I., & Keating, P. M. (1990). (Eds.). *Access to knowledge: an agenda for our nation's schools.* New York, NY: The College Board.

Government Accountability Office. (2006). *No Child Left Behind Act: Education a needed to improve local implementation and state evaluation of supplemental educational services.* Washington, DC: Author.

Heinrich, C. & Burch, P. (2009). *Preliminary findings of a multisite study of the implementation and effects of supplemental educational services.* Retrieved from http://

www.sesiq2.wceruw.org/documents/
ExecutiveSummary_Dec%20district%20briefings12.2010.pdf

Henig, J. R. (2006, November). *The political economy of supplemental education services*. Prepared for the American Enterprise Institute/Thomas B. Fordham Foundation Conference, "Fixing Failing Schools: Is the NCLB Toolkit Working?", Washington, DC.

Hentschke, G., & Wohlstetter, P. (2007). Conclusion: K-12 Education in a broader privatization context. In K. Bulkley & L. Fusarelli (Eds.), *The politics of privatization in education, The 2007 Yearbook of the Politics of Education Association* (Special double issue). *Educational Policy, 21*(1), 297-307.

Honig, M. (2006). Complexity and policy implementation. In M. Honig (Ed.), *New directions in education policy implementation* (pp. 1-23). Albany, NY: SUNY.

Koyama, J. (2011). Principals, power, and policy: Enacting supplemental educational services. *Anthropology and Education Quarterly, 42*(1), 20-36.

Lauer, P. A., Akiba, M., Wilkerson, S. B., Apthorp, H. S., Snow, D., & Martin-Glenn, M. L. (2006). Out-of-school-time programs: A meta-analysis of effects for at-risk students. *Review of Educational Research, 76*(2), 275-313.

Noam, G. (2004). *The four Cs of afterschool programming: A new case method for a new field*. New York, NY: The Robert Browne Foundation.

Potter, A., Ross, S. M., Paek, J., McKay, D., Ashton, J., & Sanders, W. L. (2007). *Supplemental educational services for the commonwealth of Tennessee: 2005-2006*. Memphis, TN: The University of Memphis, Center for Research in Educational Policy.

Stewart, M., Burch, P., Good, A., Heinrich, C., Kirshbaum, C., Acosta, R., Nisar, H., Dillender, M., & Cheng, E., (2012, April). *The implementation and effectiveness of supplemental educational services for students with disabilities and English language learners*. Paper presented at the 2012 American Educational Research Association Conference, Vancouver, CA.

Sunderman, G. L. (2006). Do supplemental educational services increase opportunities for minority students? *Phi Delta Kappan, 88*(2), 117-122.

Sunderman, G. L., & Kim, J. (2004). *Increasing bureaucracy or increasing opportunities? School district experience with supplemental educational services*. Cambridge, MA: The Civil Rights Project at Harvard.

U.S. Department of Education. (2009). *Supplemental educational services: Non-regulatory guidance*. Retrieved from http://www2.ed.gov/policy/elsec/guid/suppsvcsguid.doc

Zimmer, R., Gill, B., Razquin, P., Booker, K., Lockwood, J. R., Vernez, G., Birman, B. F., ... O'Day, J. (2007). *State and local implementation of the No Child Left Behind Act: Volume I—Title I school choice, supplemental educational services, and student achievement*. Washington, DC: U.S. Department of Education, Office of Planning, Evaluation and Policy Development, Policy and Program Studies Service.

CHAPTER 10

LOCAL COLLEGE ACCESS STRATEGIES

Examining the Equitable Distribution of Postsecondary Access in Michigan

Nathan Daun-Barnett and Irene Holohan-Moyer

The K-12 school reform agenda is seldom connected with the college access movement and yet, the two are closely related, if not explicitly linked. No Child Left Behind (NCLB), Race to the Top, and corresponding state school reform efforts movement has ratcheted up academic standards for students, teachers, and schools, as discussed previously in this volume. At the same time, colleges and universities are being asked to provide a postsecondary education to a broader cross-section of the adult population—a shift from mass higher education—a period marked by considerable expansion of access to underrepresented groups during the middle part of the 20th century—to college for all. A large number of these prospective students are not prepared academically for college level work and in many cases are asked to complete remedial or developmental courses—at their own expense. If we hope to increase equity in educational opportunity for an increasingly diverse nation, then we must begin discussing college access and the academic preparation of students for

Charting Reform, Achieving Equity in a Diverse Nation
pp. 251–272

college across the P-16 continuum —which means bringing school reform and college for all into closer alignment within states. From our perspective, that begins by examining the intersection of K-12 school reform and the movement toward universal college access.

We view the college for all movement as establishing a support apparatus in the shadows of comprehensive school reform and argue that *college access advocates have assumed a subordinate role to their K-12 reform colleagues on arguably the most important access issue today—academic preparation.* While colleges and universities rely on schools to prepare students for advanced study, they remain underinformed and perhaps apprehensive about weighing in on how high schools do their work. Proponents of the access for all agenda have chosen to push for policies likely to increase the level of preparation for all high school students—including rigorous course requirements for high school graduation and increased access to early college credit through *advanced placement* and dual enrollment opportunities—but they have not been active partners with schools to make the new standards achievable. Implicitly, they presume that too few students are prepared for college level work because they either choose the easiest path to a high school diploma or they lack access to advanced curricular options. Many of these same policy priorities may come at the expense of other important secondary outcomes, such as high school completion.

In this chapter we examine two separate strategies intended to increase access to college for students across the state of Michigan—*Promise Zones* created by state legislation and local college access networks (LCANs) that grew out of the federal College Access Challenge Grant (CACG) program. We focus on Michigan for two reasons. First, we contend that in order to appreciate the complexity of these two intersecting movements, we must take into account the state social and political contexts. While these are national issues, the policies shaping these debates operate at the state level and each state has a different mix. Second, Michigan has been on the leading edge of a growing movement to develop place-based strategies to increase college access and success. The *Kalamazoo Promise*—an economic development strategy that guaranteed a free college education for graduates of the local public school district (which we discuss in greater detail shortly)—may be the most notable example of place-based college access strategies in Michigan.

In this investigation, we consider two questions: (1) How do local communities facilitate access to college, given an existing state policy context, and (2) What are the implications of these approaches for the equitable distribution of access to college across the state? We consider how communities respond to the demands for greater access to college and how state entities, both governmental and nongovernmental organizations, influence local college access strategies using equity as a lens. We begin by providing some background regarding the role of policy to address barriers preventing access to college. Next, we utilize Deborah Stone's (2002) framework for examining equity in the context of distributive conflicts—in this case, the distribution of opportunities to attend college. In particular, we are interested in whether statewide distributive goals for equity can be achieved by leveraging state resources to develop targeted, localized approaches. In the final section we reflect upon these two different approaches to developing local access strategies relative to the equity framework.

Our conclusions resonate with those of Stone—whether equity can be achieved by either of these approaches depends largely upon how one defines the term, but in large part, neither approach currently expands opportunities equally across all communities in the state and as such, there will be winners and losers along the way. The Promise Zones tip the scales in favor of communities that are home to higher proportions of students typically excluded from access to college, but there is a risk that the anticipated benefits will not materialize because sustained funding is predicated on growing the local tax base. The LCAN model promises to reach a much larger cross section of the state population and may have the potential to utilize more levers to effect change, but it does not necessarily address the critical barrier of college cost, which may leave the same groups underrepresented in college, even within the communities served. And both approaches largely avoid the question of academic preparation for college—arguably the most important barrier to college access today—which is the piece of the access conversation most closely aligned with comprehensive school reform today.

We conduct this investigation as an embedded case study where the two separate approaches—Promise Zones and LCANs—are identified as units of analysis, with the sociopolitical backdrop of Michigan as the context. Yin (2009) suggests that this approach is appropriate when the purpose of the study is to describe the features, context, and process of the phenomenon under investigation. Census data and school enrollment data from the National Center for Education Statistics are utilized to understand the demographic context of the communities across Michigan. In order to understand how different communities plan to address the college access challenges in their communities, we examined grant proposals submitted to the Michigan College Access Network (MCAN)—which is a statewide nonprofit organization that provides coordination for many of the college access initiatives across Michigan. Finally, we administered a survey of community leadership to examine the nature of the partnerships across key stakeholders and to identify the sources of support communities identify to augment the funds available through MCAN.

COLLEGE ACCESS FOR ALL

Access to college has been a priority for state and federal policy makers for more than half a century and those concerns have grown considerably in recent years. Across the nation, most educators and policymakers recognize that postsecondary education is necessary for future generations to actively participate in a global knowledge economy. President Obama's (2010) call for the U.S. to once again lead the world in terms of the proportion of adults with a college education underscores the political and economic importance assigned to the attainment of a college credential. Students have gotten the message. According to a recent national study of postsecondary transitions, 80% of 10th graders in the U.S. plan to earn a bachelor's degree or above after high school (Ingels, Burns, Chen, Cataldi, & Charleston, 2005) and 75% of high school graduates attend college (Ingels, Planty, & Bozick, 2005).

Policymakers and educators pay particular attention to three key barriers in their attempts to address college access—academic preparation, college affordability, and access to information and support (Daun-Barnett & Das, 2011; Tierney, Bailey, Constantine, Finkelstein, & Farmer Hurd, 2009). Colleges lament that students entering college are not well equipped to complete college level work and the data are suggestive. Research over the past 40 years has shown that better prepared students succeed at higher rates (Adelman, 2006; Pelavin & Kane, 1990; Perna, 2006) and those requiring remediation are less likely to earn a degree (Calcagno & Long, 2008; Martorell & McFarlin, 2007). Currently, a third of students entering college require at least one remedial course; 42% among community college students alone (U.S. Department of Education & National Center for Education Statistics, 2011). Cost plays a substantial role in student's decisions to attend college. Low income students are particularly sensitive to price and are much less likely to attend college than their more economically advantaged peers (Heller, 2002). Finally, many college access initiatives are designed to help more students and parents navigate the college-going process. In 2012, for example, every state in the nation has developed at least one college access web-portal as a one-stop shop for students' college access information needs (Daun-Barnett & Das, 2011). While all three factors contribute to students' chances for college access, not all college access strategies address each equally well, as is true with the two place-based strategies in Michigan.

ACHIEVING EQUITY THROUGH STATE POLICY

In his address to Howard University, President Lyndon B. Johnson defended his support of affirmative action claiming,

You do not wipe away the scars of centuries by saying: "now, you are free to go where you want, do as you desire, and choose the leaders you please." You do not take a man who for years has been hobbled by chains, liberate him, bring him to the starting line of a race, saying, "you are free to compete with all the others," and still justly believe you have been completely fair. (Johnson, 1965)

Affirmative action, as controversial as it was and continues to be, was an attempt to eliminate discrimination against women and underrepresented minorities in employment and, by extension, college admissions (Ball, 2000; Orfield, Miller, & Civil Rights Project (Harvard University), 1998). This is just one of many ways policymakers have attempted to influence the distribution of opportunities for college access and equity has always been a concern among both supporters and detractors of the policy. Stone (2002) notes that policy goals like equity and efficiency are used as rationales for policy formation assuming a single, agreed upon definition, when in fact, there is little consensus regarding how these goals are best achieved. She notes that the simple, overly general definition of equity as "treating likes alike" does not fully account for who should have access, what they should have access to, and the process by which access should be granted—we use these three questions to examine the extent to which the two contrasting local access strategies in Michigan are likely to influence the equitable distribution of college opportunities. As our debates over affirmative action, admissions policies, and financial aid programs attest, there is little consensus among policymakers regarding how best to address these distributive questions.

Access to college is fundamentally a question of equity and how we think about access has everything to do with the distributive assumptions articulated by Stone (2002). The first distributive assumption suggests that everyone has access to a college education in the U.S. because many institutions are open enrollment and maintain relatively modest tuition and fees. However, if students have not completed high school, gaining access to postsecondary education is implausible if not impossible. Similarly, if a student completes their schooling in the U.S. but does not have legal citizenship in this country, they may be eligible to apply but will not qualify for state subsidized tuition in most states (Flores, 2010). Today, low-income and underrepresented minority students are less likely to attend college suggesting we have not yet settled the question of who should have access—though today's answer to this question is more inclusive of low-income and underrepresented minority students than a century ago (Bowen, Kurzweil, & Tobin, 2005).

The second and perhaps the more contentious question is what sort of education or institution students should be able to access. The establishment and expansion of community colleges in the U.S. subsequent to the end of the Second World War and the passage of the GI Bill, opened the doors of higher education to a much broader cross-section of the population than ever before (St. John & Asker, 2003; Thelin, 2004). Today, approximately 50% of undergraduate students attend community colleges (Provasnik & Planty, 2008). But does a guarantee of access to a 2-year public institution reflect an equitable distribution of postsecondary access? Stated differently, are community colleges equivalent in terms of opportunities and outcomes to public universities or private liberal arts colleges? The answer to this question is clearly no. Community colleges may represent an important minimum threshold, but economic opportunity is stratified by level of degree attained and the more advanced the educational credential, the more one is likely to earn in their lifetime (U.S. Bureau of Labor Statistics, 2011).

Finally, Stone (2002) reminds us that the process of distribution is important to consider as we define equity. Admission to postsecondary education is fundamentally based upon meritocratic principles. To attend any college, one must first complete high school or an equivalency certification. In California, arguably the most proscriptive state system of higher education, a student must graduate in the top third of their high school class to attend a 4-year college and in the top 12.5% to attend the University of California system (Kerr, 1995). This process assumes equal access to preparation for college while in primary and secondary education, which has clearly not been the case for many Americans (Kozol, 2005). The process for distributing access to postsecondary education places students from low-income backgrounds, particularly in lower performing schools at a disadvantage. If Reardon (2011) is correct, then the widening achievement gap by socioeconomic status may be particularly problematic for efforts to improve college access. Not only do these students lack opportunities to prepare for college, they are also less likely to have access to information and support to engage in the college choice process. Fewer admissions counselors pay visits to these schools and school counselors in poor performing schools are asked to spend more time on administrative roles and less on college participation (Bridgeland & Bruce, 2011; Dahir, Burnham, & Stone, 2009). At the same time, community colleges and high price for-profit institutions focus their recruitment efforts on these students.

One of the constraints on the distributive process that receives less attention than academic merit is geographic proximity (Tinto, 1973). We suspect that with more than 4,000 colleges and universities in the U.S. there is a college or university near where most people live. However, in rural communities or smaller urban centers, the numbers and types of institutions available may limit opportunity. If a student attends high school in a place were the only college is a small, private liberal arts institution, and they were not a strong student in school, they may not view college as a viable option. Alternatively, they might consider an online program or an educational program delivered in a nontraditional form (e.g., weekend classes, online and face-to-face hybrids). Stone's (2002) discussion of these distributive assumptions provide us a useful lens through which to view these place-based college access strategies and to consider the extent to which equity can be meaningfully achieved with locally developed solutions.

THE POWER OF PLACE

In his work examining regional economic growth, Florida (2004) recognized that while place has always been important to theories of economic development, it plays a different role in the knowledge economy. Florida builds upon human capital theories—which suggest that an investment in talent will fuel economic growth—and finds that the key determinant of regional economic vitality today is the presence of a creative class. This new generation of knowledge workers enters the workforce in positions that take knowledge and translate it in new, creative, and entrepreneurial ways. The places that grow their economies train highly talented workers, but they also create environments that attract the future generation of creative knowledge workers. The Kalamazoo Promise was one very successful effort to implement the ideas articulated by Florida and state policymakers across the country have taken notice. The New York State Commission on Higher Education (2007) proposed the formation of Empire Promise Zones and a million dollar promise (reflecting the estimated wage premium for a bachelor's degree over one's lifetime). In 2008, Governor Jennifer Granholm proposed and signed into Michigan law a state initiative to create 10 Promise Zones across the state (Michigan Senate Fiscal Agency, 2008). Those 10 communities are now in some stage of developing their own version of tuition guarantees to meet the postsecondary education needs of their local communities. More recently, Michigan seeded another initiative, the LCANs under the umbrella of the MCAN. The goals of each are similar to those of the Kalamazoo Promise— increase college access for all—but both models approach the task from very different perspectives.

The emphasis placed upon locally developed strategies is not surprising in Michigan. It is the only state in the nation without a formal coordinating body for public higher education—public universities enjoy constitutional autonomy and that degree of autonomy trickles down to community colleges. Until recently, Michigan was one of six states in the nation without standardized high school graduation course requirements

—leaving those decisions to school districts (Council of Chief State School Officers, 2008). Equally, Michigan has a substantial network of community foundations committed to establishing and maintaining scholarship programs as part of their work. Promise Zones and LCANs are based upon different theories of change and emanate from local models but both are informed by the experience of Kalamazoo and rely upon state level interventions—a point we discuss more closely in a moment.

THE EVOLUTION OF PROMISE ZONES

In the fall of 2005, the city of Kalamazoo, Michigan announced the creation of the Kalamazoo Promise, guaranteeing tuition and fees for every graduate of the Kalamazoo Public Schools (KPS) to any public 2- or 4-year institution across the state. This simple, powerful promise created enormous energy and enthusiasm, motivating more than 100 communities across the U.S. to express interest in beginning their own promises. A handful of communities—including El Dorado, Pittsburgh, and Denver—have launched similar initiatives and others have begun planning. The fact that educators or business leaders would eliminate the cost of college as a mechanism to improve college participation is not new. Eugene Lang employed a similar strategy 30 years ago when he promised to pay for the college education of a class of sixth graders in New York City (I Have A Dream Foundation, 2008). Policymakers in Georgia used the same lever on a much larger scale when it created the Georgia HOPE scholarship (Cornwell & Mustard, 2004). What was different in Kalamazoo was the fact that civic, business, and education leaders launched the Kalamazoo Promise as part of a larger economic development strategy for a local geographic region.

Janice Brown (personal communication, 2009), former superintendent of Kalamazoo Public Schools and executive director of the Promise, reminds aspiring Promise communities that it took more than 5 years of active conversation among key political, business, and education leaders to come to some agreement on the Kalamazoo strategy. And as Miller-Adams (2008) notes, families from outside of the KPS decried the injustice of providing this benefit to some but not others. The Kalamazoo Promise was able to overcome many of these concerns because the scholarship was underwritten by an anonymous private donor who saw the investment in KPS students as a tool to bring students and families back into the district and by extension, build the human capital potential of its residents. By most accounts, the investment paid dividends for the city of Kalamazoo in a very short time—both as a tool to increase participation in college and to fuel economic growth. Within 4 years, enrollments in KPS reversed a slow annual decline to a substantial increase of 14% (Miron & Cullen, 2007). The increases in enrollments came from an equal mix of three separate groups—students within Kalamazoo attending either a charter or a private school, families moving back into the district from adjacent communities, and families attracted to Kalamazoo from other parts of the state and the country. A larger number of KPS graduates attended college—70% of whom attended either Kalamazoo Valley Community College or Western Michigan University, located in Kalamazoo (Miller-Adams, 2008).

Shortly after the announcement of the Kalamazoo Promise, the governor's advisors on education began to explore the possibility of replicating the Promise in other communities across the state. They had identified a potential funding mechanism—a tax capture of a portion of the additional tax revenues generated by attracting more residents to a particular place and increasing property values—but the larger challenge was to identify the right "places" around the state. From a purely human capital perspective, the choice of place would not matter so long as the community could grow and attract the talent sought by potential employers.

The Granholm administration viewed the place-based approach as a strategy to both increase postsecondary opportunities while also fueling economic growth (Governor's Commission on Higher Education and Economic Growth, 2004; Granholm, 2004). In some ways, however, these two goals may be at odds. Ann Arbor for example is one such community that attracts this sort of creative synergy between education and economic development, but it is not a place that requires additional resources to motivate greater college participation. In fact, creating a tuition guarantee for Ann Arbor would be an inefficient distribution of resources because many of those students would attend college without the assistance. Flint, Michigan, on the other hand, is exactly the sort of place a state might hope to create economic development strategies, but it may not have the assets, infrastructure, or capital necessary to attract creative talent or leverage postsecondary education for economic development.

The 2008 Promise Zone Act (Michigan Senate Fiscal Agency, 2008) created 10 Promise Zones across the state of Michigan. The zones authorized under the legislation are identified in Table 10.1. Communities were eligible to apply if the proportion of families with children living in poverty exceeded the state average. Participating communities were required to create a coordinating board of community leaders and educators and establish a plan to raise funds for the tuition guarantee. Additionally, the law sets the minimum tuition guarantee at the rate of tuition and fees for the community college and requires that all students exhaust publicly available sources of financial support before being eligible for the Promise.

In exchange, once the Zone offers its first round of scholarships, it becomes eligible to capture half of any increase in the state education tax

Table 10.1. Promise Zones in Michigan

Promise Zones	Urbanicity	Percent Bachelors	Free/Reduced Lunch
Baldwin School District	Rural	7.8%	89.2%
Battle Creek School District	Urban	10.8%	72.1%
Benton Harbor School District	Urban	11.7%	92.8%
City of Detroit	Urban	11.3%	74.4%
Hazel Park School District	Suburban	14.9%	79.3%
Jackson School District	Urban	19.1%	70.1%
Lansing School District	Urban	23.0%	68.1%
Muskegon Intermediate School District	Rural	17.3%	51.8%
Pontiac School District	Urban	17.4%	87.9%
Saginaw School District	Urban	9.8%	79.3%
State		25%	41%

Source: National Center for Education Statistics (2011). Common Core of Data.

collected in the Promise Zone. The tax capture is the more complicated part of the legislation and likely the most controversial because it will only work if communities are able to replicate Kalamazoo's success of increasing taxable value—likely by bringing more residents into the community. If the Promise fails in this regard, the community will become ineligible for the state tax capture. At that point, communities will either end their programs or find alternative funding sources. The Michigan Senate Fiscal Agency (2008) points out that the law impacts the funding of schools in two ways. First it reduces the overall state school aid fund by $15.3 million annually, which is the amount expected to be captured by the 10 Promise Zones. This is a modest decrease in a total annual budget of $12 billion for K-12 education funding, but this comes on top of declining state revenues that have already placed great pressure on schools. Second, it will change the distribution of state school aid across districts (albeit modestly), with Promise Zones receiving added revenues to fund their tuition scholarships and the other districts receiving less. Based upon data from Kalamazoo, the Zones will benefit, but the surrounding communities will lose resources because 80% of the increase in Kalamazoo population was the result of movement within the state. The Senate Fiscal Agency numbers may be overly optimistic given that the Promise Zone tuition guarantees are less generous and less secure than those provided by Kalamazoo. Less movement is expected when the incentives are small. Two years of tuition at a community college under one of the Promise Zones may be worth only $3,000 per year over 2 years, while the maximum award for a student in the Kalamazoo Promise may be as much as $12,000 per year for as many as 5 years, depending upon the institution they attend. In addition, since there is no private financial backer willing to make the promise in perpetuity, the benefit could disappear, which is an additional disincentive for a family to move.

Michigan identified 10 Promise Zones and three (Baldwin, Jackson, and Muskegon) began offering their tuition benefit in 2011. As Table 10.1 indicates, most of the zones are in urban settings. Battle Creek, Benton Harbor, Jackson, Pontiac, and Saginaw are all smaller urban centers with populations ranging from 34,000 to 67,000 (U.S. Census Bureau, 2011). Hazel Park is a Northwestern Suburb of Detroit, but in many respects faces similar challenges as other urban communities. All of the communities that applied for and were selected to become Promise Zones face considerable challenges in terms of educational opportunity and stand to benefit from the program. All 10 communities post lower rates of college attainment and serve a larger proportion of low-income students than the state.

While the Promise Zone strategy more heavily emphasized urban communities with high poverty rates, several large urban centers are missing from this list. Dearborn, Flint, and Grand Rapids, for example, are all midsized cities serving a similar population. Also missing from the list of Promise Zones are any communities in the upper peninsula of the state. Chippewa and Marquette Counties, for example, are relatively small in terms of population size (36,000 to 67,000), but exhibit higher poverty rates than the state average. They may have been appropriate locations for Promise Zones, but neither chose to apply. One of the key limitations of the model is that Promise Zones only provide access to a tuition guarantee for approximately 20% of the state population meaning that many communities serving high proportions of low-income families are not eligible to participate.

MCAN AND THE DEVELOPMENT
OF LOCAL COLLEGE ACCESS NETWORKS

The LCAN were informed, at least in part, by the tremendous success of the Kalamazoo Promise, but the approach evolved to address different barriers to access. Where the Kalamazoo strategy grew from their economic development plans to invest in human capital while simultaneously seeking to attract business, invest in infrastructure, and create appealing spaces to live and work, LCAN's emerged from an earlier set of recommendations about how to leverage local assets to increase postsecondary opportunity within communities. In 2004, Governor Jennifer Granholm announced the formation of a 41-member statewide commission on higher education and economic growth. Her charge to the commission was to "identify strategies to double the number of Michigan residents with postsecondary degrees and other credentials of value within 10 years" (Lt. Governor's Commission on Higher Education and Economic Growth, 2004, p. i). The commission issued 19 recommendations in their final report to the governor; one of which suggested the creation of "community compacts for educational attainment" (p. 17). The text called for local partnerships among policymakers, business leaders, K12 educators, and postsecondary institutions to address the collective needs of local community members. The university and community college representatives on the commission made compelling arguments for a nuanced approach to improving postsecondary outcomes and by the end of deliberations among the full body, there was a consensus that local strategies had to be a part of the set of priorities for the commission. The recommendation fell short of establishing a plan for community compacts and it included no incentives for their creation. As a result, little was done to address this recommendation for nearly 4 years following the commission.

The theory of change implicit in the community compact was that local communities could substantially increase the proportion of adults with a college education if they established partnerships inclusive of key stakeholders from K-12 education, higher education, policymakers, community-based organizations and the business community. The LCAN approach recognizes that statewide systemic alignment between K-12 and higher education is difficult to achieve and that gaining access to college is more plausible for students and parents when barriers are addressed locally. The theory also places greater emphasis on the provision of information to students and parents, based upon the assumption that better informed students will make different choices regarding their educational path. The commission made no attempt to identify which communities should develop compacts, suggesting that all communities might benefit from this sort of organizing. Unlike the Kalamazoo Promise—which was based largely in human capital theory and the investment of local dollars in the development of local talent—the community compact allows local leaders to identify which barriers to address. A review of grant proposals from the LCANs reveals that most of the efforts initiated by the statewide MCAN and the LCANs addressed two barriers—(1) providing students and parents' information and support and (2) assisting students as they navigate the college choice process. The proposed work of the LCAN's often took the form of college success centers, where counselors, advisers, and peers helped students access the information they need to decide whether and where to go to college. LCAN's have helped students navigate the process largely through the use of the Michigan College Access Portal and the promotion of College Goal Sunday and College Application week—both of which emphasize completing the Free Application for Federal Student Aid and college applications, respectively. None of the proposed community-based access strategies focused meaningful attention on the academic preparation students receive in school. In a few cases, organizations offered test preparation services or afterschool tutoring, but none of these efforts attempts to tie their work to school reform.

Despite the growing momentum under MCAN in 2011, the LCAN model was slow to develop across Michigan for two reasons. First, until 2008, there was no organizing body charged with the responsibility for developing community compacts. The work of the commission was time limited and the group was disbanded once the final report was issued. Second, there were no resources identified to seed the creation of local compacts. By 2012, state appropriations to higher education had either been cut or had not received an increase in funding for eight consecutive years, effectively reducing public support for higher education by 20%, from a high of $2.07 billion in 2002 to $1.68 billion in 2012 (Palmer, 2011). State budget projections suggested that the revenue picture was not likely to improve for several years (and at the time this chapter was written in 2012, state revenues continued to decline). Given this dire revenue outlook, the federally sponsored CACG program created a window of opportunity for the state to invest in college access related initiatives.

Under the federal CACG program, governor's in each of the 50 states, DC, and the territories were eligible to receive grants of $66 million or more, allocated according to the proportion of children living below poverty in the state (U.S. Department of Education, 2011). In 2009, the total program expanded to $150 million and Michigan's share rose from $2.1 to $4.2 million. As a condition for receiving the block grant, states were required to provide a match of $1 for every $2 provided by the U.S. Department of Education. At the time the program was announced, the state had no coordinated effort to improve college access so, like many states, Michigan sought out successful models and innovative strategies from neighboring states. Michigan began by engaging key potential statewide partners but many of them maintained a proprietary interest in forming and operating the state's college access activities and no single partner could adequately meet the matching requirement for the challenge grant alone. It was also increasingly apparent that situating the network within any one of these partner organizations would come at the expense of collaborations with other partners.

One promising practice other states had employed was the creation of college access networks. Ohio had a well-established network (OCAN) and was part of the National College Access Network. OCAN connected efforts across the state and supported the work of local service providers committed to increasing access to college. The Council of Michigan Foundations (CMF) was particularly interested in the establishment of a separate organization modeled after OCAN. CMF recognized that, as a statewide organization, the creation of a Michigan version of OCAN would help to connect state-level work with community access strategies—a priority among its members.

MCAN was formed in 2009 and their primary strategy was to provide seed money for the creation of LCAN. The Kresge Foundation became a central partner in the Michigan college access strategy in 2010 and pro- vided support for MCAN and a large re-granting initiative to community foundations involved in their respective LCANs. These resources helped to satisfy the federal match requirement of the CACG but more to the point, they created an incentive for communities to engage in a common set of college access strategies. By 2012, forty-five local communities were either in the planning stages or in the process of implementing a local college access network.

In terms of equity and expanding postsecondary opportunities, the LCAN model appears to reach a much larger cross section of communities—four times as many communities as the Promise Zones and nearly half of all LCANs are located in rural communities. The statewide MCAN plays a strong coordinating role in local efforts both in terms of the expectations it sets for community participation and the role it plays connecting local providers with statewide resources and support. MCAN partners with the relevant state entities ranging from the Michigan Department of Education to the coordinating agencies for community colleges and public universities to other nonprofit service providers. MCAN is also in the process of building a statewide infrastructure including a common set of tools and access to college enrollment data. As Table 10.2 shows, LCAN's have broadened the definition of community in two ways beyond the Promise Zone. First, it extended its reach to include counties and multicounty regions in areas outside of urban centers, including the upper peninsula. LCANs were also established in several urban regions not identified as Promise Zones, including Grand Rapids (Kent County), Flint (Genesee County), and Ann Arbor/Ypsilanti (Washtenaw County). Second, the state recognized that communities may be defined at a variety of levels. For example, while Detroit is a single Promise Zone, five separate communities within the city limits could develop separate neighborhood level LCANs.

The tradeoff for a more inclusive definition of community is that the MCAN network includes a number of communities that may not serve high percentage of students in need of additional support. For example, Auburn Hills is a fairly affluent community in Southeast Michigan in Oak-

Table 10.2. Participating Local College Access Networks in Michigan

Local College Access Networks			
	Albion	*	Jackson County
	Alpena, Montmorency, & Alcona		Kalamazoo County
	Auburn Hills		Kent County
*	Baldwin		Keweenaw Peninsula
	Barry County	*	Lansing
*	Battle Creek		Mancelona
	Bay County	*	Muskegon County
*	Benton Harbor		Newaygo County
*	Brightmoor Neighborhood (Detroit)	*	North End Neighborhood (Detroit)
	Charlevoix-Emmet	*	Osborn Neighborhood (Detroit)
*	Downtown Detroit	*	Pontiac
	Eastern Upper Peninsula	*	Springwells Village Neighborhood (Detroit)
	Escanaba LCAN		St. Clair County
	Genesee County		Sturgis
	Grand Haven		Union City, Athens, & Tekonsha
	Gratiot & Isabella Counties		Washtenaw County
	Highland Park		Western Wayne County
	Holland/Zeeland		
	Ionia & Montcalm Counties		

Source: Michigan College Access Network
*Indicates that Promise Zones exist in these communities as well.

land County where the percentage of adults with a 4-year degree far exceeds the state average. Washtenaw County is similar—while opportunities may differ from Ann Arbor to Ypsilanti, more than 50% of adults across the county have attained a bachelor's degree or above. From this perspective, the MCAN approach may be inefficient because it is distributing resources to students residing in communities with comparatively low levels of demonstrated financial need.

The MCAN model does not address what sort of postsecondary education students are able to access. Promise Zones set their tuition guarantee at a minimum based on tuition and fees at a community college and allowed the money to be portable to other institutions—frequently those located within the geographic service region. In contrast, MCAN strategies emphasize access to information and a supportive network of adults and peers but offered no tuition guarantee. To the extent that student choice is a function of the knowledge and information students possess, then the LCANs may be providing greater opportunities to extend the range of institutions students might otherwise attend. However, in communities like Ionia, Montcalm, or Keweenaw, student's choice of institution remained limited, to a degree, by the communities' proximity to colleges and universities. LCANs do not limit students' choices to particular institutions but students in these communities must often choose between a college degree and remaining in their community—not a decision every student is willing to make. Like Promise Zones, LCANs have not attempted to align efforts systematically with K-12 school reform. Assuming local strategies successfully increase access to information and expand the number of supportive adults working with students, new cohorts of students will be better informed about state graduation requirements and may have more ready access to test preparation for the required ACT test (as part of the Michigan Merit Exam). Ultimately, both Promise Zones and LCAN's leave the issue of academic preparation to districts and schools.

CONCLUSIONS

Based upon our investigation of local access strategies in Michigan, we are able to make three conclusions regarding the potential contributions of these approaches to improving access to postsecondary education and the likely effects on the equitable distribution of those opportunities. First, we found that both Promise Zones and local college access networks hold some promise for addressing the unique challenges students face as they make the transition from high school to college. Second, we conclude that even under the best of circumstances, these programs are unlikely to improve the equitable distribution of postsecondary opportunities. They may have some impact in their own communities but too many students are left untouched by either approach. Third, for as promising as these approaches appear to be, our investigation suggests that both approaches will be difficult to sustain, given the uncertainty of state funding and the vagaries of federal grants and private philanthropic support. We summarize the findings for each of these three conclusions below.

The Promise of Local College Access Strategies

Michigan may be the first state in the nation to develop a systematic approach to leveraging federal, state, and local resources to address unique college access challenges at the community level. Thanks to the early success of the Kalamazoo Promise, the Michigan experience has shown that it is possible to bring new partners into the college access conversation or to redefine the roles of existing partners like the philanthropic community. Michigan has become home to the place-based scholarship suggesting that it is possible to link an investment in human capital with the economic vitality of local communities. In the process, the local access strategy movement in Michigan has led to several new contributions. First, it is testing whether or not states can create effective incentives to bring more private dollars into the college access conversation. Kalamazoo made its promise with private anonymous dollars—at a substantial investment of nearly $12 million per year. Other Promise Zones will be able to capture a modest level of state support but for these communities to enjoy successes similar to those in Kalamazoo; they will need to leverage state tax dollars with other sources of support. We suspect that one of two conditions will emerge naturally across these communities. Either, they will be successful leveraging resources to bring more dollars to the table or they will attempt to improve opportunities with less robust interventions. Both of these conditions are useful to test and policymakers, in particular, will be interested to know whether these approaches are efficient strategies for states to pursue.

Second, the local approaches have allowed for new partnerships to emerge between schools and their communities. A case in point has been the growth of the National College Advising Corps (NCAC) in Michigan. This partnership brings paid volunteers or para-professionals into schools to assist school counselors with helping students and families navigate the college choice process. The coordination necessary at the local level to participate in either the Promise Zones or the LCANs has made it possible for communities to bring these initiatives into schools where the need for additional support is high. In 3 years, NCAC in Michigan has grown from 8 members to 48. They are typically not trained counselors but they are recent college graduates who understand and have successfully navigated the college choice process. Success with this model may open the door for similar strategies including partnerships with other programs such as AmeriCorps. Third, the philanthropic community has increased its involvement in education considerably since the inception of these local access strategies. Both private philanthropies and community foundations have been involved in education programming for many years, including college scholarships. The increased participation of community foundations coupled with the substantial investment the Kresge Foundation has made in developing a statewide college access strategy suggests that new resources can be brought to bear on the college access challenge. All of these innovations are made possible in part by the development of Promise Zones and LCANs and they hold promise for other communities seeking to improve postsecondary opportunities.

Marginal Effects on the Equitable Distribution of Postsecondary Opportunities

For as optimistic as we are about the potential of local access strategies, we are equally concerned about the impact of these approaches on the equitable distribution of those opportunities for low-income, first generation, and underrepresented minority students. This study suggests the first problem may be one of geographic distribution. Promise Zones were intended to serve high need communities, and from that perspective, one might suspect that equity was a concern among policymakers. Where Promise Zones focus almost entirely on urban communities and target a critical barrier to access—college cost—the benefit is extended to as little as 20% of the state population. The process to apply for Promise Zone status was open to any community with higher than average poverty rates among children in the state, but many communities were either unable to apply or chose not to do so. LCANs, on the other hand, are likely to increase students' support to navigate the choice process and the effort will reach many more communities, but this matters less if students cannot afford to attend. The process for selecting Promise Zones considered equity by limiting participation to communities serving high proportions of low-income students, but many more communities in that same group did not participate. The LCANs extend boundaries of the program to a much broader cross section of students and communities, but the focus of the intervention was on access to information and support for students less likely to participate in college.

The second, and more serious concern from an equity perspective, is that both approaches fail to address what is arguably the most important college access barrier—academic preparation. Neither approach attempts to improve academic preparation directly—LCAN's address preparation indirectly by providing students better information about academic expectations and major choices. The Promise Zone strategy is silent on preparation. Ironically, the latter may help students overcome one of the more important obstacles to college (cost) at the expense of the other (academic preparation). As the Senate Fiscal Agency points out, under current assumptions, $15.3 million will be diverted from the state school aid fund to the Promise Zone Authorities—effectively reducing support for schools charged with preparing students for college. The amount is modest relative to the $12 billion Michigan appropriates annually to schools and the reductions will be spread across all districts. But at a time when Michigan faces persistent revenue shortfalls, every dollar counts. Even for the Promise Zones, the additional resources earmarked for scholarships cannot be used to improve the quality of the P-12 education students receive.

Lack of Sustainable Funding for Local Strategies

Finally, we conclude that, even under the best of circumstances, neither of these approaches may be sustainable over the long run—largely because both rely on unstable sources of funding. LCANs received much of their support from MCAN through the federal CACG, state appropriations, the Kresge Foundation, and local community-based foundations. The federal grant has disappeared because the state of Michigan failed to maintain its investment in public higher education at a sufficient level and, while the philanthropic community has maintained its support of these initiatives, community-based foundations are more inclined to provide start-up funding and assist with long-term sustainability planning than to maintain annual investments. The 2012 legislative appropriation offsets a portion of the loss from CACG but there are no guarantees this funding will remain from one year to the next. Promise Zones, on the other hand, redirect money from the state school aid fund and as such, are subject to competing priorities of state legislators. The resources from the tax capture are not guaranteed and the legislation requires that communities identify initial funding for their tuition scholarships before any tax capture is possible.

On balance, the limitations appear to outweigh the potential benefits. The infusion of new resources and the innovations that result from local collaboration may be fruitful and will be watched closely by researchers and policymakers but we suspect that these approaches are only likely to improve postsecondary opportunities for less advantaged students at the margins, limited both by the number of potential students served and the lack of attention to academic preparation. Without greater attention to long-term sustainability, those benefits will only last as long as funding from state and private sources and that window will close unless other sources of support are identified or more of these strategies are institutionalized as part of larger school reform efforts or state funding priorities.

REFERENCES

Adelman, C. (2006). The toolbox revisited: Paths to degree completion from high school to college. Washington DC: U.S. Department of Education.

Ball, H. (2000). *The Bakke case: Race, education, and affirmative action*. Lawrence, KS: University Press of Kansas.

Bowen, W. G., Kurzweil, M. A., & Tobin, E. M. (2005). *Equity and Excellence in American Higher Education*. Charlottesville, VA: University of Virginia Press.

Bridgeland, J., & Bruce, M. (2011). 2011 National Survey of School Counselors: Counseling at a Crossroads. In The College Board National Office for School Counselor Advocacy (Ed.), *College board advocacy & policy center* (p. 60). New York, NY: The College Board.

Calcagno, J. C., & Long, B. T. (2008). The impact of postsecondary remediation using a regression discontinuity approach: Addressing endogenous sorting and noncompliance. *NBER Working Paper Series, 14194,* 40. Retrieved from http://www.nber.org/papers/w14194

Cornwell, C., & Mustard, D. B. (2004). Georgia's HOPE scholarship and minority and low-income students: Program effects and proposed reforms. In D. Heller & P. Marin (Eds.), *State merit scholarship programs and racial inequality*. Los Angeles, CA: The Civil Rights Project.

Council of Chief State School Officers. (2008). Key State Policies on PK-12 Education: 2008 (pp. 42). Washington, DC.

Dahir, C. A., Burnham, J. J., & Stone, C. (2009). Listen to the Voices: School Counselors and Comprehensive School Counseling Programs. *Professional School Counseling, 12*(3), 182-192.

Daun-Barnett, N., & Das, D. (2011). College access and the web-based college knowledge strategy: Analysis of the know how 2 go campaign. *Enrollment Management Journal, 4*(3), 42-65.

Flores, S. M. (2010). State DREAM Acts: The effect of in-state resident tuition policies and undocumented Latino students. *Review of Higher Education, 33*(2), 239-283.

Florida, R. L. (2004). *The rise of the creative class: How it's transforming work, leisure, community and everyday life*. New York, NY: Basic Books.

Governor's Commission on Higher Education and Economic Growth. (Ed.). (2004). *Final report of the Lt. Governor's Commission on Higher Education & Economic Growth*. Lansing, MI: Author

Granholm, J. M. (2004). *Our determination, our destination: A 21st century economy*. Retrieved from www.michigan.gov/printerFriendly/0,1687,7-168--84911--,00.html

Heller, D. E. (2002). *Condition of access: Higher education for lower income students*. Westport, CT: Praeger.

I Have A Dream Foundation. (2008). *History of I Have A Dream Foundation*. Retrieved from http://www.ihaveadreamfoundation.org/html/history.htm

Ingels, S. J., Burns, L. J., Chen, X., Cataldi, E. F., & Charleston, S. (2005). *A profile of the American high school sophomore in 2002: Initial results from the base year of the education longitudinal study of 2002* (NCES 2005-338). Washington, DC: U.S. Department of Education.

Ingels, S. J., Planty, M., & Bozick, R. (2005). A Profile of the American high school senior in 2004: A first look—Initial results from the first follow-up of the education longitudinal study of 2002 (ELS:2002) (NCES 2006–348). Washington, DC: U.S. Department of Education.

Johnson, L. B. (1965). *Commencement Address at Howard University: Fulfill these rights.* Retrieved from http://www.lbjlib.utexas.edu/johnson/archives.hom/speeches.hom/650604.asp

Kerr, C. (1995). The idea of a multiversity. In C. Kerr (Ed.), *The uses of the university* (4th ed., pp. 1-34). Cambridge, MA: Harvard University Press.

Kozol, J. (2005). *The shame of the nation: The restoration of apartheid schooling in America* (1st ed.). New York, NY: Crown.

Lt. Governor's Commission on Higher Education and Economic Growth. (2004). *Final Report of the Lt. Governor's Commission on Higher Education and Economic Growth.* Retrieved http://www.cherrycommission.org/docs/finalReport/CherryReport.pdf

Martorell, P., & McFarlin, I. (2007). *Help or hindrance? The effects of college remediation on academic and labor market outcomes.* Retrieved from http://www.utdallas.edu/research/tsp-erc/pdf/wp_mcfarlin_2010_help_or_hindrance_college_remediation.pdf

Michigan Senate Fiscal Agency. (2008). Michigan Promise Zone Act—Bill Analysis. Retrieved from http://www.legislature.mi.gov/documents/2007-2008/billanalysis/Senate/pdf/2007-SFA-0861-F.pdf

Miller-Adams, M. (2008). *The Kalamazoo Promise: Building assets for community change.* Kalamazoo, MI: Upjohn Institute for Employment Research.

Miron, G., & Cullen, A. (2007). *Trends and patterns in student enrollment in Kalamazoo Public Schools: Evaluation of the Kalamazoo* (Promise Working Paper No. 4). Kalamazoo, MI: Western Michigan University Evaluation Center.

National Center for Education Statistics. (2011). *Common core of data.* Retrieved from http://nces.ed.gov/ccd/

New York State Commission on Higher Education. (2007). *A Preliminary Report of Findings and Recommendations.* Retrieved from www.suny.edu/facultysenate/CHE_preliminary_report.pdf

Obama, B. (2010). Remarks of President Barack Obama—As prepared for delivery address to Joint Session of Congress. Retrieved from http://www.whitehouse.gov/the_press_office/remarks-of-president-barack-obama-address-to-joint-session-of-congress/

Orfield, G., Miller, E., & Civil Rights Project (Harvard University). (1998). *Chilling admissions: The affirmative action crisis and the search for alternatives.* Cambridge, MA: Civil Rights Project Harvard University, Harvard Education Pub. Group.

Palmer, J. (2011). Summary Tables, fiscal year (FY) 2010-11: Table 2. *Grapevine survey of state appropriations to higher education.* Retrieved from http://www.grapevine.ilstu.edu/tables/FY11/Grapevine_Table2.pdf

Pelavin, S. H., & Kane, M. (1990). *Changing the odds: Factors Increasing access to college.* New York, NY: College Entrance Examination Board.

Perna, L. W. (2006). Studying college access and choice: A proposed conceptual model. In J. Smart & M. Paulsen (Eds.), *Higher education: Handbook of theory and research* (pp. 99-157). Memphis, TN: Springer.

Provasnik, S., & Planty, M. (2008). Community colleges: Special Supplement to the Condition of Education 2008 (NCES 2008-033). Washington, DC: National Center for Education Statistics.

Reardon, S. (2011). The widening achievement gap between rich and poor: New evidence and possible explanations. In R. J. Murnane & G. Duncan (Eds.), *Whither opportunity? Rising inequality and the uncertain life chances of low-income children* (pp. 91-116). New York, NY: Russell Sage Foundation Press.

St. John, E. P., & Asker, E. H. (2003). *Refinancing the college dream: Access, equal opportunity, and justice for taxpayers.* Baltimore, MD: Johns Hopkins University Press.

Stone, D. A. (2002). *Policy paradox: The art of political decision making* (Rev. ed.). New York, NY: Norton.

Thelin, J. R. (2004). *A history of American higher education.* Baltimore, MD: Johns Hopkins University Press.

Tierney, W. G., Bailey, T., Constantine, J., Finkelstein, N., & Farmer Hurd, N. (2009). *Helping students navigate the path to college: What high schools can do.* Washington, DC: National Center for Educational Evaluation.

Tinto, V. (1973). College proximity and rates of college attendance. *American Educational Research Journal, 10*(4), 277-293.

U.S. Bureau of Labor Statistics. (2011). *Education pays.* Retrieved from http://www.bls.gov/opub/ooq/2011/summer/oochart.pdf

U.S. Census Bureau. (2011). American factfinder. Retrieved from http://www.census.gov/

U.S. Department of Education. (2011). College Access Challenge Grant Program Retrieved from http://www2.ed.gov/programs/cacg/awards.html

U.S. Department of Education & National Center for Education Statistics. (2011). *Remediation and degree completion: The condition of education.* Washington, DC: Institute of Education Sciences. Retrieved from http://nces.ed.gov/programs/coe/indicator_rmc.asp.

Yin, R. K. (2009). *Case study research: Design and methods* (4th ed.). Los Angeles, CA: SAGE.

ABOUT THE CONTRIBUTORS

Gail L. Sunderman is a senior research fellow with the Center for Education Policy at the University of Maryland. Her research focuses on educational policy and politics, urban school reform, and the impact of policy on the educational opportunities of low income and minority students. She is a former Fulbright scholar to Afghanistan and received her PhD in political science from the University of Chicago.

Rudy Acosta is a doctoral candidate at the University of Southern California in the Rossier School of Education. His research focuses on educational policy and market-based initiatives in K-12 public schooling, access of information to educational policies in under-resourced communities, and parent and community organizing around school reform. He was a seventh-grade math and science teacher in the South Bronx.

Marian Adams Bott, following a career in municipal and corporate investment banking in New York City, shifted to pro bono public sector work, concentrating on public education. Since 2004, she has served as the education finance specialist for the League of Women Voters of New York State. She received her EdD from Teachers College, Columbia University and lives in New York City and Rye, New York.

Patricia Burch is an associate professor at the University of Southern California in the Rossier School of Education with an interest in strengthening research, policy, and practice connections. Dr. Burch is an expert in issues of privatization, district redesign, and equity in public education and has conducted major studies and evaluations of K-12 education reform across the country.

Robert G. Croninger is an associate professor and associate chair in the Department of Teaching and Learning, Policy and Leadership in the

College of Education at the University of Maryland. His current research focuses on the challenges of studying teaching and identifying instructional practices that affect learning, particularly for students who have been historically disadvantaged in elementary and secondary schools.

Nathan Daun-Barnett is an assistant professor in the Educational Leadership and Policy Program at the University at Buffalo. His research examines factors influencing student's transitions from high school to college. He served for 3 years as the state evaluator for Michigan's College Access Challenge Grant and currently serves as the director of the College Success Center at Bennett High School in Buffalo, NY.

Erica Frankenberg is an assistant professor in the Department of Education Policy Studies at the Pennsylvania State University where her research focuses on racial desegregation and inequality in K-12 schools, and the connections between school segregation and other metropolitan policies.

Annalee Good is a research associate at the University of Wisconsin-Madison where she has conducted research on the nature of the instructional landscape in federally funded tutoring programs and the role of tutoring in school reform. She was a classroom teacher for 5 years before earning her masters and doctoral degrees in educational policy studies from the University of Wisconsin–Madison.

Rebecca Holcombe is a doctoral candidate at the Harvard Graduate School of Education and the director of Teacher Education at Dartmouth College. Her research interests include teacher quality, school leadership, and test-based accountability. Her work is informed by her experience as the director of academics for a public school district, as a school principal, and as a classroom teacher.

Irene Holohan-Moyer is currently a doctoral student in the Educational Leadership and Policy Program at the University at Buffalo and Associate Registrar where she supports the university's student information systems. Her research focuses on understanding student's experiences in dual enrollment programs and student's college experiences as they relate to finishing their undergraduate degrees.

Kathleen Mulvaney Hoyer is a doctoral candidate in the Education Policy Studies program in the Department of Teaching and Learning, Policy and Leadership at the University of Maryland. Her research focuses on the creation and implementation of federal education policy and its interaction with state and district policy.

Jennifer Jennings is an assistant professor of sociology at New York University. Her research focuses on the effects of accountability systems in education and health care on racial and socioeconomic inequality in education and health outcomes, and teacher and school effects on cognitive and noncognitive skills.

Daniel Koretz is the Henry Lee Shattuck Professor of Education at the Harvard Graduate School of Education. His research focuses on educational assessment and policy, with an emphasis on the effects of high-stakes testing, including effects on educational practice and the validity of score gains. Dr. Koretz is a member of the National Academy of Education and a fellow of the American Educational Research Association. Before obtaining his degree, Dr. Koretz taught emotionally disturbed students in public elementary and junior high schools in Parkrose, Oregon.

Jaekyung Lee is a professor and interim dean in the Graduate School of Education at the State University of New York at Buffalo. In 2009-10, he was a fellow at the Center for Advanced Study in the Behavioral Sciences, Stanford University. His research focuses on educational accountability and equity, particularly the issue of assessing and closing the achievement gap among different racial and social groups of students in P-16 education.

Xiaoyan Liu is an assistant director of institutional research and planning at Bucknell University where she facilitates institutional policymaking, strategic planning, and student learning outcomes assessment by coordinating, collecting, analyzing, and reporting on a wide variety of institutional data. Her scholarly interests include student engagement, achievement gap, social skills, learning outcome assessment, and program evaluation.

Heather Schwartz is a full policy researcher at the RAND Corporation in New Orleans, Louisiana. She researches education and housing policies intended to reduce the negative effects of poverty on children. Prior to working at RAND, Dr. Schwartz consulted to public housing authorities and to HUD on mixed-income housing policies. She obtained her PhD in education policy from Columbia University.

Mary S. Stewart is a doctoral candidate at the University of Wisconsin-Madison in the department of Educational Policy Studies. Her research focuses on educational policy implementation, legal issues in education, and program evaluation. Her current work focuses on the federal supplemental education services program and other after-school and university-level tutoring programs.

CPSIA information can be obtained
at www.ICGtesting.com
Printed in the USA
BVOW06s0809190517

484354BV00003B/6/P